Different Drummers

Different Drummers

Military Culture and Its Discontents

Edited by
Tad Tuleja

Utah State University Press
Logan

© 2020 by University Press of Colorado

Published by Utah State University Press
An imprint of University Press of Colorado
245 Century Circle, Suite 202
Louisville, Colorado 80027

 The University Press of Colorado is a proud member of
the Association of University Presses.

The University Press of Colorado is a cooperative publishing enterprise supported, in part, by Adams State University, Colorado State University, Fort Lewis College, Metropolitan State University of Denver, Regis University, University of Colorado, University of Northern Colorado, University of Wyoming, Utah State University, and Western Colorado University.

∞ This paper meets the requirements of the ANSI/NISO Z39.48–1992 (Permanence of Paper).

ISBN: 978-1-60732-942-8 (paperback)
ISBN: 978-1-60732-952-7 (ebook)
https://doi.org/10.7330/9781607329527

Library of Congress Cataloging-in-Publication Data

Names: Tuleja, Tad, 1944– editor.
Title: Different drummers : military culture and its discontents / edited by Tad Tuleja.
Description: Logan : Utah State University Press, [2020] | Includes bibliographical references and index.
Identifiers: LCCN 2020024019 (print) | LCCN 2020024020 (ebook) | ISBN 9781607329428 (paperback) | ISBN 9781607329527 (ebook)
Subjects: LCSH: Insubordination. | Soldiers—Attitudes. | Soldiers—Conduct of life. | Military discipline. | Armed Forces—Regulations.
Classification: LCC UB789 .D54 2020 (print) | LCC UB789 (ebook) | DDC 306.2/7—dc23
LC record available at https://lccn.loc.gov/2020024019
LC ebook record available at https://lccn.loc.gov/2020024020

Cover illustration © Robert Burns, weareglasscutter.com.

In memory of two veterans of the
Good War who recognized the folly
of that term

Thaddeus V. Tuleja, U.S.N. and
Claude H. Nolen, U.S.A.

If a man does not keep pace with his companions, perhaps it is because he hears a different drummer.
—Henry David Thoreau

Contents

Preface
Oppositional Positioning

ONE GOAL OF MILITARY BASIC TRAINING is to replace recruits' focus on their own individuality with an unquestioned devotion to group solidarity. No military unit—whether as small as a squad or as large as an army—can survive unless its members agree to subordinate their personal desires to collective action. This "deindividualization" is evident in everything from dress codes to forms of address, from small-arms drill to a reverence for "proper channels" and chain of command. To be a member of the armed forces is to be subordinate not only to superiors but also to a vast array of protocols and regulations designed to ensure the efficient functioning of the organizational whole. So ingrained is the respect for subordination that we may consider it what Alan Dundes (1971) called a "folk idea," that is, a governing principle of belief and of behavior that is so deeply inbred in military culture that it goes without saying.

But strict obedience to this principle is only an ideal. In reality, subordination, unit cohesion, and military culture itself are constantly being challenged by human beings who insist on clinging obstinately to their noncollective personalities. Breakouts from the ideal appear in forms as minor as mock-official acronyms (SNAFU, FUBAR) and as major as desertion and the fragging of superiors. The institutions of the Military Police, the Uniform Code of Military Justice, and the "brig" hint at a history of soldierly rebellion against the ideal, while even on the everyday vernacular level, grumbling about organizational strictures—and about the perceived fecklessness of the "Army way"—seems as characteristic a feature of warrior behavior as dutiful nods to patriotism or regimental honor.

The chapters in *Different Drummers* explore this disjunction between organizational solidarity and individual pushback, seeking to examine the ways in which members of the armed forces express ambivalent or conflicted attitudes about the organizations that they serve, for the most part, with enthusiasm and pride. With few exceptions, we focus not on antimilitary or

DOI: 10.7330/9781607329527.c000a

antiwar sentiments, but on the psychological tensions expressed by soldiers who, to quote from Christina Knopf in chapter 2, "accept[ed] membership within the military community while rejecting certain aspects of its organization." We look here at people who dissent from military culture, but who do so as members of a loyal opposition.

Several of the chapters in *Different Drummers* began as presentations at American Folklore Society meetings, and I conceived the book originally as a companion volume to *Warrior Ways: Explorations in Modern Military Folklore* (2012), which I coedited with my colleague Eric A. Eliason. Lisa Gilman's chapter in that book used the term "oppositional positioning" to describe the conflicted sensibility of Iraq War veterans who, while continuing to identify strongly with military culture, just as strongly opposed our Middle Eastern entanglements. "Oppositional positioning" was a good term, I thought, and in soliciting prospective chapters for *Different Drummers*, I asked for essays showing how this type of tension had been exhibited by other warriors—active duty or veterans—in other situations.

Some of the essays I eventually accepted as chapters came from fellow folklorists, including some of the "usual suspects" from *Warrior Ways*. Angus Gillespie, Jay Mechling, Rick Burns, and Jim Deutsch, for example, are all scholars trained in my home discipline. But I was aiming in *Different Drummers* for an interdisciplinary volume, and to that end I have been happy to receive provocative essays from literary scholars Ron Ben-Tovim, Catherine Calloway, and Matt Perry. In addition, media scholar Christina Knopf has drawn on communications theory to assess the impact of World War I cartoons. Carol Burke—another *Warrior Ways* alumna—trains her journalist's eye on war-zone narratives. Mark Russell's take on military culture reveals the oppositional positioning of a clinical psychologist. And four of the book's authors—military veterans Mark, Rick, Ron Fry, and John Paul Wallis—offer the first-person perspective of their own service experience.

As editor, I have adopted the interdisciplinary focus for two reasons. First, it reflects my appreciation that, in recent decades, the American Folklore Society has been inviting other disciplines—and nonacademics—to participate in the society's meetings and publications. Folklorists' traditional focus on artistic communication in small groups has been progressively widening to encompass expressive culture more generally, including the practices of popular and even elite culture. The definition battles of the 1970s have largely subsided, and this leaves an opening for a volume in which folklorists and others come together to cast individual lights on a common problem.

My second reason for welcoming multiple perspectives relates to how I see that common problem. In considering oppositional positioning, I don't focus on "bottom-up" folk practices per se but on how both those practices and more "elite" practices (e.g., veteran Gerardo Mena's poetry) respond to the perceived false narratives of the "top-down" culture. What interests me is the dialectical exchange between the official fabric of a "total institution" and the creative impulses that nibble at its edges. That worrying of the official narrative can appear in a variety of registers, and I wanted *Different Drummers* to acknowledge that variety. As a result, this book has chapters on the vernacular genres of "bodylore" (Mechling and Wallis [chapter 3]), folk song (Tuleja [chapter 7]), personal experience narrative (Burns [chapter 9] and Burke [chapter 12]), and legend (Deutsch [chapter 8]); literary items such as soldiers' memoirs and poetry (Perry [chapter 6], Calloway [chapter 10], and Ben-Tovim [chapter 11]); the artwork of soldier cartoonists (Gillespie [chapter 1] and Knopf [chapter 2]); and the actual defiance of command by officers in the field (Russell [chapter 4] and Fry [chapter 5]).

These are very different responses to the common problem, and clearly examples of responses in different registers. What unites them, I suggest, is an ethical tension not uncommon among military professionals, forced as they are to juggle accommodation and resistance to a culture that, even in nations pledged to radical individualism, remains fundamentally conservative and collectivist. It is my hope that this survey of diverse responses to the "totalizing" challenge will do justice to the loyal opposition's creative ingenuity and to the ethical compunctions that make that ingenuity necessary.

This book concludes an ethical and professional journey that began in 1997 with my first edited volume, *Usable Pasts*. I am fortunate in having found a home for that book, for *Warrior Ways*, and now for *Different Drummers*, with Utah State University Press. For this volume particularly, I thank the anonymous reviewers whose comments helped me clarify the collection's focus; and to the good folks on the press's staff: Laura Furney, Rachael Levay, Darrin Pratt, Beth Svinarich, Daniel Pratt, and Dan Miller.

My fellow editor on *Warrior Ways*, Eric A. Eliason, has been as responsible as anyone for helping me mitigate my distaste for disciplinary regimes with an appreciation of martial values and of the men and women who, sometimes enthusiastically and sometimes reluctantly, choose to embrace them. I hope that this "companion volume" to *Warrior Ways* may serve as a tribute to our collegiality and friendship.

As always, my wife, Andrée, remains the haven in which all my scribbling gets done.

WORKS CITED

Dundes, Alan. 1971. "Folk Ideas as Units of Worldview." *Journal of American Folklore* 84, no. 331 (January–March): 93–103.

Gilman, Lisa. 2012. "Oppositional Positioning: The Military Identification of Young Antiwar Veterans." In *Warrior Ways: Explorations in Modern Military Folklore*, edited by Eric A. Eliason and Tad Tuleja, 181–201. Logan: Utah State University Press.

Different Drummers

Introduction

The Myth of the Robot Soldier

Tad Tuleja

IN FEBRUARY 1778, WITH THE RAGTAG CONTINENTAL ARMY enduring a miserable winter at Valley Forge, a Prussian Army officer, Baron Friedrich Wilhelm von Steuben, sought out General George Washington and volunteered for service. His martial bearing and sterling credentials—he had been aide-de-camp to Frederick the Great, and he carried a letter of introduction from Benjamin Franklin—so impressed Washington that he appointed the distinguished foreigner his inspector general. In that capacity von Steuben fostered major improvements in sanitation, camp layout, bookkeeping, and—most significantly—the formations and synchronized movements of military drill. The nation's first professional drill instructor, he was a vigorous proponent of putting the troops through their paces, and the handbook he wrote in 1779, *Regulations for the Order and Discipline of the Troops of the United States*, went into dozens of printings. It remained the Army's training bible until the War of 1812.

Today, with firelocks and ramrods vestiges of the past, the particulars of von Steuben's manual may seem quaint. Yet its import remains relevant, for it shows that "order and discipline" are achieved by habituating recruits to bodily movements that they must perform precisely in response to undebatable verbal commands. The instructions for cocking a firearm—part of a long "Manual Exercise" in the use of arms—provide an example. The command for this step—number 2 of 27—is "Cock . . . Firelock!" At that command, the soldier is to perform two distinct motions:

> *1st.* Turn the barrel opposite to your face, and place your thumb upon the cock, raising the elbow square at this motion.
>
> *2nd.* Cock the firelock by drawing down your elbow, immediately placing your thumb up the breech-pin, and the fingers under the guard.

DOI: 10.7330/9781607329527.c000b

A simple mechanical movement, one which would already have been familiar to any of the citizen-soldiers of Washington's army, is here broken down into a two-step algorithm, initiated by a set command and meant to be executed with reliable speed and precision (von Steuben [1779] 1966).

Von Steuben ensured that reliability by means of the constant drilling for which he became notorious, and though he would not have been familiar with the terms, what he was consciously instilling in his recruits was a conditioned reflex supported by muscle memory. "Discipline," wrote a World War I British officer, "is the long-continued habit by which the very muscles of the soldier instinctively obey the words of command; even if his mind is too confused to attend, yet his muscles will obey" (cited in Cramer 1921, 774). The habituation of obedience: the Baron would have approved.

DOCILE BODIES

For the continental soldiers von Steuben trained, the point was not simply to cock the firearm; it was to cock it in the "proper" fashion—in the "Army way," as we would say now—and in coordination with every other soldier. An army of farmers and hunters might obey their own inclinations, cocking their muskets and flintlocks in a dozen different ways. A disciplined military force, collectively obedient to an officer's order, acted in every circumstance uniformly and in unison. Drill was thus both a means of training and a demonstration of the discipline inculcated by that training.

Such discipline was a hallmark of military training in eighteenth-century Europe. Von Steuben himself had absorbed its principles while serving Prussia's most celebrated military leader, Frederick the Great. When he brought those principles to America, he was doing more than instructing farmers in small arms drill; he was transporting to a colony in rebellion the very Prussian, and very undemocratic, Enlightenment ideal: that of the human being as calibratable machine that, when properly trained and "fitted out," could serve the efficient functioning of a corporate entity such as a school, an army on the march, or a nation-state.

In the eighteenth century, Michel Foucault argued eloquently, "The book of Man the Machine" was written simultaneously on an "anatomico-metaphysical" register of doctors and philosophers and a "technico-political" register of schools and armies: the two registers reinforced each other to ensure the production and control of "docile bodies" whose obedience was the guaranty of their utility. It was just this conjunction between obedience and utility—between compliance with regulation and effective performance—that attracted von Steuben to drill and that has made "docility" theoretically essential to martial training ever since. In today's boot camps no less than at Valley Forge, "disciplinary coercion establishes in the body the constricting link between an increased aptitude and an increased domination" (Foucault [1975] 1995, 135–138).

In von Steuben's time, there were tactical advantages to this discipline. A unit whose members responded with instant precision to an officer's command enjoyed a battlefield advantage in concentration of force. When infantry units faced each other in multiple-ranked line formations, steady fire could be sustained only when the soldiers in each rank fired and reloaded simultaneously. And soldiers who had been conditioned to maneuver tightly together were less likely to scatter if suddenly attacked. In all of these situations, success could only be achieved through a habituation that made muscle memory itself instinctively responsive to an external authority.

But regulatory regimes, like legal structures, tend toward metastasis. The organization that begins by specifying the angle of a shouldered arm and the centimeters between drilling troopers' shoulders quickly expands to regulating the length of fingernails and mustaches, and it ends by specifying the permissible size, weight, shape, and color of everything from buttons and boots to footlockers, gun carriages, and bombers. Moreover, this expansion is accompanied by a blizzard of paperwork that ensures the documentation of such uniformity is itself accomplished according to implacable rules. The result, not very many regulatory generations after the Baron's opening gambit, is the paradise (or nightmare) of precision known to all personnel, grumblingly, as "the Army way."

ESPRIT DE CORPS

If discipline's pragmatic effect is to form an efficient fighting force, its psychological effect is to instill in that force a sense of common purpose, celebrated variously as unit cohesion, esprit de corps, the French élan, and the "brotherhood of arms." One might argue that this bonding effect is secondary and instrumental, a romanticized means of making regimentation attractive. There is no denying, however, that whatever its organizational logic, the group identity that military training inculcates is emotionally compelling. By becoming disciplined together—by in effect surrendering their freedom together—soldiers build allegiance to something greater than their individual selves: they learn to love each other, their units, and whatever ideals they as a brotherhood are said to be fighting for. If they are docile bodies, they are docile only in service to the greater "body," which is, literally in French, the military "corps."

In soldiers' memoirs the sense of collective identity is probably the most commonly cited appeal of military service. It is not, however, an organic given, rising out of shared values, but a mechanically defined and carefully scripted sensibility that serves organizational ends as well as personal ones. Esprit de corps is not the natural outcome of living and working together; it is the result—and the goal—of an uncompromising indoctrination that reorients the civilian toward his or her proper place in a new scheme of things.

This is not to say that collective identity is insincere or that it is imposed on unwilling youngsters. Indeed, there seems little in the military experience more deeply cherished than this sense of shared identity with one's fellows under arms. In his World War I memoir *A Student in Arms*, for example, British soldier Donald Hankey notes that, far from resenting the strictures of military life, soldiers often come to find comfort in the very restrictions that, upon entering the service, they saw as onerous. The recruit gradually accepts military discipline because he sees that, in submitting to it, he has professed his loyalty to "the regiment" and thus acquired a nobler mantle than his individual identity. He has learned

> one of the great truths of life . . . that it is not in isolation but as a member of a body that a man finds his fullest self-expression: that it is not in self-assertion but in self-subordination, not as an individual but as one of many brethren, sons of one Father, that a man finds the complete satisfaction of his instincts, and the highest form of liberty . . . He has given up his personal freedom, which was not really of much use to him, and in return he has received what is infinitely more precious—his share of the common heritage of the regiment, its glorious past, its present prowess, its honor and good name, its high resolve. (Hankey 1917, 271–272)

Hankey's description bears both a Christian stamp and the misty trappings of imperial pride. These qualities seem quaint now, but a starker version of his argument is still in play. The "sons of one Father" bit has been deleted, yet in the recruiting literature of today's American services, you can still hear this invocation of the "honor of the regiment," this old, intoxicating sense of the individual dying into something greater than himself.

In the US Army document "Army Values," for example, new service members are exhorted to honor duty, loyalty, and teamwork. The importance of subordinating oneself to the group is most obvious in the value called "Selfless Service": "Put the welfare of the Nation, the Army and your subordinates before your own. Selfless service is larger than just one person. In serving your country, you are doing your duty loyally without thought of recognition or gain." The well-known injunction to "leave no man behind," adopted by SEALs, among others, is another phrasing of the same sentiment (Wasdin 2011, 104). That this commitment to the fallen may paradoxically imperil the group in no way diminishes its ethical appeal.

The sentiment may reach its greatest intensity in the US Marine Corps. In *Making the Corps*, his fascinating look at the Parris Island boot camp experience, Thomas Ricks shows that becoming a Marine means becoming, above all else, a disciplined person. A disciplined person respects the heritage of the elite force he is joining. He responds with unabated enthusiasm to every command. Most of all, he understands the paradox that, as an elite soldier, his dedication must be to the Corps and not to himself.

Selflessness is so central a Marine virtue that in boot camp, recruits lose their first names. Ricks recalls a drill instructor telling his charges, "From now on you are no longer he, she, it, or whatever you was . . . You are now Recruit-and-your-last-name, understand?" Speaking of recruit Platoon 3086, Ricks writes, "Coming from a society that elevates the individual, they are now in a world where the group is supreme. Using 'I' raises suspicion. Why would you care more about yourself than about your unit. You are 3086" (2007, 40). One of the worst comments a recruit can get on his or her evaluation card is "Displayed an individual-type attitude" (78). Being willing to surrender one's self to the needs of the group is at the very heart of Marine Corps discipline. Being unwilling to do that puts you in the same category as "undisciplined" and "nasty" civilians (162).

To sum up, the purpose of military discipline is to create a collectivity of "docile bodies" that is able most efficiently to accomplish practical objectives. One time-tested way to create that docility is to convince individuals that they are ennobled by submitting themselves to the collective regime; in other words, their value consists only in their fealty to others. Discipline becomes both the instrument and the evidence of that fealty. It demonstrates that the individual soldier is behaving honorably toward the person next to him or her, toward the Corps (the corporate body), and toward the national agenda.

DOCILE MINDS

Given their disdain for the "me attitude," it might be supposed that military forces such as the Marines also discourage soldiers thinking for themselves—that they want not just docile bodies, but docile minds as well. And if this is so, does it not follow that the ideal soldier is a mindless robot?

For this antimilitary stereotype, there is historical support. Frederick the Great himself is reputed to have remarked, "If my soldiers ever started to think, I wouldn't have an army." It was an appropriate comment for an absolute monarch enamored of mechanical toys (Foucault [1975] 1995, 136). A century later, Henry David Thoreau—a student of history who had never shouldered arms—echoed the image in that war resisters' bible, "Civil Disobedience":

> The mass of men serve the state thus, not as men mainly, but as machines, with their bodies. They are the standing army, and the militia, jailers, constables, *posse comitatus*, etc. In most cases there is no free exercise whatever of the judgment or of the moral sense; but they put themselves on a level with wood and earth and stones; and wooden men can perhaps be manufactured that will serve the purpose as well. ([1849] 2008, 229)

Soldiers themselves recognize, even as they bridle against, this caricature. In *All Quiet on the Western Front*, for example, Erich Maria Remarque has his protagonist Paul Baumer voice this assessment of the training that German soldiers underwent during World War I: "We learned that a bright button is weightier than four volumes of Shakespeare. At first astonished, then embittered, and finally indifferent, we recognized that what matters is not the mind but the boot brush, not intelligence but the system, not freedom but drill" ([1928] 1982, 21–22). One of Remarque's enemies, Donald Hankey, echoes this sentiment. In explaining the dogma that "only officers can think," he writes, "To safeguard this dogma from ridicule it is necessary that the men should be prevented from thinking. Their attention is to be fully occupied with such mechanical operations as the polishing of their buttons, in order that the officer may think without fear of contradiction" (1917, 31). Here, as befits someone who actually experienced the giving and receiving of orders—Hankey died on the Western Front in 1916—the stereotype is described sardonically. Yet it also carries the sense that, to a casual observer, the British Tommy, well schooled in class distinctions, might well seem to be confined to "mechanical operations."

Finally, here is Foucault again, on the "precise system of command" required for the "parts" of a corporate machine to interdigitate smoothly:

> All the activity of the disciplined individual must be punctuated and sustained by injunctions whose efficacy rests on brevity and clarity; the order does not need to be explained or formulated; it must trigger off the required behavior and that is enough. From the master of discipline to him who is subjected to it the relation is one of signalization: it is a question

not of understanding the injunction but of perceiving the signal and react-
ing to it immediately. (Foucault [1975] 1995, 166)

Obedience is not a question of understanding but of responding blindly to
a signal, like an electrical current responds to a finger on the switch. In this
ideal-type description of "perfect discipline," Foucault stresses hierarchy
and domination, painting the "master" as sole active agent and his "subjects" as mindless automata. It's a characteristic turn for this philosopher of
power, and it remains a durable picture among those who have never worn
a uniform.

ROBOTS IN REVOLT

Robotic behavior has always been, however, and remains a stereotype.
Antimilitarists notwithstanding, the members of today's armed forces
are clearly not required to behave like robots. In democratic armies especially, the habit of thinking for oneself that recruits bring to boot camp is
never—perhaps never can be—totally eradicated by military custom, even
in a branch as hostile to the "me attitude" as the Marines. We may imagine
that the military is what Erving Goffman (1961) calls a "total institution,"
where everything is meticulously regulated, where commands are followed
unquestioningly, and where individual initiative—including thought—is
kept in check. But in reality this totalizing model is constantly punctuated
by transgression, as the allegedly inviolate chain of command is rattled,
stretched out of shape, and sometimes broken. We may isolate three related
reasons why this occurs.

First, disruption may arise from the vicissitudes of battle. The established chain of command is broken when an officer is suddenly taken hors
de combat—sick, wounded, or dead. In war, as Hankey explains wryly, "if
all the officers are killed, the sergeants may think, and if they are killed the
corporals may think, and so on; but this is a relaxation of strict orthodoxy,
a concession to the logic of facts which must only be permitted in extreme
circumstances" (1917, 31). In extremis (and in warfare much is in extremis),
the regulatory mechanism self-adjusts, with the "mindless" cogs suddenly
acquiring not only agency but the hitherto-unseen ability to devise their
own solutions.

Second, the chain may be disrupted, ironically, by the hierarchical system itself—a system that allows for the situations Hankey describes, where
a junior assumes the authority of a fallen superior. Unlike the binary structure of a hospital or prison, which "totalizes" the split between supervisors

and subjects, the military structure separates "those who command" from "those who obey" through a flexible and performance-based promotional system. In a given theater or field situation, a general may theoretically be running the whole show, but in practice the operation of any military unit is the result of decisions made at multiple levels, by individuals who, according to their skills and results, may move up (or down) according to performance. Furthermore, these "subaltern" decisions create information that loops back to "higher," making the command-and-response dynamic of military units resemble not rote obedience but the give-and-take of cybernetic exchange.

This exchange has implications for how the military perceives the cognitive capabilities of even its most junior members—and for how those members perceive those capabilities themselves. An Army private may aspire to a corporal's stripes, and if his superiors spot within him what the services call "leadership potential"—a major ingredient of which is the ability to think—he may end up as a master sergeant. The same potential for promotion applies to officers. Nor is it unknown for enlisted men and woman to become officers. The services even have a slang term for such individuals: mustangs. Built into the structure of command, therefore, is the potential for thoughtful individuals to work their way up the chain. As Napoleon is said to have remarked of soldiers in a far more rigid hierarchy than our own: "Every French soldier carries in his knapsack a marshal's baton."

Third, the discipline of the chain may be subverted in situations in which a subordinate receives a command that he or she sees as unjustified on practical, moral, or legal grounds. In such situations soldiers are permitted—in some cases even required—to disobey what might look like a legitimate order. In illustrating this type of scenario, let me enlist the support of someone who may at first seem to be an unlikely ally: Erving Goffman.

In his 1957 essay "On the Characteristics of Total Institutions," Goffman provided a classic analysis of institutions whose "total" character is symbolized by its residents' long-term separation from the outside world and their supervision by staff members who administer a predictable and restricted "round of life." Goffman focused chiefly on prisons and hospitals, but he also considered schools, work camps, and military installations. In an army barracks or a ship, therefore, one would expect to find many of the same "totalizing" elements that are present in hospitals and prisons, including the expectation that "those in charge" issue orders and their subordinates, robotically, carry them out.

But Goffman points to a mitigating factor. In distinguishing between voluntary, semivoluntary, and involuntary admissions, he notes a difference in attitudes toward regimented confinement among postulates in a convent, who have entered voluntarily, and inmates in a penitentiary, who are there against their will. He sees soldiers falling into a middle category, and even in an army of conscripts, he implies, one finds a higher degree of residual "personality" than among those who are under confinement merely as punishment. In such an army, "inmates are required to serve but are given much opportunity to feel that this service is a justifiable one required in their own ultimate interests" (Goffman 1961, 118). But that same principle of "justifiable service" opens the opportunity for a denial of discipline when an action stipulated by a superior is interpreted as unjustified.

The possibility of making such an interpretation, unavailable to von Steuben's recruits, is an important element of American military law, firmly established in the Uniform Code of Military Justice. While the refusal to follow an order is in general grounds for punitive action, a soldier who refuses an order that he or she deems to be illegal has, if the soldier is proved correct, a chance of vindication under the UCMJ. The challenge to the system may of course be rejected. But the fact that a protocol exists for making it means that the military's "precise system of command" is not entirely inflexible. Where privates may second-guess their lieutenants, you're no longer in Prussia.

DIFFERENT DRUMMERS

To some soldiers—perhaps to the majority—the military's disciplining of everyday life may come as a relief, even a blessing. To those who enter the service adrift, uncertain of who they are or where they are going—that is to say, those who sign up hoping to "find themselves"—to these individuals, being told what to do and precisely how to do it may provide a welcome vacation from responsibility. Like those released prisoners who cannot endure the freedom of "outside," some soldiers positively embrace the endless restrictions of military life and are relieved to find that as members of a hierarchical organization, they are freed from the perils of making incorrect or "nasty" choices. My guess, though, is that in modern democratic armies such willing functionaries are rare. In reality, despite the genuflections constantly paid to unit cohesion and chain of command, most human beings in uniform are not themselves uniform: on one level or another, they cling obstinately to their civilian inclinations, pushing back against the rigors of corporate uniformity as a way of saving "self" from being devoured by the group.

In "The Underlife of a Public Institution," a companion piece to his more famous "Total Institutions" essay, Goffman studies the ways that mental patients "make out," that is, carve out private shelters within their totalizing worlds. That process, he argues, is as necessary to our humanity as the sense of "belonging." "Our sense of being a person can come from being drawn into a wider social unit; our sense of selfhood can arise through the little ways in which we resist the pull. Our status is backed by the solid buildings of the world, while our sense of personal identity often resides in the cracks" (1961, 315).

If inmates of mental institutions can find "little ways" to resist discipline and regimentation, it would be strange indeed if soldiers—members of an only partially "totalized" environment—did not yearn for an equivalent sense of individuality. And so they do. As organic, cognitive beings, not mechanical toys, soldiers are routinely searching for gold "in the cracks." They break out from Foucault's ideal-type norm in a myriad of ways, from the creation of mock-official acronyms (SNAFU, FUBAR) to chronic grumbling, from going AWOL and deserting to, in the most extreme cases, turning their frustration lethally against despised superiors. Creative insubordination is as deeply important a feature of military culture as the by-the-book protocols that officially govern it. The "Army way" is a kind of grammar. What soldiers say and do, in and out of the cracks, is a different, and less disciplined, thing entirely.

In *Different Drummers*, we seek through a variety of case studies to analyze creative dissent by individuals whose military identity is ambivalent or conflicted. Our intended focus is not antimilitary practices (like civilian marches) but versions of what Lisa Gilman (2012) has called the "oppositional positioning" of service members themselves. We are interested in the experiences of folks who are in the military but not completely of it—of folks who, while loyal to the uniform, may still sometimes feel themselves (to borrow Thoreau's famous phrase) marching to a "different drummer." These are stories of loyal (or mostly loyal) soldiers who, for a variety of reasons, resist the myth of the robot soldier to embrace their humanity.

The book is divided into four sections. Part I, "Weapons of the Weak," focuses on what anthropologist James Scott (1985) has called "weapons of the weak": small acts of verbal and physical resistance through which regimented soldiers proclaim their individuality. Drawing on Bill Mauldin's cartoons and other examples from World War II, in chapter 1 folklorist Angus Gillespie examines the military tradition of "griping," concluding that, contrary to the services' official line, humorous complaining about intractable situations can have an ironically positive effect on troop morale. In chapter 2, media scholar Christina Knopf offers a similar analysis of visual humor in the Dominion forces of the world wars, showing how ostensibly subversive "back chat" against officers helped to promote enlisted men's unit solidarity. In the third chapter, folklorist Jay Mechling and Marine veteran John Paul Wallis show how American troops today utilize their own bodies as sites of creative resistance against a "total institution."

In part II, "Rattling the Chain of Command," two American military officers, drawing on personal experiences, show how blind obedience to an institutional hierarchy can have baleful impacts on mission success. In chapter 4, US Navy psychologist Mark Russell, hindered by institutionalized machismo and hierarchical rigidity from giving combat veterans the care they deserved, shows how ignoring an official reporting protocol became his only means of budging an unresponsive bureaucracy. US Army captain Ronald Fry explains in chapter 5 how, as a Special Forces commander in Afghanistan, he was obliged to disobey an order that he believed would get his men killed.

The studies in part III, "Questioning the Patriotic Crusade," reveal oppositional positioning during World War I—that grim crusade that, as Woodrow Wilson put it, the United States joined to make the world "safe for democracy." In chapter 6 Matthew Perry examines the case of poet E.E. Cummings, who volunteered as an ambulance driver for the French, was arrested for suspected subversion, and spent several months in a French military prison. Perry show how Cummings's bitterly humorous memoir *The Enormous Room* revealed his growing disillusionment with the Allied cause and eventually with the war itself. In my essay (chapter 7) on the British Army's trench songs, I show how the sardonic embrace of victimization in occupational folk songs such as "Hanging on the Old Barbed Wire" may have served as a morale booster and a shield against despair. In chapter 8, folklorist James Deutsch explores variants of the wartime legend that deserters from both sides of the conflict were living like animals together under No Man's Land. He argues that this tale, in embellishing the horrors of the war itself, may have served also as a fantasy of escape and even an ironic index of internationalist cooperation.

The essays in part IV, "Messing with the Narrative," analyze the disconnect between military "master narratives" and the more complicated stories that soldiers tell themselves. Folklorist and Marine veteran Richard Burns, interviewing veterans who had seen a friend die in Vietnam, explores in chapter 9 the gaps between personal memories and the heroic rhetoric of an official citation. In chapter 10, literary scholar Catherine Calloway calls attention to the marginalized genre of women's war narratives, showing how two female veterans became military activists, inspiring other women warriors to tell their stories and working to improve veterans' benefits for all. In chapter 11, drawing on Foucault's notion of the "soldier-weapon complex," Ron Ben Tovim shows how an Iraq War veteran and poet, Gerardo Mena, attempts to reclaim the humanity of comrades who have become "things" by remembering them in the "speaking objects" of his poems. The final essay (chapter 12), by English professor and journalist Carol Burke, looks at the reluctance of deployed soldiers to regale their juniors with war stories and the willingness of civilian contractors, most of them veterans, to satisfy the desire with embroidered tales of their own "high-speed" pasts.

In the conclusion, I respond to the themes raised by the book's chapters, and especially to those of the final section, by defining a "master narrative" that governs behavior in many militaries. I show how the US military honors a virtuous triad of hardiness, brotherhood, and self-sacrifice and how the power of these folk ideas (Dundes 1971) functions to augment the traditional discipline of the total institution. In exploring the tension between two forms of solidarity—operational cohesion and emotional cohesion—I argue that weapons of the weak such as griping can serve to increase rather than threaten solidarity and that some of the attacks on discipline by military dissenters may be read as attempts to defend emotional cohesion against those who are seen as undermining its integrity. In this sense, those who express discontent with armed forces culture might be seen as paradoxical defenders of its noblest intentions.

WORKS CITED

Army Values. n.d. Accessed June 17, 2020. https://www.army.mil/values.

Cramer, Stuart. 1921. "Disciplining Americans." *North American Review* 214 (793): 774–785.

Dundes, Alan. 1971. "Folk Ideas as Units of Worldview." *Journal of American Folklore* 84, no. 331 (January–March): 93–103.

Foucault, Michel. (1975) 1995. *Discipline and Punish: The Birth of the Prison.* New York: Vintage.

Gilman, Lisa. 2012. "Oppositional Positioning: The Military Identification of Young Antiwar Veterans." In *Warrior Ways: Explorations in Modern Military Folklore*, edited by Eric A. Eliason and Tad Tuleja, 181–201. Logan: Utah State University Press.

Goffman, Erving. 1961. *Asylums: Essays on the Social Situation of Mental Patients and Other Inmates.* New York: Anchor Books.

Hankey, Donald. 1917. *A Student in Arms.* New York: E. P. Dutton.

Remarque, Erich Maria. (1928) 1982. *All Quiet on the Western Front.* Translated by A. W. Wheen. New York: Ballantine.

Ricks, Thomas E. 2007. *Making the Corps.* New York: Scribner.

Scott, James C. 1985. *Weapons of the Weak: Everyday Forms of Peasant Resistance.* New Haven: Yale University Press.

Thoreau, Henry David. (1849) 2008. "Civil Disobedience." In *Walden, Civil Disobedience, and Other Writings*, 3rd ed., edited by William Rossi. New York: W. W. Norton.

von Steuben, Friedrich Wilhelm, Baron. (1779) 1966. *Regulations for the Order and Discipline of the Troops of the United States.* Facsimile in *Baron von Steuben and His Regulations*, by Joseph R. Riling. Philadelphia: Riling Arms Books.

Wasdin, Howard E., and Stephen Templin. 2011. *Seal Team Six: Memoirs of an Elite Navy Seal Sniper.* New York: St. Martin's.

Part I
Weapons of the Weak

1

On the Griping of Grunts

Angus Kress Gillespie

IN THE LATTER YEARS OF WORLD WAR II, a baby-faced artist from
Mountain Park, New Mexico, was among the most famous soldiers in the
American army. Bill Mauldin, born in 1921 into a military family, joined the
US Army in 1940, served with the Forty-fifth Infantry Division in North
Africa and Italy, and left the service at the end of the war with a Legion of
Merit. His fame rested not on battlefield heroics, but on the cartoons he
drew, beginning in February 1944, for the service newspaper *Stars and Stripes.*
In six of these a week, he depicted ordinary combat infantrymen—those we
today would call "grunts"—not as the ramrod-stiff stalwarts of regimental
fantasy but as tough, disheveled, grumbling, plucky souls making the best
they could of terrible situations. Mauldin's "Up Front" cartoons, often featuring the haggard foxhole buddies Willie and Joe, were enormously popular with American troops, who saw him as their spokesman and defender
against an impersonal military system (Severo 2003).

Mauldin did have detractors, especially among the brass whose privileges he sometimes mocked. According to one Mauldin biographer, the
cartoonist ran into trouble with three-star general John Lee when Mauldin
ridiculed Lee's management of gasoline supplies (DePastino 2008, 185).
And his cartoons so offended another general, George S. Patton, that for
a time the survival of "Up Front" seemed in jeopardy. Famously devoted
to spit-and-polish discipline, Patton saw in the chronically unshaven Willie
and Joe examples of scruffy and potentially insubordinate laxity—griping,
"unsoldierly" characters who were bad for morale. They were not as disrep-
utable, perhaps, as the two battle-weary soldiers whom Patton had slapped
during the Sicilian campaign—an action that brought him a reprimand
from General Eisenhower (Blumenson 1985, 209–210). But to Patton
being bearded and sardonic was bad enough, and in 1944 he threatened to

DOI: 10.7330/9781607329527.c001

block distribution of *Stars and Stripes* to his troops unless the paper dropped Mauldin. At that point his superiors arranged a meeting between him and the cartoonist, where, it was hoped, some compromise to the morale question might be achieved.

The meeting took place at Patton's Luxembourg headquarters in February 1945. Mauldin describes it vividly in his memoir *The Brass Ring*. After greeting Mauldin with disarming cordiality, he writes, Old Blood and Guts quickly launched into a tirade that came close to equating "Up Front" with Bolshevik propaganda. What on earth did Mauldin mean, Patton demanded to know, by drawing "those god-awful things you call soldiers."

> You know goddamn well you're not drawing an accurate representation
> of the American soldier. You make them look like goddamn bums. No
> respect for the army, their officers, or themselves. You know as well as I do
> that you can't have an army without respect for officers. What are you try-
> ing to do, incite a goddamn mutiny? (Mauldin 1973, 312)

"Sergeant," he concluded, "I don't know what *you* think you're trying to do, but the krauts ought to pin a medal on you for helping them mess up discipline for us" (315).

Patton then produced copies of two Mauldin cartoons, which he claimed had no discernible purpose but to "create disrespect for officers." I'll look at other Mauldin cartoons later in the chapter, but these two provide a useful starting point, as they illustrate nicely why Mauldin's grumbling grunts—so beloved among GIs themselves—offended old-school disciplinarians such as George Patton.

In the first cartoon, US Army jeeps driving through a liberated French town are being "deluged by flowers, fruit, and wine," while some American soldiers, "taking advantage of the general confusion," are "pelting the convoy commander . . . with riper examples of the fruit" (Mauldin 1973, 315). "My, sir," says a junior officer in the caption, "what an enthusiastic welcome." In the second (uncaptioned) cartoon, GIs wait to enter a USO show featuring "Girls, Girls, Girls" while officers wait at the stage door, ready to take the girls out after the performance. In both drawings, the overt theme is resentment of rank and the subtext the grunts' understanding that the hardest workers in the war—the Willies and Joes—are not being given the respect their privations should have earned them.

To Mauldin, this unequal privilege was not only unjust; it was damaging to morale. As he explained to Patton in a remarkable passage, he saw his drawings as in a sense *restoring* morale, by letting soldiers see that at least somebody sympathized with them and was able to express their grievances in a humorous format. Here's what he told the general:

> The soldier is back in his foxhole stewing about officers and thinking he's got the short end of the stick in everything, even women . . . He feels there's been an injustice, and if he stews long enough about this, or about any of the other hundreds of things soldiers stew about, he's not going to be thinking about his job. All right, sir, he picks up a paper and he reads a letter or sees a cartoon by some other soldier who feels the same way, and he says, "Hell, somebody else said it for me," and he goes back to his job. (1973, 317)

This explanation was lost on Patton, who retorted, "You can't run an army like a mob." But it's a sensitive and pragmatic explanation, and in proposing that soldiers' griping provides a restorative or "venting" function, it clarifies a great deal more than Bill Mauldin's cartoons.

I will return to this idea in a moment, as I examine other examples of World War II grumbling. But let me first clarify the scope of this inquiry by saying what I mean—and what I think Mauldin meant—by "griping." To George Patton, it seems, *any* objection to authority opened the road to mob rule. In daily practice, though—and not just in the military—it is worthwhile to distinguish among different forms of complaining, since not all complaints have the same gravity, the same impact on morale, the same ability to relieve frustration, or the same expectation of achieving positive results.

THREE MODES OF OBJECTION

Mauldin's cartoons, like many other satires, are a form of objection—a behavior that expresses dissatisfaction with mistreatment. I would suggest separating such objections into three main types: Complaining, Whining, and Griping. I borrow these terms from Robin Kowalski's work on "positivity in the negative," where they are used interchangeably along with other terms such as grumbling, venting, and kvetching (2002, 1024). In the military context, it's useful to see these behaviors not as interchangeable but as distinct forms of objection to official mistreatment. Here is how I would define the distinctions.

The first type of objection, *Complaining*, I see as a legitimate observation about injustice or stupidity, directed against an authority that is violating its duty to treat one fairly. When soldiers say that they haven't been paid in three months, that they have filled out paperwork and received no response, or that they have been issued Kevlar vests that do not stop bullets, they are saying that are being victimized by a military system that is failing to provide some benefit that is required by law or at least by commonly accepted understandings of service protocol.

Because it identifies a clear violation of established practice, Complaining of this sort is meant seriously and is expected to be taken seriously. When the complainer mounts such an objection, even though official channels may be slow to respond, he or she still has the right to expect a response. If one is lacking, the complainer may issue a formal complaint with his or her commanding officer or, if that doesn't work, with higher authorities such as the IG or a congressional representative. For example, when Navy psychologist Mark Russell (chapter 4) "jumps the chain" of command to seek better treatment for returning combat vets, he is engaging in this first type of legitimized Complaining.

Complaining is thus at the "high end" of the objection continuum. At the opposite end—the less legitimate end—fall those objections that I would call *Whining*. Psychologist Guy Winch draws the distinction clearly: "Complaining involves voicing fair and legitimate dissatisfactions with the goal of attaining a resolution or remedy . . . And when the dissatisfactions we voice are trivial or inconsequential and not worthy of special attention, we are whining." Experiments have shown that even children as young as three years are able to distinguish between these legitimate and trivial forms of complaining (Winch 2012).

Whining tends to be less focused on violations of justice than on affronts to what the Whiner considers his dignity or comfort. As with Complaining, humor rarely enters the picture here. The whiner, primed to take offense at the least provocation, sees the system's intrusions on his or her perceived well-being as evidence not of the system's general oppressiveness but as inconveniences designed especially for him or her. "My shoes are the wrong size." "Why do I always get guard duty on weekends?" "Sergeant Brady has it in for me." These are the complaints you hear from a chronic whiner. They are generally not taken seriously either by the brass or by the whiner's fellow soldiers. Like three-year-olds, they too can see what complaints are trivial.

This is not to say that are trivial to the whiner. Indeed, it's reasonable to see Whining as a cry of distress. It's an expression of frustration, fatigue, dissatisfaction, or discontent but one that lacks any stoical acceptance of a common situation and any humorous sense of self-awareness. Whiners do not, like Mauldin's readers, see that "someone else" has aired their grievances for them. Rather, they feel themselves to be singularly abused and alone. That is why they are shunned rather than embraced.

The third type of objection is what I call *Griping*. A kind of middle ground between Complaining and Whining, Griping tends to be lighter than the former, more serious than the latter—and yet much more resigned to a difficult situation, so long as someone acknowledges that it *is* difficult. Thus Griping usually takes the form of "humorous complaining," a social strategy adopted by those who feel abused and yet are able to accept the abuse as a "benign violation." This is the paradox of humorous complaining. It comes into play "when something that is perceived to threaten a person's well-being, identity, or normative belief structure (i.e., a violation) simultaneously seems okay or acceptable (i.e., benign)" (McGraw, Warren, and Kan 2015, 1154).

It is Griping that was represented in Mauldin's cartoons and that also provided the spark for other creative efforts by the long-suffering dogfaces of World War II. In reviewing some examples of these efforts here, I will show how they reveal the "venting" function that Bill Mauldin himself so clearly defined and that—General Patton's outrage notwithstanding—may have actually improved American troops' morale.

GRIPING: A CLOSER LOOK

Griping has probably been a feature of military life for as long as there have been militaries. Soldiers in all centuries and all places have had difficult, often perilous, jobs, and it would be surprising if members of even crack units such as the Roman legions did not at moments give way to venting their frustrations. So it must have been throughout history. During the American Civil War, Southern troops referenced their meager diet of boiled peanuts in the sardonic folksong "Goober Peas." During World War I, one doughboy, Corporal Adel Storey, illustrated the joking resignation to misery that is characteristic of griping: "It is so muddy," he wrote to his parents, "that I think I am getting web-footed . . . for we eat in mud, sleep in mud, and live in mud, and if there is anything else to do, I guess we do it in mud too" (cited in Cowing and Cooper 1919, 56–57). At about this same time, *Stars and Stripes*, then the official newspaper of the American Expeditionary Force, began to include items of humorous dissatisfaction, such as the story "People We'd Like to Meet," which ran on February 15, 1918. Among the people the writer wanted to pummel for transgressions were "the composer who wrote the Reveille call," "the contractor who made those field shoes," and "the packer who concocted that 'canned Willy'" ("People" 1918)—a trio of villains responsible not for injustice but for creating an uncomfortable world that had to be humorously endured.

If the miseries of the trenches created the twentieth century's first wave of colorful griping, World War II brought this soldierly tradition to full flower. Its ubiquity among GIs is suggested by a 1943 photograph from a Virginia army camp. It shows a sergeant named John Haar registering a grievance in a "machine" called a "Gripe-o-Graf" (Virginia Press Photo 1943). The machine label lists typical sources of grumbling including no dough, no date, bad chow, bad weather, no gas, no butts, no Cokes, no pass, no furlough, hikes, and miscellaneous. The idea behind the machine—in fact a cardboard box decorated with lights and wires—was that a soldier could insert a written criticism into a slot on the top, and the machine would register on a dial the soldier's degree of dissatisfaction. The machine is not designed to correct the soldier's problem, only to acknowledge it, and this makes it an appropriate instrument for the "management" of griping. Unlike the whiner, the military griper does not take bad chow personally, and he does not expect the machine to feed him steak. It is enough that the phony instrument takes notice of the hardship that the GI is putting up with.

This is exactly what Mauldin's cartoons were doing, even though many of the gripes he noted were more serious than bad chow, and the whole point of his work was to recognize that fact. In his autobiographical account *Up Front*, he wrote, "I'm convinced that the infantry is the group in the Army which gives more and gets less than anybody else. I draw pictures for and about dogfaces because I know what their life is like, and I understand their gripes" (Mauldin 1944, 5). In giving voice to the soldiers' frustrations, Mauldin also tried to give the reader at home some idea of what the infantry goes through. "Dig a hole in your back yard while it is raining," he wrote. "Sit in the hole until the water climbs up around your ankles. Pour cold mud down your shirt collar. Sit there for forty-eight hours, and, so there is no danger of your dozing off, imagine that a guy is sneaking around waiting for a chance to club you on the head, or set your house on fire" (143–144). That clearly was written by somebody who had been there.

In many of his cartoons, Mauldin walked a thin line between satirizing the Army and celebrating the average soldier's stoicism. Consider, for example, his drawing of a weary and bedraggled GI, rifle strung over his shoulder, marching through the mud and rain as he escorts three similarly exhausted German prisoners to a prison camp. The caption repeats a line from a recent news item: "Fresh, spirited American troops, flushed with victory, are bringing in thousands of hungry, ragged, battle-weary prisoners" (Mauldin 1983, 174). The contrast between Mauldin's depicted reality and the official fiction could not be starker.

In another drawing, two soldiers hunker down in a foxhole as tracer bullets fly through the night sky. One soldier says to the other, "I feel like a fugitive from th' law of averages." Although he is acutely aware of the danger, rather than overtly complaining he is offering a blunt and clever assessment of the shared situation (Mauldin 1983, 145). In a third example, a bedraggled and unshaven soldier is about to receive an immunization shot from an overweight and bespectacled Army doctor. "Got anything for lead poisonin'?" the patient asks (206). Again, Mauldin sees the difficulty, even the absurdity, of his situation. He knows there is no immunization against enemy bullets. Yet he is not complaining or whining, but making a wry, grisly joke out of deadly peril. In both of these cases, we see the combination of stoicism and humor that constitutes Griping.

The Army was not oblivious to the extent of the Griping, and it apparently believed that such attacks on its protocols and authority had the potential for undermining unit cohesion and imperiling the war effort. Not all officers were as hostile as General Patton was to "unsoldierly" behavior, but there was a recognition in some senior circles that even humorous bitching, if left unchecked, might somehow divert enlisted personnel from doing their jobs. Patton himself snapped at cartoonist Mauldin: "If this soldier you're talking about is stewing it's because he hasn't got enough to do" and is therefore free to "bitch and beef and gripe and run around with beards" (Mauldin 1973, 317–318). That wasn't an official Army line, but it reflected a real fear.

To alleviate that fear, the Army in 1943 enlisted the combat grunt's own weapon, satirical humor, in a series of short animated training films featuring "Private Snafu." "The cartoon antithesis of Bill Mauldin's seasoned dog faces," Snafu was a good-hearted but lazy griper who represented "a potential threat inherent in the average GI, if he were not vigilant and did not play by the rules" (Birdwell 2005, 203). The films were the brainchild of the Oscar-winning director Frank Capra, a US Army major, and the scripts were supervised and often written in verse by Army captain Theodore Geisel, who was later to achieve fame as Dr. Seuss. Private Snafu was voiced by Warner Brothers' Mel Blanc (TCM Spotlight).

The Private Snafu films were designed to deliver with humor a message that conventional training films did more ponderously: by doing things obediently "the Army way," soldiers would ensure victory. By questioning the protocols or privations that came with the territory, as Private Snafu did in every episode, soldiers opened our boys up to risk and gave advantage to the enemy. The second film in the series, entitled "Gripes," focused specifically on how grumbling invited such disaster. In this short, directed by

Warner Brothers' Fritz Freleng (1943), we first see Private Snafu assigned to KP duty, doing dishes and peeling potatoes. He objects that KP duty was not what he had in mind when he joined the Army.

> I joined this here Army to join in the fun,
> A jab to the Japs and to button the Hun.

He resents having to clean up the camp, he resents standing in line, he resents having to submit to inoculations. Totally fed up with his situation, he muses aloud:

> If I ran this army, boy, I'm telling you,
> I'd make a few changes. That's just what I'd do.

Snafu then becomes sick and is hospitalized. In a delirious state, he has a dream that his troubles have disappeared. He is visited by a small, winged creature chomping a cigar and wearing socks, shorts, and a hat. This creature, he learns, is Technical Fairy, First Class. And the fairy has a "good notion: to give you some help, and a promotion." So Snafu is promoted to Master Sergeant Super Star, and he is told to take command. We next see him lounging in a recliner with a box of cigars as he announces over the public address system, "This camp is under new management."

Under Snafu's direction, all discipline is suspended. There is no more drill, no more saluting, no more cleaning latrines. Snafu is shown reclining in a king-sized bed, surrounded by beautiful women who cater to his every need. It is a Griper's dream come true. But then the scene is interrupted by the sound of airplanes, and the Technical Fairy appears with dire news:

> I beg pardon, sir, but you hear all that humming,
> I got a suspicion the Germans are coming.

He's right. The Germans mount an invasion. But the soldiers, lulled into inactivity under Snafu's lax regime, are unprepared and they scatter. Snafu, left alone, is killed by a German bomb. (His foolishness gets him killed in every episode.) The film ends with Private Snafu waking up from the dream and returning immediately to KP with new enthusiasm. This gives the Technical Fairy the opportunity to have the last word:

> The moral, Snafu, is the more that you work,
> The sooner we'll beat Hitler, that jerk.

And not only the more you work, but the more you do so willingly, smilingly, unquestioningly. The implicit lesson, here as in all the Private Snafu shorts, is that deviation from accepted practice can get you killed—and even complaining about that practice carries risks, because it lures soldiers away from the heads-down approach which is the "proper" soldier's attitude and the key to victory.

AN ATTACK ON MORALE?

The implicit assumption of the Private Snafu shorts was that if you were griping about your job, you weren't doing it effectively. They also seemed to suggest that gripers—at least extreme examples such as Private Snafu—were serious about wanting their sorry situations to be corrected: they didn't see the point of peeling potatoes or sleeping in mud and wanted the Army to make these unpleasantries go away. Griping, in other words, was a serious demand for change. And in demanding change, in voicing discontent with things as they were, the griper threatened that state of military bliss known as good morale. By pointing out things that everyone knew were distasteful (who wants to peel potatoes?), gripers would make others feel alienated from their jobs, from the system that required these jobs, and from their duties as US soldiers. According to this perspective, Patton may have been extreme, but he wasn't wrong. Griping wasn't harmless; it demoralized the troops.

That was the reasoning behind the Army's distaste for Griping. It sounds logical enough, and yet I believe it was wrong. In fact, a good case can be made for seeing Griping—not all Complaining, and certainly not Whining—not as a morale-buster, but as a morale-booster. This sounds counterintuitive, but there's good social science research that suggests it is true.

A benchmark of that research is a study done shortly after the war by sociologist Henry Elkin. Elkin, who had served both an enlisted man and as an officer during the war, argued that the Army is a classic example of a bureaucracy. In the military, soldiers were expected to uncomplainingly carry out orders given by superiors, even if the superiors were neither liked nor respected. Off duty, the soldiers were under no such constraints and were free to give expression to their true feelings. Thus their everyday, unmonitored speech revealed "a general rebelliousness, expressed in various shades of negativism, from mildly cynical humor to scathing denunciation." But this negativism, he noted, was purely verbal. In expressing it, soldiers were achieving the emotional satisfaction that Mauldin tried in vain to explain to Patton. But the soldiers were neither expecting nor demanding change. Griping and general negativism "were symbolic affirmations of independence and strength, showing that the G.I. did not want to be considered a mere cog in the Army machine" (Elkin 1946, 409). Rather, they were making those small acts of resistance to bureaucratic conformity that Erving Goffman (1961) would later see at work among "total institution" inmates.

In addition, Elkin noted, Griping among World War II GIs was a standard means of establishing social contact. When one soldier met another, a Gripe could be a conversational gambit, a bonding tactic. Much as civilians might talk about unpleasant but "unfixable" weather, soldiers would talk—often disparagingly, often humorously—about those aspects of Army life that were unpleasant, unchangeable, and shared by everyone in an enlisted person's uniform. The Gripe became a kind of mild, in-group "war story"—a bitching but not bitter reflection that "We're in this together." Griping may have registered alienation from the military system, but on the personal level it brought buddies together. For that reason, I would argue, we should see it as an important means of improving morale.

A half century after Elkins wrote his article, psychologist Robin Kowalski (2002) published a paper in the *Journal of Clinical Psychology* that confirmed that complaining could have positive benefits, both for the complainers and for those around them. Coming from the perspective of "positive psychology," Kowalski made the point that, despite its bad reputation, complaining can sometimes exhibit a "positivity in negativity." She noted that, in a process she called "cathartic complaining," people are allowed to vent, "to get their frustrations off their chests" and that they "typically feel better after expressing the complaints," in other words that they enjoy an experience of "improved affect" (2002, 1028–1029).

In addition, confirming what Elkin had said at the end of the war, Kowalski stressed the interpersonal benefits of complaining. Some complaining, she wrote, can serve as a "social lubricant" or "icebreaker" that makes it easier for people to bond and establish relationships. This tool can be particularly beneficial "when the state of affairs is truly dissatisfying." "Complaining allows people to start conversations with others with whom initiating conversation might otherwise be difficult. Complaining provides a script for an interaction that would otherwise, at least initially, be scriptless" (2002, 1032). It's not hard to conclude from this observation that griping might help soldiers bond more easily with their comrades, thus contributing to unit cohesion and good morale. This finding seems even more likely to be the case when the sharing of grievances is not expected to yield changes in the system—that is, when soldiers understand their griping as an expression rather than a challenge.

The discipline of folklore may provide some additional insight to this situation. We might think of the exchange of complaints as a military unit's folk activity, an example of what the eminent folklorist Dan Ben-Amos once identified as a type of "artistic communication" within small groups (1971, 12). Seen in this way, griping is both an outer-directed and an inner-directed activity. It mounts an attack, often humorous, against overweening authority as it solidifies the bonds of those oppressed by that authority by allowing them to circulate jibes that are their own form of resistance. And yet this resistance, as Elkin and Kowalski understood, remains symbolic, providing less a threat to institutional order than a strengthening of bonds.

The pioneering Elkin paper postdated the war, but even during the war, common sense might have led some observers to reach similar conclusions. Common sense was indeed a factor in the Bill Mauldin case, in terms of what came after his meeting with Patton. Shortly after that encounter, Mauldin's friend Will Lang, another combat journalist, described the meeting in a story for *Time* magazine, reporting that the general and the cartoonist had been unswayed by each other's arguments. "After forty-five minutes with Old Blood & Guts," Lang wrote, "Young Gags & Grime emerged grinning, reporting last week: 'I came out with all my hide on. We parted good friends, but I don't think we changed each other's opinions.' Mauldin's GIs remained unwashed, unsquelched" (Lang 1945, cited in DePastino 2008, 195).

Patton heard of the *Time* story from Harry Butcher, a Navy captain who was an aide to Allied supreme commander Dwight D. Eisenhower. Patton did not take it well. He reminded Butcher of how (in his view) Bruce Bairnsfather's cartoons had hurt British morale in World War I, and he fumed, "If that little s.o.b. ever comes in the Third Army area again, I'll throw him in jail" (Hirshson 2002, 607). He had made this threat before without effect, but this time there was reaction from Ike himself, who had already reprimanded Patton over the slapping incidents. In April, two months after the Luxembourg meeting, Eisenhower "forbade any general from interfering with or criticizing anything in *Stars and Stripes*" (607). Hands-off material of course included Willie and Joe cartoons, which led Butcher to comment in his diary that General Patton had "lost the battle of Mauldin" (607).

In the end, then, it was another hard-driving general, not a psychologist or a civilian soft on discipline, who came to Mauldin's aid. Eisenhower, who was a fine reader of men and who had a better sense of humor than did Patton, evidently understood that in a military context Griping can serve a real purpose—a military purpose. It can act as a social safety valve to ventilate frustrations, and it can create solidarity among those in harm's way more effectively than peeling potatoes or shining buttons.

Ike understood that low-level, humorous griping was not mutiny and that tolerating it might actually improve morale. Patton, who (we should not forget) was deeply respected by his men, did not understand this, so he went down in history not as a soldier's soldier but as a by-the-book martinet and a "flamboyant nut" (Mauldin 1973, 185). And the man who went down in history as the champion of the dogface, the beleaguered GI, the griping grunt, was a stubborn little SOB who drew cartoons.

ACKNOWLEDGMENTS

I first began to work out some of these matters in discussions with Richard Burns, Carol Burke, and Eric A. Eliason as we worked together on a panel of military folklore at the 2015 Annual Meeting of the American Folklore Society (AFS). I presented an early version of this chapter at the Annual Meeting of the AFS in 2017. My colleague Nikolai Burlakoff was of valuable assistance in refining the contents of this chapter, and for this I am grateful. Thanks also to Tad Tuleja for weighing in with a strong editorial hand.

WORKS CITED

Ben-Amos, Dan. 1971. "Toward a Definition of Folklore in Context." *Journal of American Folklore* 84 (331): 3–15.

Birdwell, Michael. 2005. "Technical Fairy First Class: Is This Any Way to Run an Army? Private Snafu and World War II." *Historical Journal of Film, Radio, and Television* 25 (2): 203–212.

Blumenson, Martin. 1974. *The Patton Papers 1940–1945.* Boston: Houghton Mifflin.

Cowing, Kemper F., and Courtney Ryler Cooper, ed. 1919. *Dear Folks at Home.* New York: Houghton Mifflin.

DePastino, Todd. 2008. *Bill Mauldin: A Life Up Front.* New York: W. W. Norton.

Elkin, Henry. 1946. "Aggressive and Erotic Tendencies in Army Life." *American Journal of Sociology* 51 (5): 408–413.

Freleng, Fritz, director. 1943. *Gripes.* https://www.youtube.com/watch?v=wFI7WvwpGJQ.

Goffman, Erving. 1961. *Asylums: Essays on the Social Situation of Mental Patients and Other Inmates.* New York: Anchor Books.

Hirshson, Stanley. 2002. *General Patton: A Soldier's Life.* New York: Harper Collins.

Kowalski, Robin W. 2002. "Whining, Griping, and Complaining: Positivity in the Negativity." *Journal of Clinical Psychology* 58 (9): 1023–1035.

Lang, Will. 1945. "G.I. Mauldin v. G. Patton." *Time*, March 26, 1945.

Mauldin, Bill. 1944. *Up Front.* New York: Henry Holt and Company.

Mauldin, Bill. 1973. *Bill Mauldin: The Brass Ring.* New York: Berkley Medallion.

Mauldin, Bill. 1983. *Bill Mauldin's Army: Bill Mauldin's Greatest World War II Cartoons.* New York: Presidio Press.

McGraw, Peter, Caleb Warren, and Christina Kan. 2015. "Humorous Complaining." *Journal of Consumer Research* 41 (5): 1153–1171.

"People We'd Like to Meet" 1918. *Stars and Stripes*, February 15. http://frontiers.loc.gov/service/sgp/sgpsas/1918/191802/19180215/07.pdf.

Severo, Richard. 2003. "Bill Maudlin, Cartoonist Who Showed World War II through G.I. Eyes, Dies at 81." *New York Times*, January 23, 2003.

TCM Spotlight. "Private Snafu Shorts." 1943–1946. http://www.tcm.com/this-month/article.html?isPreview=&id=1112957%7C1111753&name=Private-Snafu-Shorts.

Virginia Press Photo. 1943. "World War II Doughboys Gripe O Graf." March 19. https://i.pinimg.com/564x/5d/58/10/5d58103e3521a7bfbbf91d8584a64f49.jpg.

Winch, Guy. 2012. "The Difference between Complaining and Whining." October 10. *Psychology Today*.com. https://www.psychologytoday.com/blog/the-squeaky-wheel/201210/the-difference-between-complaining-and-whining.

2

Back Chat

Subversion and Conformity in Dominion Cartoons of the World Wars

Christina M. Knopf

IN WORLD WAR I, NEARLY 9 MILLION MEN of the United Kingdom and British Empire served in the British Army. Officers were present in the trenches—indeed, part of the platoon officer's job was to care for the welfare of his troops, including daily inspections of their feet for health—but familiarity was discouraged, and, because of the size of the military, higher-ranking officers, despite their presence, were not readily visible (Buff 2014). The large numbers of men were organized and coordinated through strict military hierarchy and discipline, which enabled soldiers to endure the horrid conditions of trench warfare. From brutal training to severe field punishment, and from the reward of food to the penalty of dangerous duty, conformity and obedience were both encouraged and enforced. Mutiny—rebellion against authority—was the worst military offense, punishable by death, because it was a direct assault on military discipline (Sheffield 2014).

In this situation of rigid control, even soldiers who were devoted to their officers could sometimes feel oppressed by the military hierarchy. Their resentment was often expressed not in direct rebellion but in acts of creative insubordination couched in humor. A good example appears in a wartime cartoon drawn by the Australian soldier Frank Dunne (1919, 29). In the sketch, one of Dunne's fellow "diggers," having endured months of regimentation, finally stands up to an abusive officer. "I want none of your back chat," says the officer, and the soldier responds with a raised fist, "Well, take one from the front." The double entendre of "front" shows both that the soldier is willing to confront his abuser face-to-face and that, perhaps unlike the officer, he has seen the horrors of battle.

Such insubordination in a live interaction could have earned the belligerent soldier harsh punishment, as he would have been seen as a threat to the strict authority that was required to train and mobilize thousands

DOI: 10.7330/9781607329527.c002

of troops for the prolonged conflict. But in cartoons and other forms of humor, such resistance was permissible, as military leaders came to understand that humor provided soldiers a means of coping not only with the brutality of war but also with the strict military lifestyle (Shaw 2014).

In 2008, recognizing that a sense of humor gives soldiers this advantage, one British officer, Brigadier J. Nazareth, published *The Psychology of Military Humour* as a resource for the service officer wishing to use humor strategically to alleviate the strain of military life. He noted specifically that humor had allowed British soldiers to extend their bravery through massive defeats—during the Battle of the Somme, the offensive at Passchendaele, and the Battle of Aubers in the First World War—and that in World War II the Germans tried to replicate that emboldening humor. In his study of soldier cartoons from the World Wars, moreover, historian Jay Casey revealed that the British Empire's involvement in World War I resulted in realistic comic images that "traded in war's brutality and insanity" (2009, 07.4). Casey also noted that Allied cartoons of World War II, by "subvert[ing] the visual etiquette applied so rigidly with other editorial decisions" in military publications, allowed soldiers to accurately portray attitudes "about the circumstances of war in which they found themselves" (07.8). So the utility of humor in wartime, and of cartoons in particular, is well established.

HUMOR AS RESISTANCE AND CONTROL

To the extent that military humor may be seen as a special case of workplace, or occupational, humor, sociologist Erving Goffman's (1959, 1969) work can help us to understand it as a type of strategic interaction that can be used to influence the behavior of others and to establish and maintain individual and group identities through conformity to or deviation from social expectations. Such studies add theoretical confirmation to Nazareth's anecdotal accounts of humor in the military. Nazareth indicated, for example, that "in the military environment," though "the subordinate has a feeling of respect for his seniors, at the same time he has many occasions to resent their authority"; sometimes the resentment is expressed in the guise of humor, which allows the subordinate to safely release nervous energy (2008, 75). In his view, humor has a unifying effect "important in building up *esprit de corps*" and in making organizational frustrations tolerable without undermining authority.

Owen Hanley Lynch's investigations of workplace humor make a similar point by demonstrating that organizational humor can serve functions of resistant subversion and of "concertive" control. Lynch notes that "safety

valve resistance humor" (2009, 456) is humor used to create distance from
the constraining effects of hierarchy and "concertive control humor occurs
when ingroup members use humor discourse to ensure all . . . activity con-
forms to ingroup members' standards and norms" (453). Just as resistance
humor "reduces the sting of control . . . but does not directly undermine
it" (456), control humor "is masked as ingroup, specialization humor, but it
still contains effective control measures" (453). This idea is reaffirmed in Jay
Black's (2010) study of comic strips of the 1950s, such as *Li'l Abner*, where
parodic and satiric humor offers a safe venue for sociopolitical dissent,
making criticism palatable. And, because parody imitates recognized con-
ventions or characteristics, as Helene A. Shugart (1999) argues, it implicitly
and inherently *reinforces and supports* the focus of its mockery. In this analysis,
even subversive humor—such as the digger's threat of violence against his
superior—may subtly ensure that colleagues conform to the group's norms,
thus preserving in-group self-identity.

In this chapter, building on such findings, I consider how cartooning
provided Dominion soldiers with an opportunity to oppose strict military
authority and give officers "back chat," while also sustaining them as members of an organization doing the business of war. Using critical dramaturgical thematic analysis (inspired by Boje 2004), I consider both semantic/
explicit and latent/implicit themes in Dominion soldier cartoons to consider
the manifest and inherent features of soldier humor (for more on thematic
analysis, see Boyatzis 1998). Analysis focuses on cartoons created by and/or
for members of the military in trench newspapers, regimental journals, and
souvenir books. This material is a proven valuable resource for understanding the soldier experience (see Chapman 2016; Chapman and Ellin 2012),
and a broad representation of publications helps to more fully capture soldier culture in Dominion forces. Although every effort was made to ensure
adequate representation of British and Dominion soldier cartoons from the
world wars in this study, sources were ultimately selected based on availabil-
ity. The ephemeral nature of wartime military publications—their localized
audiences, limited circulation, and cheap production—has resulted in a kind
of data decay that is compounded by the logistical limitations of research
access, such as cost and location. Appendix 2.A, at the end of this essay,
provides a complete list of the primary sources considered.

THEMES OF SUBVERSION: FOUR COMPLAINTS

In the cartoons I've analyzed, those that directly mock the officer class are
pointed in their distinction between those in command and those under

command. Four main themes appear with regard to the representation of military authority, and each of them presents the officer class as radically deficient in qualities admired by the soldier. To the cartoonists reflecting the views of the frontline fighters, officers differ from enlisted soldiers in appearance, common sense, temperament, and sensitivity, as well as in actual battlefield experience.

APPEARANCE: THE "BROWN TYPE"

Officers and soldiers are not the same; they are built and look differently. A World War II cartoon by Bing Coughlin (1946) has the diminutive and hapless hero, Herbie, reporting for sick parade. The medical officer informs him, "A pain in your abdomen! . . . Young man, officers have abdomens, sergeants have stomachs, . . . you have a bellyache!" (31). In this example, even anatomically, officers are different. In other cartoons, they are frequently depicted as tall, barrel-chested men, with chiseled, square-jawed faces sporting neat moustaches. They carry canes or riding crops. Their uniforms are crisp and clean. They are what David Langdon illustrated as a "Brown Type" or Army man (cited in Ward-Jackson 1943, 16). By comparison, the average enlisted man is short and slouched, with skinny legs and a paunchy belly inside a rumpled, dirty uniform. His face is either youthful and free of facial hair or covered in unkempt moustaches or beard stubble. For example, see figure 2.1: This cartoon by Cottrell in the Summer 1918 issue of *Blighty* is typical of the contrast between the polished and proper appearance of officers and the "dilapidated" appearance of enlisted soldiers.

At the semiotic level of analysis, this difference in appearance may seem minor, especially because comic art depends on the use of stereotypes to quickly convey information to readers (see, e.g., Strömberg 2010). At the latent level, however, this is one of the most subversive elements in soldier cartooning. The uniform is a key feature of military identity and discipline. Therefore, cartoons that portray shabby or repurposed uniforms, such as Cecil Hartt's (1917, n.p.) illustration of shrapnel helmets being used for cooking, are a direct sign of disrespect to the military order. Moreover, soldiers who strictly conform to military dress codes are viewed by other soldiers as naive outsiders, strictly adhering to a sartorial ideal that has no place in the real world of war. The contrast is drawn expertly in a World War II cartoon by Coughlin (2008), where Herbie and his friends look suspiciously over their shoulders at "the new reinforcements comin' up with their brass all shined" (82).

The imagery of the disheveled soldier is part of what Tim Cook (2008) referred to as a theme of antiheroism in the culture created by the

Figure 2.1. Cottrell (Summer 1918). Cartoon in *Blighty*. Retrieved
January 13, 2019, from https://digital.nls.uk/91026994 (archived at
the National Library of Scotland; see appendix 2.A).

civilian-soldiers of the Canadian Corps. "In a war where soldiers were elevated to heroes by civilians, the soldiers often chose to emphasize the antiheroic qualities in their cultural products. These anti-heroes, characters who
lacked traditional heroic qualities such as courage or self-sacrifice, became
the soldiers' heroes" (174). However, even though the antiheroes' rejection
of heroic attributes was an act of resistance to military propaganda, the
creation of the antiheroic characters relied on soldiers' intimate familiarity
with proper military behavior. Therefore, depicting the sloppy soldier as
an antihero may be simultaneously a show of subversion and a strategic
reminder of how a good soldier dresses.

COMMON SENSE: THE "BRAINLESS" OFFICER

Officers may look sharp, but they often act quite dull. In one Frank Dunne cartoon archived at the National Library of Australia, an officer directs a digger on a trench telephone to not "curse so much." It goes on, "Use tact and speak politely so they'll think an Officer is talking." The digger responds, "This cow must thing [*sic*] that already. 'ees just called me brainless" (Dunne n.d.). In another, Dunne (1919) depicts one digger asking another, "And did the O.C. know that the trench had fallen in?" The answer speaks to the perception of officers' obliviousness when the second digger replies, "No; we had to dig him out to tell him" (14). A cartoon by Burke Goffney in the June 1918 edition of *The Kia Ora Coo-ee* demonstrates such brainlessness when a commanding officer tells a quartermaster to "dig a hole and bury" the heap of sand behind the stores (in Kent [1918] 1981, issue 18). Such a lack of logic is likewise reflected in a World War II cartoon by Bing Coughlin (1946) in which soldiers unloading heavy ammunition from a truck—a task under which the physical labor is obvious—are commanded, "Drop wot yer doin' an' get over here fer P.T. [physical training]" (103). David Langdon (n.d.) depicted officers as little more than experts in clichés (52), and Coughlin (1946) implied they are incapable of making decisions without the assistance of their military-assigned servants (101). Military bureaucracy has been called "organized anarchy" that inhibits military efficiency and success because of its reinforced ambiguities, misdirection of problems, misuse of participants, overabundance of information, excessive demands, and selectivity (Sabrosky, Thompson, and McPherson 1982). Thus, expressions of officer idiocy via absurd adherence to protocol in comparison to the savvy wit of soldiers simultaneously subvert authority while celebrating empowering the practical knowledge and experience of subordinates. (For more on the strict adherence to regulations, see Tuleja's discussion of "robot soldiers" in the introduction of this volume.)

TEMPERAMENT: THE "CALLOUS COW"

Officers' lack of common sense segues easily into a lack of commiseration with the enlisted. Frank Dunne (1919) indicates this with a tongue-in-cheek cartoon in which one soldier is relaying communication from a trench phone to another soldier, who asks, "Who's at the other end?" The phone operator replies, "He says, 'An officer and a gentlemen,'" to which the first exclaims, "Well, tell them that they can't both speak at once" (3). Another Dunne cartoon is far more direct, describing a sergeant as a "callous cow": "when Fritz [the German military] sends over tear gas it only makes him laugh" (1919, 8). Bruce Bairnsfather (1927) wonders, "Do colonels eat their young?" as one directs a terrified private to reconnoiter an old barn for enemy machine guns and, if found, to draw their fire (100). In actuality, attrition warfare in World War I is thought to have provided justification and rationalization for losses sustained by the British Expeditionary Forces (Strachan 2014).

A World War II cartoon by David Langdon (n.d.) emphasized officer cruelty with a drawing of an officer who shoots the thumb off a saluting soldier, berating him with "perhaps that'll teach you to keep your thumb in line with your hand when you salute" (9). Such a cartoon allows soldiers to achieve solidarity in shared commiseration at their plight. But it also has a more subtle subversive subtext. The salute, a customary way of recognizing an individual of superior rank, is the most basic of military courtesies integral to establishing military discipline. The poor execution of a salute, such as improper placement of the thumb, is, therefore, a rejection of military discipline—and, as noted by Alexandra Jaffe (1988), manipulation of the standard rules of saluting may be used for expressing individual attitudes toward the establishment. For such subversion to be enacted, one, of course, must first know the rules in order to know how to bend them, and so this cartoon reinforces proper behavior in the act of violating it.

Inexperience: "One Long Loaf"

The alleged mean streak in officers is exacerbated by the perception of their distance from the front lines. Those in command are observed, and thus portrayed, as having the easy jobs of war. Throughout the Great War, European *poilu* (soldier) humor was very critical of the *embusqués* (the shirkers), chiefly wealthy civilians on the home front and the military officers with posts safely away from the trenches (see Daughton 2000). The perceived idleness of officers and staff is a prominent theme in Frank Dunne's (1919) cartoons. In one, a quartermaster tells a griping digger that everyone gets corns in war including him, and the digger retorts, "But—blast yer!—I've gotta walk on mine!" (2). The implication is that officers do not march. In another cartoon, a digger puns that if "bread is the 'staff of life'" the "life of the staff" is "one long loaf" (32). Dunne also comments on the seeming detachment of officers from the war when "The Genial Brass Hat" remarks to a couple of diggers that things are pretty quiet today and a "Candid Digger" answers, "What with the birds singin' 'en you blokes strollin' 'round, a man'd hardly know there wuz a————war on!" (21). Bruce Bairnsfather (1917, n.p.) refers to officers as "Birds of Ill Omen," implying they are only seen in the

Bill— on leave from the trenches—meets
a pal on the Staff in London ——
Which is which?

Figure 2.2. Cecil Hartt
(1917). *Humorosities by an
Australian Soldier.* Archived at
the State Library of Victoria
(see appendix 2.A).

trenches prior to an offensive, and when one of Dunne's (1919) cartoon officers inquires, "Have you sufficient volunteers for the raid to-night?" a sergeant, similarly, quips, "No, you're just in time for it" (15).

Hartt (1917) noted officers as embusqué with an illustration of a smiling, clean-shaven man in a crisp, pristine uniform shaking hands with a bearded man, cigarette hanging from his mouth, wearing a rumpled uniform, rifle slung over one shoulder and satchel over the other, weighted down by a pack on his back and a bayonet on his hip (see figure 2.2). The caption reads, "Bill—on leave from the trenches—meets a pal on the Staff in London——Which is which?" (n.p.).

The December 1, 1917, edition of the *Listening Post* similarly describes the sergeant as someone who "never does anything he can get out of" (19), and the captain as one who commands a company by seeing that the " 'Subs' [Lieutenants] do all the work," who rides a horse while the men march, and who "doesn't carry a pack, but sees that everyone else carries one" (20). Similarly, "An Anzac Alphabet" proclaims, "M is the Major *observing from latitudes* / Tending to strained and discomforting attitudes" (J.W.S. Henderson in AWM 2010, 136; emphasis added). A Bing Coughlin (1946) cartoon in World War II revisited the class distinctions of the poilu and embusqué of the previous war with an officer in the chow line; though the available food consists of stew, prunes, and tea, this officer requests a ragout of beef with chestnut sauce, providing the confused cook with a small bag of chestnuts for the sauce (97).

RESISTANCE AND OPPOSITION

Whether comparing the appearance, intelligence, temperament, or experiences of the officers to the enlisted, these cartoons present a stark contrast between the official imagery and ideas of the military and the lived experiences of war. The phrase "The ideal and the real" is a sentiment repeated throughout British and Dominion cartoon humor of the World Wars; the wording is not only found in *Fragments from France* (Bairnsfather 1917, n.p.) and *The Anzac Book* (in AWM 2010, 13) but is also a concept echoed in cartoons that compare dreams of home to the horrors of the front, the illusions of war films to the actualities of warfare, the attitudes of wealthy shirkers to the experiences of beleaguered warriors, and the ideas of officers to the truths of the soldiers. For example, see figure 2.3, a cartoon by F. Paget Hewkley, included in *The Anzac Book* by soldiers in the Gallipoli campaign, that highlights the disconnect between the ideal of the military hero and the reality of the citizen-soldier antihero. Such cartoons are a passive confrontation with the military hierarchy, resisting both its propaganda and its hubris, though not undermining its authority.

Most cartoon subversion is achieved indirectly, through such means as the representation of rumpled uniforms and other forms of self-efficacy that undermines the patriotic, propagandized, ideals of a well-trained, disciplined, and devoted royal military. For example, a cartoon entitled "The 'Ric'" in *The Anzac Book* features a "New Arrival" asking, "Strewth! Wot's that?" as something hums past his parapet. The officer replies, "Only a ricochet," and the recruit naively wonders, "An' d'we use 'em, too, sir?" (in AWM 2010, 25). Indeed, the antiheroism of the citizen-soldier is considered in studies of trench publications to be one of the most important themes running through Dominion trench culture

Figure 2.3. F. Paget Hewkley (1915). "The Ideal and the Real" in the Ottoman Empire: Turkey, Dardanelles, Gallipoli. Archived at the Australian War Memorial (see appendix 2.A).

of the Great War, exemplified through archetypes of malingerers, "old soldiers," and the grumpy Tommy (Cook 2008; see also Chapman and Ellin 2012 and 2014; Chapman et al. 2015). Bruce Bairnsfather's (1917) work epitomizes this, not only through his grumpy character of Old Bill but also through a series of "Other Times, Other Manners" cartoons that compare the romantic heroism of wars past, as exemplified through a knight in chain mail or a stoic Napoleon, to the modern indignities of mere survival.

Some cartoons, however, are more direct in their resistance and provide the occasional opportunity for soldiers to speak and act freely, which they could or would not do in real interactions. For example, in the December 15, 1918, edition of *The Kia Ora Coo-ee*, a cartoon conversation has an officer asking a soldier, "What were you before the War, Jones?" and Jones replying bluntly, "'Appy, Sir" (in Kent [1918] 1981, 4). Such confrontational humor is most evident in the Frank Dunne (1919) cartoon, seen in figure 2.4, in which a soldier threatens to punch the officer who wants "none of your back chat" (29).

Figure 2.4. Frank Dunne (1919). *Digger Days: Laughing through the Great War.* Archived at the National Library of Australia (see appendix 2.A).

A *Herbie* cartoon by Bing Coughlin (1946) similarly featured a soldier wanting to give a commissioned officer "one swift kick" because, as he puts it, "I used to be his batman [personal servant]" (58). Another creation by Coughlin (1946) also disrespects officers, referring to them as "the high priced help," but includes the consequences of such insubordination with the cheeky Herbie, held by an MP (military police), receiving a lecture on the proper way to address officers (80). The same sentiment appears in another Coughlin cartoon (1946) in which Herbie finds himself in the detention barracks remarking, "So the army can't make us do anythin' we don't wanna do! . . . They sure can make us wish we had!" (142).

Whether the subversion was latent, through rejection of the spit-polish heroic soldier in favor of the disgruntled and disheveled antihero, or semiotic, through cartoon threats of physical violence, the humor relied on accepting membership within the military community while rejecting certain aspects of its organization. This could be just a side effect of the nature of the humor; the parody only works when it resembles the things it mocks, but given Nazareth's (2008) observations about the importance of humor in the military, it is likely also part of the process of group identification. In describing what she calls "oppositional positioning," Lisa Gilman (2012) notes that a military group's identity can be established through the "simultaneous identification with and rejection of (or differentiation from) a larger cultural community of which they are also members" (182). The Dominion soldiers of the world wars solidified their group identity as Dominion soldiers by differentiating themselves from the officer class through a particular set of experiences (e.g., hardship), attitudes (e.g., shrewdness), and symbols (e.g., scruffiness).

CONCLUSION

Of the Great War, Bruce Bairnsfather wrote, "The whole of the thing made me laugh. I could not refrain from smiling at the absurdity, the stark, fearful predicament" (1927, 31). Brigadier Nazareth agrees that because "the British have suffered so many disasters in battles, and yet have been victorious in so many wars" (2008, 204), they developed unshakeable faith in their might that allowed them to trivialize crises and direct humor against themselves. Furthermore, British military humor was shaped by its long history, which engendered a deep regard for tradition. Nazareth also noted that within the royal militaries, humor was influenced by such generalities as the English's steadiness, the Scot's bloodthirst, the Canadian's daring, the Irish's impetuousness, the Australian's aggressiveness, and the Indian's loyalty—but that a strong team spirit pervaded the entire system. This tendency is clear in the ways in which the cartoons simultaneously serve the functions, as described by Lynch (2009), of resistant subversion *and* concertive control. As acts of resistance, the cartoons subvert military authority by belittling it. In so doing, they exert concertive control among the enlisted ranks through instructive guidelines about acceptable and inacceptable team behavior—or what Goffman (1959 and 1969) conceived as strategic interaction for negotiating group norms. For example, mocking officers for indolence was a means both of questioning their authority and of reminding fellow soldiers that shirking was not acceptable within the group. Their esprit de corps is reflected in the enlisted soldiers' unification as a group that is different from that of the officers.

As a kind of oppositional positioning (Gilman 2012), the cartoons accept the authority of the military even while berating it, with creators and readers simultaneously identifying as both soldiers and as civilians. Cartoons may have provided a reprieve from the rigors of military discipline in the British and Dominion militaries of the world wars, but lives still depended on obedience. Jokes about unpolished buttons or about incorrect salutes distinguished the citizen-soldier from the commissioned officer, but they also reminded citizen-soldiers about their duties to the Crown. This junction made cartoon humor an officially acceptable outlet for criticizing the military establishment. The cartoons reinforced the very structures they mocked, even going so far as to remind readers about the real-world consequences for such insubordinate behaviors. And yet, through the thematic demonstrations of the differences between enlisted and officers, the cartoons provided a kind of subversive reinforcement. Cartoon humor allowed the citizen-soldiers of England and the Dominions to maintain their humanity and to endure the horrors of war by embracing an identity that was simultaneously oppositional to and respectful of order. It was, and is, what Lieutenant-General Sir Alexander Godley called "eloquent testimony to the unfailing good humour and cheerfulness of the troops under conditions which require conspicuous qualities of fortitude, endurance, and patience" (in "New Zealanders in France" 1916).

Appendix 2.A

PRIMARY SOURCE MATERIAL (SOLDIER CARTOONS)

WORLD WAR I

ENGLAND

Bairnsfather, Bruce. 1927. *Carry on Sergeant!* Indianapolis: The Bobbs-Merrill Company.
Bairnsfather, Bruce. 1917. *Fragments from France.* New York: G.P. Putnam's Sons.
Walbrook & Co. and the Committee of Blighty. *Blighty.* 1917–1918. Archived at the National Library of Scotland / Leabharlann Nàlseanta na h-Alba. http://digital.nls.uk/blighty-and-sea-pie/pageturner.cfm?id=75253030.

AUSTRALIA AND NEW ZEALAND

Australian War Memorial (AWM), ed. (1916) 2010. *The Anzac Book.* 3rd ed. Sydney: UNSW Press.
Dinkum Oil, The. Retrieved March 6, 2016. https://www.awm.gov.au/blog/2010/09/30/the-dinkum-oil/.
Dunne, Frank. 1919. *Digger Days! Laughing through the Great War.* Reprinted by courtesy of the Proprietors of Smiths Weekly. Archived at the National Library of Australia. http://catalogue.nla.gov.au/Record/2241149.
Dunne, Frank. n.d. *Digger Days.* Archived in the Stan Cross Archive of Cartoons and Drawings, 1912–1974 at the National Library of Australia. Accessed January 13, 2019. http://nla.gov.au/nla.obj-6053840.
Hartt, Cecil L. 1917. *Humorosities by an Australian Soldier.* Australian Trading & Agencies Co. Archived at the State Library Victoria. http://handle.slv.vic.gov.au/10381/109083.
Kent, David. 1981. Introduction. In *The Kia Ora Coo-ee: The Magazine for the Anzacs in the Middle East, 1918.* Sydney: Cornstalk Publishing.
"New Zealanders in France." 1916. *Shell Shocks by the New Zealanders in France.* Archived in the Europeana Collections. http://www.europeana.eu/portal/en/record/9200140/BibliographicResource_3000073964269.html.

CANADA

Brazier, The. 1916–1917. Printed and published at the Front for the Canadian Scottish, 16th Battalion, C.E.F. 1916–1917. Archived at Early Canadiana Online. http://eco .canadiana.ca/view/oocihm.8_06780.

In & Out. 1918. Published in France. Archived at Early Canadiana Online. http://eco .canadiana.ca/view/oocihm.8_06652.

Listening Post. 1915–1918. Published in France for the British Expeditionary Force. Archived at Early Canadiana Online. http://eco.canadiana.ca/view/oocihm.8 _06774.

Vie Canadienne. 1916–1918. Published in Rouen, France. Archived at Early Canadiana Online. http://eco.canadiana.ca/view/oocihm.8_06751.

WORLD WAR II

ENGLAND

Langdon, David. n.d. *"All Buttoned Up!" A Scrapbook of R.A.F. Cartoons.* London, UK: Sylvan Press.

Ward-Jackson, C. H., with David Langdon. 1943. *It's a Piece of Cake or R.A.F. Slang Made Easy.* n.p.: Google Books.

CANADA

Coughlin, Bing. 2008. *Herbie Wuz Here! A Collection of WWII Canadian Military Cartoons 1944–1946.* Almonte, ON: Algrove Publishing.

Coughlin, Bing, with J.D.M. 1946. *Herbie!* Canada: Thomas Nelson & Sons.

Coughlin, Bing. 1944. *This Army: Maple Leaf Album.* Rome, Italy: No. 2 Canadian Public Relations Group.

WORKS CITED

Australian War Memorial (AWM), ed. (1916) 2010. *The Anzac book.* Third edition. Sydney: UNSW Press.

Bairnsfather, Bruce. 1927. *Carry on sergeant!* Indianapolis, IN: The Bobbs-Merrill Company.

Bairnsfather, Bruce. 1917. *Fragments from France.* New York: G.P. Putnam's Sons.

Black, James Eric. 2010. "Amoozin' but Confoozin: Comic Strips as a Voice of Dissent in the 1950s." *ETC: A Review of General Semantics 66* (4): 460–477.

Boje, David M., Grace Ann Rosile, Rita A. Durant, and John T. Luhman. 2004. "Enron Spectacles: A Critical Dramaturgical Analysis." *Organization Studies* 25: 751–774.

Boyatzis, Richard E. 1998. *Transforming Qualitative Information: Thematic Analysis and Code Development.* Thousand Oaks, CA: Sage.

Buff, Jonathan. 2014. "Military Structures and Ranks." *British Library: World War One, Articles.* January 29. https://www.bl.uk/world-war-one/articles/military-structures -and-ranks.

Casey, Jay. 2009. "'What's So Funny?' The Finding and Use of Soldier Cartoons from the World Wars as Historical Evidence." In *Drawing the Line: Using Cartoons as Historical Evidence*, edited by Richard Scully and Marian Quartly, 07.1–07.23. Clayton, Australia: Monash University ePress.

Chapman, Jane. 2016. "The Aussie, 1918–1931: Cartoons, Digger Remembrance and First World War Identity." *Journalism Studies* 17 (4): 415–431.

Chapman, Jane, and Dan Ellin. 2012. "Multi-panel Comic Narratives in Australian First World War Trench Publications as Citizen Journalism." *Australian Journal of Communication* 39 (3): 1–22.

Chapman, Jane, and Dan Ellin. 2014. "Dominion Cartoon Satire as Trench Culture Narratives: Complaints, Endurance and Stoicism." *Round Table* 103 (2): 175–192.

Chapman, Jane, Anna Hoyles, Andrew Kerr, and Adam Sherif. 2015. *Comics and the World Wars: A Cultural Record.* New York: Palgrave MacMillan.

Cook, Tim. 2008. "Anti-Heroes of the Canadian Expeditionary Force." *Journal of the Canadian Historical Association / Revue de la Société historique du Canada* 19 (1): 171–193.

Coughlin, Bing. 2008. *Herbie Wuz Here! A Collection of WWII Canadian Military Cartoons 1944–1946.* Altmonte, ON: Algrove Publishing.

Coughlin, Bing with J.D.M. 1946. *Herbie!* Canada: Thomas Nelson & Sons.

Daughton, James P. 2000. "Sketches of the *Poilu*'s World: Trench Cartoons from the Great War." In *World War I and the Cultures of Modernity,* edited by Douglas Peter Mackaman and Michael Mays, 766–1152. Jackson: University Press of Mississippi.

Dunne, Frank. 1919. *Digger Days! Laughing through the Great War.* Reprinted by courtesy of the Proprietors of Smiths Weekly. Archived at the National Library of Australia. Retrieved May 1, 2016. http://catalogue.nla.gov.au/Record/2241149.

Gilman, Lisa. 2012. "Oppositional Positioning: The Military Identification of Young Antiwar Veterans." In *Warrior Ways: Explorations in Modern Military Folklore,* edited by Eric A. Eliason and Tad Tuleja, 181–201. Logan: Utah State University Press.

Goffman, Erving. 1959. *The Presentation of Self in Everyday Life.* Woodstock, NY: Overlook Press.

Goffman, Erving. 1969. *Strategic Interaction.* Philadelphia: University of Pennsylvania Press.

Hartt, Cecil L. 1917. *Humorosities by an Australian Soldier.* Australian Trading & Agencies Co. Archived at the National Library of Australia. Retrieved March 27, 2013 from http://handle.slv.vic.gov.au/10381/109083.

Jaffe, A. 1988. "Saluting in Social Context." *Journal of Applied Behavioral Science* 24 (3): 263–275.

Kent, David. 1981. "Introduction." In *The Kia Ora Coo-ee: The Magazine for the Anzacs in the Middle East, 1918.* Sydney: Cornstalk Publishing.

Langdon, David. n.d. "All Buttoned Up!" A scrapbook of R.A.F. cartoons. London: Sylvan Press.

Listening Post, The. (1915-1918). Published in France for the British Expeditionary Force. Archived at Early Canadiana Online. Retrieved March 5, 2016. http://eco.canadiana.ca/view/oocihm.8_06774.

Lynch, Owen Hanley. 2009. "Kitchen Antics: The Importance of Humor and Maintaining Professionalism at Work." *Journal of Applied Communication Research* 37 (4): 444–464.

Nazareth, Brigadier J. 2008. *The Psychology of Military Humour.* Olympia Fields, IL: Lancer Publishers.

Sabrosky, Alan Ned, James Clay Thompson, and Karen A. McPherson. 1982. "Organized Anarchies: Military Bureaucracy in the 1980s." *Journal of Applied Behavioral Science* 18 (2): 137–153.

Shaw, Matthew. 2014. "How Did Soldiers Cope with War?" *British Library: World War One, Articles.* January 29. https://www.bl.uk/world-war-one/articles/how-did-soldiers-cope-with-war.

Sheffield, Gary. 2014. "Military Discipline and Punishment." *British Library: World War One, Articles.* January 29. https://www.bl.uk/world-war-one/articles/military-discipline.

Shugart, Helene A. 1999. "Postmodern Irony as Subversive Rhetorical Strategy." *Western Journal of Communication* 63 (4): 433–455.

Strachan, Hew. 2014. "The Strategic Consequences of the World War." *American Interest* 9 (6). June 2. https://www.the-american-interest.com/2014/06/02/the-strategic-consequences-of-the-world-war/.

Strömberg, Fredrik. 2010. *Comic Art Propaganda.* New York: St. Martin's Griffin.

Walbrook & Co. and the Committee of Blighty. 1917–1918. *Blighty.* Archived at the National Library of Scotland/Leabharlann Nàlseanta na h-Alba. Retrieved March 21, 2016 from http://digital.nls.uk/blighty-and-sea-pie/pageturner.cfm?id=75253030.

Ward-Jackson, C. H., with David Langdon. 1943. *It's a Piece of Cake or R.A.F. Slang Made Easy* N.P.: Google Books.

3

Warriors' Bodies as Sites of Microresistance in the American Military

John Paul Wallis and Jay Mechling

FOLKLORISTS, ANTHROPOLOGISTS, PSYCHOLOGISTS, and other scholars who study culture understand how humans make the body a site of resistance. This resistance begins early in humans, as caretakers attempt to "socialize" (i.e., control) the basic bodily functions of the child, including eating, urinating, and defecating, the three primary bodily systems. The infant and the older child soon discover how the struggle over the socialization of these systems provides one of the few sources of power available to them. Later, prepubescent and adolescent youth discover (again) how control over their own bodies (hair, adornment, body modification, clothing) provides material for fashioning an identity and, as a bonus, for resisting adult control by parents, teachers, and others. Memory of the power of control over one's own body lasts a long time.

Most institutions engage in what sociologists Peter Berger and Thomas Luckmann (1967) call "secondary socialization," socialization that assumes and builds on the "primary socialization" in the family. There are a few adult institutions, however, that reproduce the primary socialization of the family in order to build in the new member the same powerful bonding the family enjoys. Typically these adult institutions (the military and fraternities are the best examples) separate the novices from their everyday lives, strip them of their former accoutrements of identity (names, hair, clothing, etc.), and construct a new identity bonding the initiates to the new institution. Basic Training in the military, for example, cuts the recruit's hair, gives the recruit a new nickname, dresses the recruit in a uniform quite distinct from civilian dress, and immerses the initiate in the sort of "total institution" (Goffman 1961) that reproduces the dependence originally experienced in the primary socialization of the family. Basic Training infantilizes the recruit, controlling

DOI: 10.7330/9781607329527.c003

every bodily function, including eating, urinating, defecating, sleeping, and having sex.

Like the child and adolescent, however, warriors come to understand that they have some residual control over the body, that they can engage in what we call "microresistances" against the constraints of the total institution. This chapter examines these small acts of resistance in the American military, based upon our reading of veterans' memoirs, reporters' accounts of warriors' lives, fictions (novels and theatrical films), documentary films of warriors' lives, vernacular photography by the warriors, official press photography, and Wallis's own experiences in the Marine Corps (two tours of duty in Iraq). Maximillian Uriarte's comic strip *Terminal Lance* (referring to a Lance Corporal who never advances in rank) provides much needed, often humorous detail, based on his experience in the Marines.

Our work here contributes to the study of "bodylore," as Katherine Young (1993) dubbed it, but our topic really is the struggle that ensues when a powerful institution attempts to control and repress folk expressions of individual and collective identity. Thus, although our case study is of recruits' and warriors' uses of the body for resistance in the American military, the dynamic here resembles what happens when employers ban expressive folklore in the workplace, when teachers ban expressive folklore among students, when prison authorities try to suppress expressive folklore among the inmates, and so on.

We focus primarily on men in the American military, in large part because most of our evidence involves male warriors and their uses of their bodies, but also in part because the male body of the warrior plays such a powerful role in the iconography of the nation (Jarvis 2010). The increasing presence of women in the American military, especially in combat roles barred to them until 2016, raises some interesting questions about the female recruit's and female warrior's body and her resistances to the "good order and discipline" in the overwhelmingly male institution. Unfortunately our evidence of the uses of the female body is scant and very speculative, but it seems obvious to us that the presence of female bodies in the smaller military units (e.g., a platoon) changes in some significant ways the masculine folk cultures of those units. Clearly we need good ethnographic accounts of women warriors' uses of their bodies as sites of resistance.

ON MICRORESISTANCE AND BODILY FIXATIONS

We use the word "microresistance" to describe the small ways members of the American military can perform acts of protest and resistance in a "total institution" that controls most elements of their lives. We distinguish these acts from larger acts of resistance, such as the antiwar movement within the military during the Vietnam War (see the documentary film *Sir! No Sir!* [Zeiger 2005]) and the antiwar coffeehouses that have appeared on the outskirts of military bases in the United States during the recent wars (see *Grounds for Resistance* [Gilman 2011]).

The small acts we focus on here can be both individual and collective. Some acts we write about may seem idiosyncratic, individual expressions of resistance, but, as Mechling argues in "Solo Folklore" (2008b), even individual acts with no audience other than oneself can have the qualities we see as traditional and folkloric. For example, when a warrior, male or female, writes some graffiti on the wall of a Porta Potty or wood-walled latrine, that is an individual act but also a folkloric act. Other expressive acts that we count as microresistance have audiences for the performance.

Folklorists, anthropologists, sociologists, sociolinguists, literary critics, and historians, among others, note that the body is a perfect metaphor for the society, with an inside and outside and a border "crossed" by dangerous materials—air, food, and drink crossing into the body, with a range of excretions (including urine, feces, blood, milk, saliva, and semen) crossing in the other direction (Douglas 1966). As Susan Sontag (1978, 1989) observes in her essays on illness as metaphor, the metaphors of the body and of the society bleed into one another.

Basic to our approach is the principle that the strict control of the recruit's body by the total institution, intense during Basic Training (boot camp) but continuing throughout the warrior's experience, tends to create bodily fixations (oral, anal, genital) that find their expression in the folklore. A psychoanalyst would focus on an individual patient's experiences in childhood socialization of the oral, anal, and genital systems, for example, toward understanding related symptoms in the adult patient. As folklorists, though, we focus on a pattern of socialization in Basic Training and continuing in the battle zone that is shared by the group, a common experience that is part of the "high context" folklorists expect when they study folklore. The "symptoms" the folklorist deals with are the performances of folk traditions. Thus, we expect that the stressful experiences recruits have with food, urination, and defecation in Basic Training will provide their folklore with highly charged symbolic material (food, piss, shit, to use the folk terms) for their acts of resistance.

THE MALE BODY

For some time now masculinity studies have understood the basic paradox of the male body in American culture—namely, that, despite aggressive performances of manliness, masculinity really is a very fragile construction (Chodorow 1978; Frosh 1994; Mechling 2005), and the male body is a vulnerable element in that construction (Bordo 1999). In Western societies, where mothers take primary responsibility for raising the child in its early years, the psychological development of the male child requires a separation from the mother, from the feminine, which is not the appropriate figure for identification. Masculinity is defined as "not female." Male friendship cultures in boys and young men create, maintain, and repair (when needed) the performance of male heterosexuality, primarily through the denigration of the feminine (misogyny), including the feminine side of males (homophobia).

The male body is at the center of this paradoxical fragility of the social construction, performance, maintenance, and (when necessary) repair of masculinity. Writ large, the body serves as an apt symbol of the society, strong and hard (Jarvis 2010). This analytical tool serves well in anthropology (Douglas 1966), sociolinguistics (Lakoff and Johnson 1980), history (Sontag 1978), and folklore studies (Young 1993). When used in visual communication, notably advertising and propaganda, the male body signals strength and agency. But, as Susan Bordo (1999, 95) says, "the phallus . . . haunts the penis," by which she means that the actual penis is vulnerable and undependable, really not up to the symbolic strength and potency of the symbolic phallus, adding to the anxiety the male feels in constructing his masculine performance.

In psychoanalytic theory, severe socialization of any of the bodily systems—oral, anal, and genital—can lead to a fixation, which can emerge as a symptom. Psychological anthropologists long ago fashioned and tested hypotheses about cultures and core personalities based on the severity of the socialization of these systems (Whiting and Child 1953; Whiting and Whiting 1974). Psychological anthropology's insights still have some explanatory power as we come to understand puzzling human behavior.

THE BODY AND THE CORPS, THE INDIVIDUAL AND THE GROUP

We begin with the "two bodies" in the military—the actual male body of the recruit and warrior and "the corps," adopting the Marine Corps term for that military organization, but meaning really every branch of the service and the American military as a large government institution. Individual bodies have "members" (arms, legs) and the collective corps has "members." And, like body parts, the individual as a body part can quite literally be lost or destroyed and then replaced by another, uniform part.

The military institution must socialize the individual's body severely to make it conform to the demands of the organization. Traditional forms of military discipline, as emphasized in recruit training, requires uniformity and unquestioning obedience to authority. Toward that end, the military works at controlling the individual's body as much as possible.

These generalizations are true for all military organizations across time and space, but in the case of American culture, we have to recognize the strong forces reinforcing a competitive individualism that affects both men and women in their socialization. The relationship between the individual and the group in the United States varies according to ethnicity and other factors, such as religion, of course. The basic drama in a total institution such as the military, then, is this enduring tension between the norms of individualism in American culture and the absolute requirements of the total institution for conformity and uniformity.

Basic Training (boot camp) aims to strip the recruit of his previous identity and, by reproducing the intense levels of emotion and dependence experienced in the primary socialization in the family, build a new identity suitable for a warrior. The first third of Kubrick's theatrical film *Full Metal Jacket* (1987), captures that experience, and Thomas Ricks's (1997, 122–123) report on his time at Parris Island as a journalist describes similar scenes of recruits feminized and infantilized.

Basic Training infantilizes and feminizes the recruit. Paradoxically, this strategy aims, ultimately, to create the adult heterosexual male warrior. The infantilization creates the circumstances for building a whole new set of family-like relationships and emotions (a "band of brothers," a "fratiarchy") based in the new identity as a warrior. The feminization (a verbal tactic commonly used by DIs—drill instructors) taps and enhances the young recruits' misogyny and homophobia, which they learn in preadolescent and adolescent male friendship groups. The social construction of heterosexual warrior identity requires a distancing from the feminine, even a disgust of the feminine, whether the feminine appears as real women or as behavior deemed "feminine" in men.

What follows is a brief look at the conditions of bodily socialization in Basic Training and the folklore of resistance we see resulting from the fixations created by that severe socialization.

ORAL

From his first meal in Basic Training, the recruit eats under stressful conditions. The documentary film *Black Friday: Dark Dawn* (2012) confirms the experience Wallis had in Basic Training in the Marine Corps at the same camp, Pendleton, in San Diego, California. Recruits are instructed in regimented ways how to line up at the food line, how to hold the tray, how to extend the tray for food, how to carry the tray to a table, how to sit at the table. Once permission to eat is granted, the recruits typically have mere minutes to eat as fast as they can. The dining experience thus functions to infantilize soldiers, as if the mere act of feeding themselves requires detailed instructions.

The fixation with food continues in the war zone, as the MREs (Meals Ready-to-Eat), typically unpalatable fare, become rich material for conversation and play. In Wallis's mortar platoon in northern Iraq, the warriors invented a game they called "Iron Chef MRE," reproducing the popular television cooking show with the challenge of making MREs palatable. Maximillian Uriarte, whose comic strip *Terminal Lance* and commentary provide a great deal of evidence about the male culture of the Marines, posted on Facebook a photo of a Marine who had a tattoo on his calf, an illustration of an MRE (Meal Ready to Eat) leaning against an outline of a rock that has "rock or something" written on it, a reference to the instructions for heating and eating MREs—"lean it against a rock or something." Another post on Uriarte's TL website reproduces a comical chart of jelly bean "flavors" from MRE meals. In fact, MREs are a common topic for the humor in Terminal Lance (Uriarte 2016a).

Folklorists often find food contamination legends in institutions such as the military. George Rich and David Jacobs (1973) analyzed the well-known legend from World War II that the military puts saltpeter (potassium nitrate) in the food to dampen the male sex drive, and there is some evidence that similar legends persist. Maximillian Uriarte mentions a legend that must have circulated during his deployment. In his graphic novel *The White Donkey: Terminal Lance* (2016b), he has a medic in the platoon warn the warriors against eating the MREs, and in particular he tells them that the chewing gum in the MREs is a laxative.

In the military, food contamination legends such as these address both social and psychological anxieties. Because the performance of masculinity depends deeply upon the health and strength of the male body, contaminated food poses not just a practical threat to health but also a symbolic threat to the military body.

ANAL

Just as eating in Basic Training causes great stress and oral fixation, so the institution's control over the time, place, and frequency of urination and defecation causes fixation on the genital and anal systems. Typical in Basic Training is an order from the DI, "attack the head," followed by a countdown of two minutes, during which time the recruits are expected to "shit," an experience that almost certainly results in an anal fixation. Uriarte, in his *Terminal Lance* comic strips (and the book collection of his strips), makes frequent mention of the "thumb in the other's butt" play among the Marines he served with, and the essay by Mechling (2012) on vernacular photography by warriors notes the frequent photos of soldiers on latrines or of naked soldiers and sailors bathing (just butts showing, no genitals). Dian Hanson's (2014) large collection of snapshots of men's bodies taken by warriors in World War II suggests a fascination with the naked male butt, a fascination bordering on fixation. Diarrhea has been a chronic problem for warriors in the field, so the anal system is constantly on the warrior's mind. Wallis recalls that one fellow Marine used to plug his anus with toilet paper when he had the runs, prompting the platoon to start joking about "manpons" (male tampons).

The Marine Corps has its own specialized version of a fixation on the anal system. A nickname for the Corps among recruits and Marines after Basic Training is "the Green Weenie," and the colorful metaphor to describe having the Corps do something unpleasant to the individual or group is to have the "Green Weenie" slip into the anus, as male anal sex and rape are the ultimate version of domination, "putting down" the male in the female position for sex (Dundes 1997, 27). The speech play about the "Green Weenie" in the Corps, of course, is all in fun—see Terminal Lance strip #181, "Easy Access" (Uriarte 2018, 84), for a humorous explanation for why cammies (camouflage pants) constantly split at the crotch, thereby providing easy access for the "Green Weenie." Mickey Weems (2012, 152) sees the Marine folk speech, such as "Big Green Weenie up your asshole," as an expression of solidarity in submission to the Corps. Marines also warn each other, "BOHICA," meaning "bend over, here it comes again."

Wallis and Mechling (2015, 289–290, 303n7) point to the Marine folk-phrase, "butt hurt," to describe a Marine who is acting unmanly in response to a tease or insult or other event, and the folk phrase doubtless feminizes the sulking Marine with reference to his inability to take the pain of symbolic anal intercourse (again, Dundes 1997, but also Mechling 2008a). Wherever one looks in Marine oral and material lore (e.g., latrinalia), then, the vulnerability of the anus rivals the vulnerability of the penis as a threat to the male warrior's construction of normative heterosexual masculinity. We have the best evidence of this from Marine sources, though some of the comments by active and veteran Army members on *Terminal Lance* discussion threads suggest that men in all the services have this same anal fixation in their folklore.

Another male, total institution might help us understand the Marine fixation on the anus. Mechling (2001) accounts for the anal fixation in the speech play and other play at a Boy Scout camp by invoking Freud's Wolfman Analysis, wherein Sigmund Freud argues that the patient's anal symptoms derived from his repression of the feminine side of his psyche. Mechling reasoned that the anal fixation prominent in the folklore at Boy Scout camp was a symptom of the necessary repression of the feminine in that all-male, total institution, the goal of which is to fashion a normative, heterosexual masculinity in the pubescent and adolescent boys at camp. Similarly, the anal fixation evident in so much of the Marine Corps and other male military lore likely amounts to a cluster of symptoms grounded in the repression of the feminine in Basic Training and beyond.

Warriors' anal fixations evident in their folklore and folk customs count as microresistance in the general sense that the graffiti, the jokes, and the other traditions potentially disrupt "the good order and discipline" the institution expects. At the same time, the institution can tolerate this relatively harmless behavior.

GENITAL

The genitals, as everyone knows, serve two functions—urination and sex. In Basic Training the officers strictly control the timing and duration of urination of the recruits. Ricks (1997, 122–123) observed a DI deny a recruit's request to "hit the head" for a "piss" and the recruit urinated in his pants, adding humiliation to the total control of his body. Beyond boot camp, when the warrior has relatively more freedom yet is still within a total institution, the consequence of the strict control of urination is the use of urination to express domination and disgust. The folk phrase "piss on it" captures this use of urination, and a dramatic example of this use of urine is the video of American warriors urinating on the bodies of dead enemy Taliban fighters (Mechling 2014; Wallis 2012).

If urination plays a role in the warrior's use of the body for microresistance, masturbation plays an even more satisfying, if usually hidden, role, largely because it is against military regulations. A query on AskReddit (now reddit), for example—"Does masturbation occur in the military? Is it

non-existent?"—yielded thirty-nine comments by mid-March 2016, mainly
comments from active and veteran military men who testify that, yes, they
masturbated in the military, and some offer examples of folklore. One com-
menter explained that he and his buddies called it "crying": "Some of us
cried in the shower, some of us cried while watching a movie. One guy told
me he would use a sock to wipe away his tears. We all cried in the military."
A submariner (Proud Turtle) reports "jerkoff contests" recorded in notes,
and another submariner notes that there was a chart of the wall beside the
Weapons Launch Console keeping track of how many times which crew
members masturbated, a story similar to one collected by Ray Raphael (1988,
76) about a "BTMS—Beat the Meat Sheet"—teen boys started at a summer camp to record the number of times each boy in a cabin masturbated.
Another comment offered this motto: "Pooping in a porter [*sic*] john is strong,
masturbating in a porter john is army strong." Men in the military often masturbate with socks, and another commentator refers to the "patrol sock."

The following was posted in porta potties and latrines in a combat zone
in Afghanistan (Jones 2013):

> **ATTENTION MARINES**
> Stop using the porta-potties as a masturbation facility. There have been
> several reports in RC (SW) of illness caused by bodily fluid discharge in
> these facilities. Any male or female caught masturbating in this facility will
> face disciplinary action under Article 92 UCMJ.
> COMPLIANCE IS MANDATORY

Aside from the questionable claim that bodily fluids pose much of a risk
in the latrine, the invocation of Article 92 of the Uniform Code of Military
Justice ("Failure to Obey Order or Regulation") is meant to frighten the
warriors. Sometimes the military will cite Article 134, "the general article,"
to threaten punishment for masturbation, as that article mentions "all dis-
orders and neglects to the prejudice of good order and discipline in the
armed forces."

Of course, even the threat of court-martial does not keep men and
women in the military from masturbating. Wallis reports that most Marines
in his unit had pornography on their personal cell phones and referred to
porta potties as "jack shacks." Especially in the war zones in the Middle
East, where access to consensual sex with women is more limited than it
was during the Vietnam War, for example, masturbation is the most common activity to satisfy sexual drives (e.g., Buzzell 2005, 39–41).

Doubtless the military has reasons for making masturbation against
regulations, as futile as that sounds. It seems that the institution does not

enforce the regulation very vigorously, though masturbating while on guard duty would be a serious breach of rules; even then, Buzzell (2005, 41–42) insists that warriors often masturbated on guard duty to stay awake. We believe that the military's regulations about masturbation stem more from symbolic meanings than from practical reasons having to do with distractions. Thomas Laquer's (2003) cultural history of masturbation makes clear the meanings of masturbation after the early eighteenth century, when objections to masturbation changed from moral (Onanism) to ethical and even political (2003, 18–19). Masturbation, argues Laquer, was threatening to the ideas of the Enlightenment because masturbation valued secrecy in "a world in which transparency was of a premium" (21), masturbation invites excess, and masturbation has no base in reality (actual intercourse) because "it was a creature of the imagination" (21).

Those elements and values—imagination, excess, solitude, and privacy—also threaten an institution such as the military. From Basic Training on, the institution suspects privacy and solitude, expects conformity to the reality created by the institution, and expects self-control. What complicates the situation even more for the military is that, as Laquer explains, beginning "in the 1970s, solitary sex was regarded as a way of reclaiming the self from the regulatory mechanisms of civil society and of the patriarchal sexual order into which the Enlightenment and its successes had put it. It became a sign of *self*-governance and *self*-control instead of their collapse" (2003, 277).

In terms of generations and generalizations, we might say that the Baby Boomers (born 1946–1964) grew up in a transitional era including the "sexual revolution" of the 1960s. By the time the Gen Xers (b. 1964–1981) and then the Millennials (b. 1982–2000) came along, attitudes toward sex and, in particular, toward masturbation changed considerably, as young people talk comfortably about these matters.

This progression of comfort with masturbating and talking about masturbating means that the young men entering the military now tend to see masturbation as a healthy expression of the individual self, as a liberation from social controls on sexual behavior and on other forms of individual expression. For these young men, masturbation is not just about the pleasure and release. Masturbation, unconsciously most likely, is about liberation from control, including self-control. A common military story is about the soldier who tries to get sent home or otherwise released from the military by seeming to be "crazy" by openly masturbating in front of an officer. Michael Herr (1977, 119–120) recounts the story of a soldier in Vietnam who "jerked off" thirty times a day.

In short, while masturbation in the military is a short-term solution to the sexual drives of the young man and may even have some values as a short-term therapy for the stress of living and fighting in the combat zone, masturbation also serves as a prime example of the individual warrior's using his own body to resist the control and uniformity of a total institution.

SKIN

The skin is the largest organ in the human body and serves extremely important physiological functions. The skin does more than biological service, though; the skin is highly cultural. "In a culture where surfaces matter," writes Margot Mifflin (2013, 4) in the introduction to her book on women and tattoos, skin is "the scrim on which we project our greatest fantasies and deepest fears about our bodies."

Tattooing has a long and interesting history in the military, most notably in the Navy and Merchant Marine and in the Marine Corps. The histories of tattooing in the American military document the sorts of tattoos soldiers and sailors and Marines have had inscribed on their bodies over centuries. The long history of sailor's tattoos shows us the role of tattoos as charms against drowning (H-O-L-D F-A-S-T across the fingers of both hands). In general, the older tattoos connected the individual to some larger collective entity. American flags and eagles and anchors signaled the individual's allegiance to the nation and to such values as liberty and patriotic strength. The traditional EGA (Eagle-Globe-Anchor) Marine insignia graced a Marine's chest or arms and signaled belonging to that service and its values.

We believe that a cultural change between the Vietnam War and the Gulf War shows up in the change in tattoos worn by young men and women, tattoos they get before enlisting in the military, tattoos they get while in the military, and tattoos they get upon leaving the military. Put simply, the tattoos now serve as very personal, individualized chronicles of the individual's experiences rather than a more general allegiance to the country or to the specific military institution. The individual tattoos resist the master narrative so important to the institution.

We found the best evidence of this change in the hour-long documentary film *Tattooed under Fire* (Schiesari 2008), which focuses on a single tattoo parlor in Killeen, Texas, home of the Army's Fort Hood. We see male and female soldiers getting tattoos just before their deployment to Iraq, and we see many of the same soldiers getting tattooed upon their return from their tour of duty. We see the tattooing, eavesdrop on the conversations between the soldiers and the tattoo artists, and see the soldiers speaking to the film-makers in direct response to questions.

As Travis, one of the soldiers we see before and after his deployment as a medic, puts it: "[my tattooed body] is my storyboard." Even before they are deployed, the men and women featured in the film want "one of a kind" tattoos, sometimes designed by themselves, combining bits of images meaningful only in relation to their experiences. One soldier, showing off his tattoo of a skull flying through a thunderstorm, explains, "This represents my life up to this point. When in uniform, I have to be like everyone else . . . my tattoos are a way of expressing myself and telling everyone that when I am out of uniform I am me."

Travis, the medic, designed a unique tattoo just before his deployment to Iraq. The disturbing tattoo on his upper arm is a fetus in a blender. Although some of the noncommissioned officers objected to Travis's tattoo—explaining that they had children—he defended it as a metaphor for the experience he was about to have in Iraq; he identified with the innocent fetus being chopped up in a blender. Jonathan, a twenty-seven-year-old soldier, comes to the parlor with his wife and new son. He wears a unique tattoo of a baby grim reaper with a pacifier in its mouth and carrying a reaper's scythe. At the same time, he tells the filmmakers and those in the tattoo parlor that he had to kill a child in Iraq and that memory haunts him in his nightmares almost every night.

Examples of black, gallows humor of the sort represented by Travis's and Jonathan's tattoos can be found more often on men than on women, it seems, but both men and women want tattoos that reflect very personal experiences, including the deaths of close friends. In 2016 the Marine Corps changed its tattoo policy to permit more tattoos, but not tattoo sleeves covering the whole arm. Commandant General Robert Neller said that the most common topic when he talked with Marines was tattoos, including those who want sleeve tattoos. "I ask them why," says Neller in an interview for the Marine Corps Times, and they tell him "Because I want to memorialize a friend." Army Reserve drill sergeant Victoria Parker, one of the warriors featured in a Clark County Historical Museum (Vancouver, Washington) exhibition *Vet Ink: Military-Inspired Tattoos*, has "Honor The Fallen" tattooed in an arc at the top of her left bicep and below that a tattooed battlefield cross (rifle upside down in boots, helmet on top) and the initials and death dates of five fallen comrades. Consuelo, who worked on a bridge crew in Iraq, tattooed, "What doesn't kill you makes you stronger" on her upper arm in memory of a friend who died in Baghdad (Clark County Historical Museum 2013).

Army chief of staff General Ray Odiero, interviewed for the same story, explained that the Army was changing its tattoo policy because attitudes toward tattoos has changed among the young people being recruited for the military. "Soldiers have grown up in an era when tattoos are much more acceptable," he said, "and we have to change along with that." The Navy recently loosened its tattoo policy along with the other services, actually going beyond the Marine Corps in permitting sleeve tattoos visible in short-sleeve uniforms and neck tattoos not exceeding a certain size. The new Army regulations permit sleeve tattoos but do not permit tattoos on the neck or hands, where they would be visible in long-sleeve uniforms.

Sometimes disillusioned warriors will have tattooed on their bodies some direct criticism of the institution or of the larger war machine. Charley, a cavalry soldier in *Tattooed under Fire*, has "Rats get fat while good soldiers die" on his upper arm, a comment on the people who profit from war without taking any risks. And we see in progress a peace symbol being tattooed on a male soldier's arm. In Vietnam Herr (1977, 103) saw this phrase written on flak jackets and even worn as a tattoo: "Eat the apple, fuck the Corps."

This too-brief examination of warriors' uses of tattoos on their bodies should make clear enough the point we made regarding masturbation and the relatively new emphasis on individual expression as a resistance against societal conformity. The new generation of recruits in the volunteer military services are late Gen Xers and Millennials and the military's demand for uniformity prompts them to use their bodies to resist control, even in small gestures.

The military permits tattoos but forbids most other forms of body modification, such as branding (burning a design into the skin with a very hot metal object, like a wire hanger). Anthony Swofford (2003, 50–51) recounts a prank played on him in Basic Training, in which his friends pretended they were going to brand him with a hot wire hanger. Much of the branding in the military after recruitment is hidden from officers. In Wallis's mortar platoon, some of the Marines gave themselves brands resembling Ruffles potato chips, searing their flesh on the cooling fins that ring the hot mortar tube, a visible sign of belonging to the fraternity of the mortar platoon. Branding is punishable in the military (article 134), but such brands are easily dismissed as "accidents," an account a superior officer can accept if, in fact, he knows of the practice and approves of it.

CLOTHING: UNIFORMS

Although not a biological part of the body, clothing is a "second skin." The "good order and discipline" in the military rely a great deal on the uniformity of appearance, represented best by the "uniform." Even so, warriors find ways to modify the uniform—especially in the more permissive environment of the combat zone. Warriors sometimes put unauthorized patches and other things on their uniforms. In Matt Gallagher's novel *Young Blood* (2016), based on his tours of duty in Iraq (see *Kaboom* 2010, his memoir), one of the soldiers wears an unapproved belt (2016, 117) and the entire unit wears patches of a dark scorpion in place of the official unit patch, a lightning bolt (2016, 123, 169). In May 2016, a photo of American Special Commandos fighting in Syria showed that one American had put a blue Kurd forces patch on his right shoulder, a show of solidarity with those fighters (Schmitt 2016, n.p.) Visible on one soldier's uniform in the documentary film *Grounds for Resistance*, a film about the antiwar coffeehouse movement, is a patch, "Death Dealer," which certainly is not approved. And in Stanley Kubrick's 1987 film *Full Metal Jacket*, the main character, nicknamed Joker by the DI in Basic Training at Parris Island, South Carolina, wears a peace symbol button on his battle fatigues and the words "Born to Kill" scrawled on his helmet.

Vernacular photos and a few press photos taken in combat zones prove that Joker's wearing a peace symbol on his uniform is not a fiction by the filmmaker. Musing on the sad and ironic variations of the soldier's "I'm not even supposed to be here today" lament, including the case where a soldier gets killed just before he is scheduled to be sent home, Buzzell observes that

> if this was Vietnam, I'd probably have FTA (Fuck the Army) inked in
> black pen all huge on my helmet in protest of having my leave canceled,
> but since this isn't Vietnam, I decided to put a black and white peace
> pin on my flak jacket in "peaceful" protest of having my leave canceled
> instead . . . It's the exact same pin that Private Joker wore in the Vietnam
> movie *Full Metal Jacket*. (2005, 234)

CLOTHING: DRAG

Photographic evidence—snapshots taken by men in the Army, Marines, Navy, and Air Force—reveals yet another way warriors use clothing to resist the "good order and discipline" expected in the military organization. In this case, the male warriors do not modify the uniform; instead, they create informal, folk "drag performances" in which one or more of the warriors fashion some version of women's clothing and hair to entertain himself and his fellows. We do not mean here the more formal "drag theatricals" one might find at all-male schools, male clubs, and other scripted, approved theatrical productions for members of the organization (Garber 1993). The theatrical performances that are part of the "Crossing the Line" ritual are examples of official military versions of theatrical drag, and other shows (USO shows in combat zones for example) sometimes have featured men in drag.

We have in mind here the folk versions of play in drag, those instances in which a warrior dresses up like a woman for his entertainment and for the entertainment of his male friends. Everyone is smiling in the photographs recording these folk performances, and the smiles and gestures (e.g., one of the male friend's squeezing the fake breasts of the one in drag) signal clearly that this is play. The play frame for the formal, approved theatricals is one thing; these informal play frames are quite another. As Gregory Bateson (1972) taught us, inviting others to play and having them accept the play frame for their interactions signals a close, trusting relationship between the players.

The spontaneous, brief, folk drag performances may be fun, but as instances of microresistance they have the potential to threaten the military institution's project of creating, maintaining, and repairing (as necessary) the identities of the warriors as heterosexual males (regardless of their personal sexual identities, which can be far more flexible than the military desires). Judith Butler notes that "in imitating gender, drag implicitly reveals the imitative structure of gender itself—as well as its contingency" (1990, 187). Butler points to Esther Newton's (1979) study of female impersonators in America as evidence of the ways "drag fully subverts the distinction between inner and outer psychic space and effectively mocks both the expressive model of gender and the notion of a true gender identity" (Butler 1990, 186). In short, the folk drag events remind the warriors that gender and sexual identity are performative, fluid and not fixed, as the military institution would have it, and in this sense the folk drag performances by male warriors can be subversive.

On the other hand, one line of functionalist thinking in anthropology, sociology, and history sees deviance as, paradoxically, actually reinforcing the norms of the group, in this case, male heterosexual identity. Inversion is comical because it is absurd nonsense (Stewart 1979), and nonsense takes its meaning from the contrast with sense or common sense. As framed play (Bateson 1972), folk drag performances share the paradox of all play—namely, that the male performance of "female" is safe because it is "not real"; the performance does not mean in the play frame what it would mean in everyday life. The folk drag performances are limited to a particular play time and play place, but the men in the group always return to everyday life, to the performance of heterosexual masculinity (again, often despite their actual sexual orientation). Some men performing folk drag and some men in the audience may actually take sexual pleasure in the performance, but regardless the performance momentarily disrupts the "good order and discipline" of the military unit.

CONCLUSION

Psychological anthropology alerts us to the ways humans use their bodies to deal with social and psychological anxieties, and we know from sociolinguistics and history (Lakoff and Johnson 1980; Sontag 1978) that the body is a perfect symbol for society. Add to this research all the attention to the male body in gender studies, especially masculinity studies (Bordo 1999), and we can see how rich and complex the male body is as a site for resisting the pressures of a total institution. Beginning with the psychoanalytic principle that harsh socialization of the oral, anal, and genital systems in the infant and child results in "symptoms" in the adult, we described the harsh socialization of the body in the total institution and pointed to the "symptoms" resulting from bodily fixations, taking the folklore as symptoms. Most of these symptoms are about control, power over the body.

The question that tantalizes us is whether and how women warriors use their bodies to resist the total institution of the military. The presence of women in the military is not new (Solaro 2006). Several thousand women served in the combat zone in the Gulf War (1991) and later that decade President Clinton opened some combat roles to women (Holmstedt 2007, xviii). Women warriors were participating in missions in Iraq and Afghanistan even before the policy changed to open up most combat roles to them (Biank 2013; Lemmon 2015; Williams 2005). Women go through the same Basic Training as the men and are subject to the same strict control of their bodies in that training. We might expect the same range of uses of the female body for microresistance in the total institution.

Women in the military face a more complex set of body issues than do the men. We focused here on male bodies because the evidence, from Wallis's experiences to the memoirs by veterans to the photographic evidence, mostly documents the male warriors' use of their bodies for microresistance. The memoirs and reportage on women in the military provide scant evidence of the sort of microresistance we write about here, though we did see above how women use tattoos in ways similar to the men's resistance. We have to wait for more evidence to flesh out how women warriors use their bodies to resist the control of the total institution.

The further complication for women in predominantly male institutions is that they are often the target of "the male gaze" and may even be sexually assaulted. Consequently, women warriors tend to present their bodies not as sexual objects but as bodies not far different from the bodies of their male comrades. Do female Marines talk about "the Green Weenie"? Female warriors masturbate, certainly, but do they talk about it and draw graffiti on the latrine walls? We saw how some female warriors personalize their tattoos, and in 2014 African American female warriors won the right to wear their hair in braids, cornrows, and twists. These tantalizing questions and examples of women's uses of their bodies for the expression of microresistance against the military institution will have to wait for more evidence and a new analysis.

WORKS CITED

Bateson, Gregory. 1972. *Steps to an Ecology of Mind*. San Francisco: Chandler.

Berger, Peter L., and Thomas Luckmann. 1967. *The Social Construction of Reality: A Treatise in the Sociology of Knowledge*. Garden City, NY: Doubleday.

Biank, Tanya. 2013. *Undaunted: The Real Story of America's Servicewomen in Today's Military*. New York: New American Library.

Black Friday: Dark Dawn. 2012. Los Angeles, CA: Moto Entertainment.

Bordo, Susan. 1999. *The Male Body*. New York: Farrar, Straus and Giroux.

Butler, Judith. 1990. *Gender Trouble: Feminism and the Subversion of Identity*. New York: Routledge.

Buzzell, Colby. 2005. *My War: Killing Time in Iraq*. New York: Putnam's Sons.

Chodorow, Nancy. 1978. *The Reproduction of Mothering: Psychoanalysis and the Sociology of Gender*. Berkeley: University of California Press.

Clark County Historical Museum. 2013. "Vet Ink: Military-Inspired Tattoos." Exhibit, February–September. http://www.cchmuseum.org/vet-ink-military-inspired -tattoos/.

Douglas, Mary. 1966. *Purity and Danger: An Analysis of Concepts of Pollution and Taboo*. London: Routledge and Kegan Paul.

Dundes, Alan. 1997. "Traditional Male Combat: From Game to War." In *Alan Dundes, From Game to War and Other Psychoanalytic Essays on Folklore*, 25–45. Lexington: University Press of Kentucky.

Frosh, Stephen. 1994. *Sexual Difference: Masculinity and Psychoanalysis*. London: Routledge.

Gallagher, Matt. 2010. *Kaboom: Embracing the Suck in a Savage Little War*. Cambridge, MA: DaCapo Press.

Gallagher, Matt. 2016. *Youngblood*. New York: Atria Books.

Garber, Marjorie. 1993. *Vested Interests: Cross-Dressing and Cultural Anxiety*. New York: HarperPerennial.

Gilman, Lisa. 2011. *Grounds for Resistance*. Done Did Productions. https://groundsfor resistance.com.

Goffman, Erving. 1961. *Asylums: Essays on the Social Situation of Mental Patients and Other Inmates*. Garden City, NY: Anchor Books.

Hanson, Dian. 2014. *My Buddy: WWII Laid Bare*. Cologne, Germany: Taschen.

Herr, Michael. 1977. *Dispatches*. New York: Knopf.

Holmstedt, Kristen. 2007. *Band of Sisters: American Women at War in Iraq.* Mechanicsburg, PA: Stackpole books.

Jarvis, Christina S. 2010. *The Male Body at War: American Masculinity during World War II.* DeKalb: Northern Illinois University Press.

Jones, Brian. 2013. "US Military Cracks Down on Troop Masturbation in Afghanistan." *Business Insider.* October 8. http://www.businessinsider.com/military-cracking-down -on-masturbation-in-afghanistan-2013-10.

Kubrick, Stanley. 1987. *Full Metal Jacket.* Warner Brothers.

Lakoff, George, and Mark Johnson. 1980. *Metaphors We Live By.* Chicago: University of Chicago Press.

Laquer, Thomas W. 2003. *Solitary Sex: The Cultural History of Masturbation.* New York: Zone Books.

Lemmon, Gayle Tzemach. 2015. *Ashley's War: The Untold Story of a Team of Women Soldiers on the Special Ops Battlefield.* New York: HarperCollins.

Mechling, Jay. 2001. *On My Honor: Boy Scouts and the Making of American Youth.* Chicago: University of Chicago Press.

Mechling, Jay. 2005. "The Folklore of Mother-Raised Boys and Men." In *Manly Traditions: The Folk Roots of American Masculinities,* edited by Simon J. Bronner, 221–227. Bloomington: Indiana University Press.

Mechling, Jay. 2008a. "Paddling and the Repression of the Feminine in Male Hazing." *THYMOS: Journal of Boy Studies* 2 (1): 60–75.

Mechling, Jay. 2008b. "Solo Folklore." *Western Folklore* 65 (4, Fall): 435–453.

Mechling, Jay. 2012. "Soldier Snaps." In *Warrior Ways: Explorations in Modern Military Folklore,* edited by Eric A. Eliason and Tad Tuleja, 222–247. Logan: Utah State University Press.

Mechling, Jay. 2014. "Pissing and Masculinity." *Culture, Society and Masculinities* 6 (1): 19–34.

Mifflin, Margot. 2013. *Bodies of Subversion: A Secret History of Women and Tattoo.* Brooklyn: Powerhouse Books.

Newton, Esther. 1979. *Mother Camp: Female Impersonators in America.* Chicago: University of Chicago Press.

Raphael, Ray. 1988. *The Men from the Boys: Rites of Passage in Male America.* Lincoln: University of Nebraska Press.

Rich, George W., and David F. Jacobs. 1973. "Saltpeter: A Folkloric Adjustment to Acculturation Stress." *Western Folklore* 32 (3): 1644–1679.

Ricks, Thomas. 1997. *Making the Corps.* New York: Scribner.

Schiesari, Nancy, director. 2008. *Tattooed Under Fire.* Documentary released on DVD 2009.

Schmitt, Eric. 2016. "US Commandos Work with Syrian Fighters in Push toward ISIS Stronghold." *New York Times* May 16, n.p. Accessed at https://www.nytimes.com /2016/05/27/world/middleeast/us-commandos-work-with-syrian-fighters-in-push -toward-isis-stronghold.html?_r=0.

Solaro, Erin, 2006. *Women in the Line of Fire.* Emeryville, CA: Seal Press.

Sontag, Susan. 1978. *Illness as Metaphor.* New York: Farrar, Straus and Giroux.

Sontag, Susan. 1989. *AIDS and Its Metaphors.* New York: Farrar, Straus and Giroux.

Stewart, Susan. 1979. *Nonsense: Aspects of Intertextuality in Folklore and Literature.* Baltimore: Johns Hopkins University Press.

Swofford, Anthony. 2003. *Jarhead: A Marine's Chronicle of the Gulf War and Other Battles.* New York: Scribner.

Uriarte, Maximillian. 2016a. Terminal Lance Facebook page. https://www.facebook.com /terminallance/?fref=nf.

Uriarte, Maximillian. 2016b. *The White Donkey: Terminal Lance.* Boston: Little, Brown and Company.

Uriarte, Maximillian. 2018. *Terminal Lance: Ultimate Omnibus.* New York: Little, Brown and Company.

Wallis, John Paul. 2012. *Reborn to Kill: American Warriors and Digital Trophies.* Senior honors thesis in American Studies, University of California, Davis.

Wallis, John Paul, and Jay Mechling. 2015. "Devil Dogs and Dog Piles." *Western Folklore* 74: 275–308.

Weems, Mickey. 2012. "Taser to the 'Nads: Brutal Embrace of Queerness in Military Practice." In *Warrior Ways: Explorations in Modern Military Folklore*, ed. Eric A. Eliason and Tad Tuleja, 139–160. Logan: Utah State University Press.

Whiting, Beatrice, and John W. M. Whiting. 1974. *Children of Six Cultures: A Psycho-Analysis.* Cambridge, MA: Harvard University Press.

Whiting, John W. M., and Irving L. Child. 1953. *Child Training and Personality: A Cross-Cultural Study.* New Haven, CT: Yale University Press.

Williams, Kayla, with Michael E. Staub. 2005. *Love My Rifle More than You: Young and Female in the U.S. Army.* New York: Norton.

Young, Katherine, ed. 1993. *Bodylore.* Knoxville: University of Tennessee Press.

Zeiger, David. 2005. *Sir! No Sir!* Displaced Films.

Part II
Rattling the Chain of Command

4

Jumping the Chain
A Military Psychologist's Story

Mark C. Russell

IN FEBRUARY 2003, THE RUN-UP TO WAR in the Gulf was in high gear. CIA intelligence said that Saddam Hussein, the brutal Iraqi ruler, was concealing biological and chemical weapons—the dreaded Weapons of Mass Destruction (WMDs)—that he might turn at any moment against our regional allies. If the intel was accurate, Saddam would be in violation of a UN disarmament resolution that the United States was intent on supporting, with force if necessary. A few optimists maintained that conflict could be averted, but for most of the country—certainly for most of us in uniform—it was clear that, whether the WMDs were real or not, it was only a matter of time before the United States, leading a multination "coalition of the willing," would be invading Iraq.

Since Saddam commanded the largest army in the Middle East and possessed a stubbornness equal to his brutality, the invasion was not expected to be a cakewalk. The coalition anticipated casualties, and in preparation for responding to them the Army's Regional Medical Center at Landstuhl, Germany—the major receiving hospital for troops wounded in the Middle East—was put on high alert. In addition, the medical capabilities of the US Naval Air Station at Rota, in southern Spain, were expanded, with support flown there from the United States to staff a new facility known as Field Hospital 8 (FH8). FH8 was to be a main receiving area for casualties from Iraq. As head of neuropsychiatry at Bremerton Naval Hospital, in Washington State, I was ordered to take over that position at FH8, heading a staff of ten at the Rota location.

I looked forward to the assignment with both personal and professional excitement. As a career military man—I had joined the Marine Corps as a youngster and was now a Navy commander—I was eager to do my part for

DOI: 10.7330/9781607329527.c004

the war effort. In addition, as a clinical psychologist who had done his PhD dissertation on combat-related PTSD, I wanted to help soldiers returning from Iraq deal with the emotional turmoil that war would inevitably throw at them. The posting to NAVSTA Rota seemed exactly what my career had been pointing me to.

But the excitement was tempered with apprehension. This concern had to do partly with the concern that any reasonable person feels on the eve of war, but mostly with a sense of uncertainty about how well prepared I was as a psychologist to deal with the emotional wounds that combat would create. I was an ostensibly well-educated young officer with a professional interest in PTSD, but in the military psychology circles of my Bremerton posting, there wasn't a lot of talk about treatment methods. I was familiar, for example, with CBT—cognitive behavioral therapy—but I didn't know if it was an appropriate tool to use with a stressed-out combat vet, and neither did any of my fellow trauma "experts." The DOD medical bureaucracy in which we served had not seen fit to make PTSD treatment part of our training.

As a result, I had become a PTSD specialist with a nearly empty toolbox. What's worse, as far as I could tell, nobody else in the military—certainly, nobody I knew personally—knew anything more than I did about managing combat stress. So being apprehensive about going to Rota wasn't unreasonable. I was worried that I might be in the position there of inventing a stress-response system from the ground up.

If I had any lingering optimism that the medical brass was on top of the situation, it was whisked away at Camp Pendleton in California during a simulation exercise conducted a few weeks before we shipped out to Rota. This exercise was designed to prepare FH8 medical personnel for the challenges we would find in receiving the wounded. In a mock triage scenario, each specialty got to hone its response measures by practicing on local Marines who played incoming casualties. On one Marine's arm would be a Magic Marker sign saying "fracture," on another one's stomach the phrase "grenade wound," and around a third one's neck a sign saying "BC," for biochemical. It all looked taut and professional until we were introduced to the "representative" combat stress victim. It was a young female Marine dressed not in battle fatigues but in a Bat Girl costume—cape, mask, the whole bit.

Using Bat Girl to represent victims of combat stress was insultingly wrong in more ways than I cared to count. As if the cartoon connection wasn't trivializing enough, the training gurus had selected a character whose name suggested a "batty" (and thus amusing) mental patient, and they had added a sexist twist by dressing their war stress victim in a provocative costume. We went through the motions of interviewing Bat Girl, but we were embarrassed by the farce, and so was she. I couldn't believe that this was the best the military could do to give my staff training in dealing with trauma. The experience didn't make me confident about what we would find in Spain.

"YOU'RE NOT ON THE LIST"

We arrived at NAVSTA Rota on February 17, 2003. With SEABEE help, we cleared and leveled a dirt field and then pitched numerous large medical field tents that would serve as the initial 116-bed facility. Our morale was high, with our enthusiasm boosted by urgency. We had no way of knowing when the expected invasion would begin, but we knew we had to be ready when the first wounded arrived. With the clock ticking at T minus "Who knows?" we had Fleet Hospital 8 up and ready for business in two days. Our director of medical services (DMS), here in Spain as at Bremerton, was a no-nonsense MD, Captain Greg Hoeksema.

Once the sprawling tent complex was up, Hoeksema called a meeting to give department heads their work station assignments. I arrived raring to go, but the meeting itself quickly changed my mood. It gave me the first of several stark revelations about just how little value our military field commanders were placing on mental health services for their returning troops.

There were several dozen department heads and enlisted leaders attending the meeting, standing in a large semicircle around Captain Hoeksema. Standing on a crate and reading from a clipboard, he barked out the assignments. One by one he called out the assigned areas for surgery, pharmacy, nursing, patient administration, and so on. But there was no mention of mental health, psychology, or trauma. When he finished he paused and said simply, "Ladies and gentlemen, you have your assignments. Get to it."

The area began to empty as department leaders corralled their staff and left to set up shop in the appropriate tent sections. Hoeksema was about to leave himself when I stepped forward. "Sir, what about mental health? Where are we to set up?"

His response floored me at the time, and even today it strikes me as unbelievable. "Mark," he said, "I don't see mental health anywhere on my list, and to be honest I'm not quite sure what you're supposed to be doing here in the first place."

For a moment I couldn't think of anything to say. This wasn't some brash kid from the backwoods who thought that psychological care was sissy stuff. It wasn't a blood 'n' guts general such as George Patton who didn't believe in battle fatigue. This was the DMS at a major receiving facility for soldiers who had just returned from combat. For someone in that position to wonder aloud what a psychologist was doing on his staff was simply mind-boggling.

If I had had more time, I might have reminded the DMS of the 1988 study that found 60 percent of wounded Vietnam veterans to be suffering the effects of PTSD (e.g., Kulka et al. 1990). I might have shared the findings from my own doctoral dissertation and numerous other studies, which showed that an even higher percentage of combat vets display a wide range of stress-related problems, including grief, anger, depression, substance abuse, and suicide (e.g., Glass and Bernucci 1966). I might have emphasized how critical it was to screen for the most common manifestation of war stress injury, the dissociative response called acute stress disorder (ASD), to lessen the chances of it developing into PTSD (Department of Veterans Affairs and Department of Defense 2004; Institute of Medicine 2008). I might have mentioned the vast array of returning vets' medically unexplained conditions that can be just as debilitating as PTSD but that have historically been dismissed as "psychosomatic" or "fake" (E. Jones and Wessely 2005). I might have said that those who provide care to wounded veterans—like his own medical staff—often endure an emotional wrenching of their own and that my staff and I were also here to deal with this secondary traumatization.

In my stunned state, all I could come up with was a boilerplate comment that even the DOD and VA could have endorsed. I was here, I told him, to document the medically evacuated soldiers' mental health needs and address them, just as his medical staff would be addressing their physical needs. According to the military's own textbook on war psychiatry and a robust scientific literature, I said, we needed to identify stress responses and stabilize mental health patients as quickly as possible after battle to prevent acute stress from developing into more severe, long-term disabling conditions (F. D. Jones 1995).

Hoeksema listened politely but was obviously unmoved. "Well," he said. "You're not on the list. You'll just have to ask around on the wards and see if they can find you a corner."

I watched the good doctor walk away, no doubt musing about what he evidently considered the "real" work of a postcombat receiving zone: patching up broken bodies. At Bremerton, I had already encountered a certain amount of resistance to the mental health field—the old "If you can't see it, it ain't there" prejudice. I had also witnessed the clownish insensitivity to mental illness that keeps stand-up comics in business. But I had never before experienced from a fellow health professional such a blatantly dismissive attitude toward my specialty—and, more important, toward the psychologically wounded warriors we were in Rota to serve.

Coming away from that meeting, I wanted to think of the DMS's dismissiveness as idiosyncratic, but I couldn't manage it. Practically fresh off the plane, I was already beginning to wonder: What if this archaic attitude was common here? What if, three decades after the end of the Vietnam War, combat stress was still considered a minor or fictional malady, not to be treated as aggressively as physical wounds? Even worse, what if the standard military view of combat stress remained Patton's (1947) idea that it was something "unmanly" that "real" soldiers don't talk about?

We were getting ready for war's inevitable casualties. We knew from a century and a half of dealing with them that some would be what the RAND Corporation would later call the "invisible wounds of war" (Tanielian and Jaycox 2008). Yet despite knowing how debilitating those unseen wounds could be, here we were, at the opening of the twenty-first century, consigning the mental health care of our wounded warriors to the same marginalized status as it had had during previous wars.

And it got worse. A couple of days after FH8 had officially opened for business, Captain Hoeksema instituted a morning meeting so department heads could report on the previous day's accomplishments and lay out a plan for the coming day. On the first such meeting I attended (as head of neuropsychiatry), Hoeksema had not called out my name. I had marked that up to oversight. When the same thing happened the next day, it became obvious that something was wrong. When I raised my hand to indicate that I was present, the DMS looked puzzled.

"Russell," he said, "I'm not sure why you're here. You don't really need to attend these meetings. I'm reassigning you to Urgent Care, under Dr. Schlegel. You can get the information you need from him."

To anyone who knew anything about mental health, this was a mystifying decision. Urgent Care, at Rota as at civilian hospitals, is what happens in the emergency room, as critical cases come in the door to be triaged. You might have a mental health specialist on hand in such a venue, to provide expert advice on the occasional psychiatric admission, but that person would not be subordinate to the ER staff. Nor in a well-run hospital would that person be permanently assigned to a triage entry point while psychiatric patients needed his or her attention elsewhere. There was no medical rationale to the DMS's decision.

Back in my office, I undertook the thankless task of informing my staff about what had transpired. "In effect," I said, "we have all been demoted.

Mental Health now has no official function at NAVSTA Rota. We are a support team for the ER."

"What do they think we're doing here?" my chief corpsman asked. "What does the DMS think is going to happen when kids are coming in from the desert with the thousand-yard stare?"

I didn't have an answer for him. All I knew was that the four of us were now an ancillary operation, with a dramatically reduced official standing. I also knew that I wasn't going to take this nonsense lying down.

JUMPING THE CHAIN

My hiatus from the leadership ranks lasted two weeks. It was a period in which we were still waiting for the first casualties to arrive, so I had time to plan my next move. I decided that rather than buck Hoeksema directly, I would put together a list of mental health agenda items that I thought should be part of the Rota blueprint and would present this list to Hoeksema's superiors as an informal Point Paper for a combat stress initiative. From my dissertation interviews, readings, and stateside experience with trauma victims, I had a good idea of what the initiative should look like, and since FH8 obviously had zero idea, starting from scratch was a logical option. I wouldn't be attacking somebody's else's plan of action, because nobody had one.

With assistance from a sympathetic head nurse, I put the Point Paper together in the first week of March. We began by noting that 40 to 60 percent of the combat casualties we were anticipating could be expected to sustain some stress-induced injury and that to deal with those casualties we would need a "reconditioning" program to determine which of them could be returned to duty (RTD) and which could not. We also recommended that we should screen *all* combat evacuees for stress-related problems, not just those presenting as psychiatric cases: this step would catch "nonpresenting" injuries and also destigmatize mental health issues by making the screenings a normal part of hospitalization. And we recommended that all patients admitted to FH8 attend a "homecoming debriefing" designed to ease their transition back to civilian life (Russell, Shoquist, and Chambers 2005).

Viewed from seventeen years down the line, these recommendations seem like common sense. In 2003, in the era of "Bat Girl" and "Find a corner," they constituted a revolutionary proposal. I knew that, and I knew too that taking the Point Paper to my direct superior, Captain Hoeksema, would be like asking him to add astrology to his medical kit bag. So I did something that military protocol tells you never to do: I jumped the chain of command.

Hoeksema's superior was FH8's commanding officer, Captain Patrick Kelly, an approachable guy whom I had first met lifting weights in the Bremerton gym, when he was the hospital's executive officer. He worked out daily in the Rota gym too, and I took the opportunity of joining him there one day, to pitch the combat stress initiative. I told him I was troubled at how ill equipped we were to handle our returning troops' mental health issues. I pointed out that while only 3 to 5 percent of combat evacuees are typically identified as psychiatric casualties, probably 40 percent are in danger of developing PTSD (Kulka et al. 1990). I told him that in a war with the threat of biochemical poison hovering over the battlefield, that rate was likely to rise to 60 percent. I noted that NAVSTA Rota's absence of a social support system put everyone—caregivers and soldiers alike—at risk. And I urged that at the very least we ought to establish a screening program, a reconditioning program, and a debriefing program.

"At present, Sir, unbelievable as it may seem," I said, "we've got no such programs in place anywhere else in the DOD medical system. In my professional opinion, we're going into this war completely unprepared to deal with the psychological damage of battlefield trauma."

That got the CO's attention, and it turned out that he was not a man to mince words or waste anyone's time. He asked me what I felt was needed to turn the situation around, and I said that I had already prepared a Point Paper that, if he wished, I could have on his desk that afternoon.

"Do that," he said. "But what about the DMS? Haven't you brought your concerns to the attention of Captain Hoeksema?"

It was a moment for diplomacy. I had already circumvented military protocol by reaching around Hoeksema, and I didn't want to aggravate matters by admitting why.

"Captain Hoeksema has been incredibly busy setting up the medical side of things, Sir. I thought he had enough on his plate. But with your permission I'll show him the Point Paper too. I realize that for something like this to work, all command levels have to be on board."

"They will be, Commander. I'll look for your report this afternoon."

Thanking Kelly for his attention, I rushed back to my quarters to put some finishing touches on the paper and had it on his desk that afternoon. The next day, I sought out Hoeksema to bring him into the loop. He had every right to resent me going around him, and I had every right to expect a chewing out, but that wasn't the way it went. By the time we met, he had already gotten a copy of the Point Paper from the CO, and he was as open to my suggestions as a few days before he had been dismissive. It's amazing what a gentle nudge from upstairs will do to military intransigence. Or maybe Hoeksema had just studied the paper himself and seen the light.

In any event, Captain Hoeksema soon became one of my staunchest supporters. He helped us distribute copies of the Point Paper, defended my recommendations in team meetings, and even reinvited me into the leadership circle. Within another day I was out of the shadow of Urgent Care and back in the saddle as head of psychiatric services—an area that, for the first time since we had landed in Spain, was now designated as a specialty functional area.

On March 15, I briefed the leadership staff—the circle I had once been banned from—on the combat stress initiative we were in the process of implementing. On March 16, the program itself went live, complete with full command approval, an RN training officer, a staff of five, and a ten-bed mental health ward functioning not as an Urgent Care sideshow but as the "key component" of the mission that my Point Paper had asked for. After a frustrating month of battling traditional attitudes, I was finally able to breathe a sigh of relief. When the casualties started coming in, we were ready.

When the war began and Rota began receiving its wounded, we made the "to do" list of the Point Paper an action agenda. Of the 1,500 medically evacuated battlefield casualties that came to us from the Middle East, we screened 96 percent of them for combat stress—whether or not they presented with psychiatric symptoms. We identified roughly 400 of them who we believed would profit from a psychiatric follow-up, and we arranged for individual debriefings of those individuals before they were sent back to the States (Russell, Shoquist, and Chambers 2005). Measured against the prevailing standard of care, these were revolutionary advances. And they had been made possible only because I had violated disciplinary protocol and jumped the chain.

SCREAMING INTO THE STORM

I'd like to say that the successful implementation of my Point Paper bore fruit beyond the 2003 Gulf War. I'd like to say that the good sense shown by my superiors Hoeksema and Kelly was shared by brass further up the hierarchy and that, working with DOD, we implemented universal screening, reconditioning, and debriefing. I'd like to say, too, that we broke down the traditional attitude that soldiers with traumatic experiences should "suck it up" and that my small contribution to common sense at NAVSTA Rota was the first step in a long overdue transformation of military psychiatry. But none of this happened.

In fact, my jumping the chain of command at Rota was the first step in a long, thankless struggle against the same entrenched attitudes that had created the "Bat Girl" scenario in the first place. The struggle began in 2003, when I returned from Rota to Bremerton and, painfully aware of my own lack of training, conducted a pioneering survey of 133 mental health specialists to determine the level of their training to handle combat stress casualties (Russell and Silver 2007). I found that 90 percent of DOD providers had received *no* training at all in any of the therapies recommended by the VA and the military itself (Department of Veterans Affairs and Department of Defense 2004; Russell and Silver 2007). This and other findings clashed dramatically with DOD's own public pronouncements that it was providing veterans "the highest quality of mental health services available" (Department of Veterans Affairs and Department of Defense 2004).

In August 2003, I sent DOD the first of many memos and Point Papers detailing my concerns that veterans' health was being put at risk by a combination of this inadequate training, a lack of research, staffing shortages, clinician retention problems, and poor access to providers (Russell 2006). As each of my pleas was passed dutifully up the chain of command, what ensued was a tragic farce of lip service, misdirection, and outright lying, at the end of which my findings disappeared into a black hole of apathy. Before long, repeated frustration led me to conclude that military medicine's leadership had mastered the arts of inaction, window dressing, cover-up, and denial. In Rota I had "jumped the chain" successfully to one sympathetic officer. Moving further up the chain to those who might actually change the system started to feel to me like screaming into a storm.

By January 2006, I had had enough. I filed a formal complaint against military medicine with DOD's inspector general (IG), asking for an expedited review of the issues I had been raising for the previous three years (Russell 2006). The responses included further foot-dragging; the appointment of a do-nothing Task Force (Department of Justice Task Force on Mental Health 2007); an invitation to give a talk entitled "Broken Promises" (Batdorff 2006), which was praised by my superiors but led to nothing; a pointless photo-op with Congresswoman Barbara Boxer; and a deeper black hole. At one point in the midst of this windmill tilting, I was quoted by *USA Today* as describing a "perfect storm" of rising veterans' needs meeting inadequate caregiver training and impediments to access (Zoroya 2007). Without setting out to do so, I had evolved from a concerned military officer and clinician to an outraged whistleblower, on a crusade to end the tragic cycle of preventable crises by transforming the military and national mental healthcare systems.

The system reacted as one would expect a threatened bureaucracy to react. Even as I was receiving praise and official commendations for my work on veterans' behalf, the brass was telling me, bluntly, to hold my tongue. I first received some subtle hints about speaking more softly. Then a Public Affairs Guidance memo came from Navy headquarters, dictating that despite all evidence to the contrary, no one in uniform should say anything publicly about the existence of a mental health crisis (Department of Navy 2007). Finally, I received a direct order not to speak to the press.

And one more thing. In 2006 and again in 2007, after receiving glowing praise on my annual fitness reports (FITREPs), I was inexplicably passed over for promotion to captain. Although the obvious reason was retaliation, I formally requested that the IG investigate the circumstances leading to the decision not to promote me (Russell 2007). The IG refused, and I left the military after twenty-six years of service. The status quo had won. I had lost, but so had millions of combat-damaged veterans, victims of invisible wounds that the Pentagon, loyal to "tradition," would prefer to remain invisible.

Unfortunately, proper treatment of war stress victims is still inhibited, if not actively blocked, by traditional attitudes, archaic policies, and in many cases political agendas that do not include a concern for veterans' rights. In official releases, the military claims that it is providing "aggressive treatment for all our veterans' mental health issues" (Department of Navy 2007). That's not the reality as finally confirmed by the DOD task force (Department of Defense Task Force on Mental Health 2007). The chronic delays in treatment long associated with this bureaucracy—notoriously exemplified in the "secret waiting list" scandal of 2014—are exacerbated for veterans suffering from combat stress because the military has not yet made mental health a priority. And it is the military's own institutional culture that perpetuates this situation.

A chief cause of the neglect, ironically, is the very mindset that is intended to produce good warriors—the "suck it up" attitude that is ingrained in boot camp, glorified in popular culture, and embraced by the services as a mark of honor. Although undeniably useful in promoting a martial spirit and the will to fight, this attitude can easily harden into disdain for "weakness," including the vulnerability revealed in PTSD and other war stress conditions. As a psychologist, I am obliged to take a compassionate approach to stress victims, but the obligation is not felt by all military officers, and there remains some Patton-like suspicion of psychiatry as a mysterious enterprise whose practical effect is to "coddle" malingerers. Given this common attitude, it's no wonder that mental health services had no place in the Rota field hospital blueprint—or that, in trying to make a place for it in the system overall, I was seen as disruptive of conventional respect for the hierarchy.

Like all bureaucracies, the military has a tendency to close ranks against criticism. Those who identify flaws in the system are seen as offering not improvement but disruption. Demands for change are seen as threats to the status quo or, even worse, as attempts to "make us look bad." The interplay of institutionalized machismo, lack of accountability, and bureaucratic defensiveness creates a military culture of evasion and denial. As a result, the very institutions that have approved the use of stress-mitigation therapies have not come through with the financial, training, or logistical changes required to put those therapies into operation (Russell 2008). Since the system puts protocol ahead of people, the ship keeps steaming fast in the wrong direction, and nobody has the will to change the course.

But the fight goes on. Today, as a civilian psychologist and the founder of the Institute of War Stress Injury, Recovery, and Social Justice, I continue the battle for common sense on combat veterans' behalf, while the system that is supposed to be honoring them seems committed to the denial of mental health's importance. There is really only one way to turn that around: to recognize that the goal of discipline isn't discipline itself but the more effective functioning of the military organism. If that organism is malfunctioning, as our current military mental health system is malfunctioning, the good soldier's job isn't to continue following orders. It is to point out flaws, to complain, to suggest improvements. I believed in 2003, and I still believe now, that if the only way to fix what's broken is to jump the chain of command, doing so isn't a violation of duty. It is the fulfillment of a warrior's highest duty: concern for your comrades.

WORKS CITED

Batdorff, Ann. 2006. "Officer Sees 'Perfect Storm' Brewing in Military's Mental Health Care System." *Stars and Stripes Pacific*, September 22. http://www.stripes.com/news /officer-sees-perfect-storm-brewing-in-military-s-mental-health-care-system-1.54480.

Department of Defense Task Force on Mental Health. 2007. "An Achievable Vision: Report of the Department of Defense Task Force on Mental Health." Falls Church, VA: Defense Health Board.

Department of Navy. 2007. "Mental Health Public Affairs Guidance of 23 January 2007." Unpublished document. US Navy Medical Department, Navy Medicine West, Bureau of Medicine and Surgery, Washington, DC.

Department of Veterans Affairs and Department of Defense. 2004. "VA/DoD Clinical
    Practice Guideline for the Management of Post-Traumatic Stress." Office of Quality
    and Performance publication 10Q-CPG/PTSD-04, Veterans Health Administration,
    Department of Veterans Affairs and Health Affairs, Department of Defense,
    Washington, DC.
Glass, Albert J., and Robert J. Bernucci, 1966. "Medical Department United States Army.
    Neuropsychiatry in World War II." Volume I, "Zone of Interior." Washington DC:
    Office of the Surgeon General, Department of the Army.
Institute of Medicine. 2008. *Gulf War and Health.* Vol. 6, *Physiologic, Psychologic and Psychosocial
    Effects of Deployment-Related Stress.* Washington, DC: The National Academies Press.
Jones, Edgar and Simon Wessely. 2005. *Shell Shock to PTSD: Military Psychiatry from 1900 to
    the Gulf War.* New York: Psychology Press.
Jones, Franklin. D. 1995. "Psychiatric Lessons of War." In *Textbook of Military Medicine:
    War Psychiatry,* edited by Franklin D. Jones, Linette R. Sparacino, Victoria L. Wilcox,
    Joseph M. Rothberg, and James W. Stokes, 1–34. Washington, DC: Borden Institute.
Kulka, Richard A., William E. Schlenger, John A. Fairbank, Richard L. Hough, B. Kathleen.
    Jordan, Charles R. Marmar, Daniel Weiss, and David. A. Grady. 1990. *Trauma and
    the Vietnam War Generation: Report of Findings from the National Vietnam Veterans
    Readjustment Study.* New York: Brunner/Mazel.
Patton, George. C. 1947. *War As I Knew It: The Battle Memoirs of "Blood 'N Guts."* New York:
    Bantam Books.
Russell, Mark. 2006. "Mental Health Crisis in the Department of Defense: DOD Inspector
    General Hotline Investigation #98829." Report submitted by Commander Mark
    Russell, USN on 05JAN2006. Available upon request via Freedom of Information
    Act (FOIA) at Department of Defense, Office of Freedom of Information, 1155
    Defense Pentagon, Washington, DC 20301–1155.
Russell, Mark C. 2008. "Scientific Resistance to Research, Training and Utilization of
    EMDR Therapy in Treating Post-war Disorders." *Social Science and Medicine* 67 (11):
    1737–1746.
Russell, Mark, and Steve M. Silver. 2007. "Training Needs for the Treatment of Combat-
    Related Post-Traumatic Stress Disorder: A Survey of Department of Defense
    Clinicians." *Traumatology* 13 (3): 4–10.
Russell, Mark, Devin Shoquist, and Chris Chambers, 2005. "Effectively Managing the
    Psychological Wounds of War." *Navy Medicine* (April–March): 23–26.
Tanielian, Terri, and Lisa H. Jaycox, 2008. *Invisible Wounds of War: Psychological and Cognitive
    Injuries, Their Consequences, and Services to Assist Recovery.* Center for Military Health
    Policy Research MG-720-CCF. Santa Monica: RAND. http://www.rand.org/pubs
    /monographs/MG720.html.
Zoroya, Gregg. 2007. "Navy Psychologist: Navy Faces Crisis." *USA Today,* January 17,
    2007. http://usatoday30.usatoday.com/news/health/2007-01-16-ptsd-navy_x.htm.

5

A Captain's First Duty
Managing Command Disconnect in a Combat Zone

Ronald Fry

SOLDIERS FOLLOW ORDERS.

THIS IS A CARDINAL—ARGUABLY *THE* CARDINAL—TENET of military discipline, considered indispensable for maintaining unit cohesion, professional decorum, and the integrity of the command chain, which in turn is considered indispensable to operational success. In modern armies, it is only by subordinating themselves to the plans of "higher" that individual soldiers cohere into fighting units dedicated to each other and to common purposes. That is why disobeying orders and, more broadly, insubordination are so strongly condemned in military law. When a modern soldier denies the authority of his chief, he becomes, by that action, a self-indulgent anachronism, more akin to an ancient berserker than a disciplined service member. We may admire soldiers' daring in asserting themselves, but we understand why the system must condemn them: they threaten the stabilizing principle of hierarchical control.

But "obedience to higher" is not an absolute principle. In the US military particularly, soldiers are not encouraged to be mindless automata but rather thoughtfully willing agents of *legitimate* authority. The Uniform Code of Military Justice, which defines infractions against discipline, is specific about this. Violations of the "obey orders" principle are covered in UCMJ Articles 90 through 92, which stipulate courts-martial for failure to obey the order of a commissioned officer (Article 90) or that of a noncommissioned officer (Article 91) or for failure to obey a general order (Article 92). Disobedience to commissioned officers "in time of war" may subject the offender to the death penalty (Article 90.2). But military courts have discretion in these matters, especially when the offended party is not an officer. In addition, the code's wording explicitly notes that soldiers may only

DOI: 10.7330/9781607329527.c005

be punished for "willfully disobey[ing] a *lawful*" command. The GIs who obeyed their captain's order to kill civilians at My Lai had no legal obligation to do so. On paper, at least, the code asks for disobedience in such cases.

But it is not only illegal orders that can sometimes appear questionable. In a war zone, operational orders are often passed down to troops on the ground from "higher" authorities billeted far away, in air-conditioned staff rooms behind the wire. No matter how well meaning these distant planners may be, their Situation Awareness can never be as precise as that of the men in harm's way, and so it sometimes happens that the orders they send down the chain are disconnected from reality. From time to time, therefore, a field commander receives orders that, while they may be perfectly legal, are also perfectly stupid—stupid because they misconstrue the situation and imperil his men.

When that happens, I would argue that the field commander is allowed, even required, to disobey the legal order so he or she can fulfill the higher duty of protecting his fellow soldiers. In this chapter, I will make this some-what unconventional case by describing an incident that happened to me in a war zone when, as a field commander I received a perfectly legal order whose implementation, I was convinced, would get my men killed.

A DEADLY VALLEY

The incident happened in Afghanistan's volatile Pech Valley during that early phase of the War on Terror known as Operation Enduring Freedom (OEF). As Alexander the Great, the British, and the Russians had discovered earlier, this area of Nuristan and Kunar Provinces breeds some of the toughest and most brutal fighters the world has ever known. In 2003, as an American-led coalition was attempting to pacify the region, it was the only known enclave in the country where an active Al-Qaeda group was operating. A shadowy network of enemy forces also included Taliban and other fighting groups who were either native to the area or seeking refuge there. The villagers, who were as hard as the terrain that surrounded them, protected or tolerated these groups in their midst. Between 2003 and 2011, 75 percent of the ordnance dropped in the entire conflict in Afghanistan was dropped in this area. Of the thirteen Medals of Honor earned by US troops there, eleven went to men fighting in these hills. The Pech, in short, was a turbulent and deadly Area of Operation.

In November 2003, a huge conventional and Special Operations mission entered the Pech Valley, attempting to hunt down terrorists and High Value Targets. As the mission wound down, Army planners decided that one Special Forces Operational Detachment Alpha (ODA) would remain behind to hold the ground gained in the operation. The ODA was to construct an A-Camp near Manogay Village deep in the Pech, build an army out of local villagers, befriend the local government and tribes, and destroy the enemy or deny them sanctuary. A platoon of forty infantrymen and a mortar team were tasked to help secure the new A-Camp. As the commander of ODA 936, code-named Hammerhead Six, I was put in charge of this critical mission, and on December 4, I assumed control of US forces in the Pech.

As we began fortifying the camp and engaging with the locals, we found them very curious about the new Americans, who bore little resemblance to the "helmeted ones"—Russian and American—with whom they had had contact up to that point. Green Berets in the field are permitted latitude in appearance, and because of our beards and our nonregulation attire, we became known for a time, erroneously, as the "Muslim Americans." We knew that being well received in this way would cause ire among our enemies, and so we expected that they would mount a display of force. They would want to reestablish their relevance not only to threaten us but to impress the local people upon whom they depended for moral and material support.

That display came a week after our arrival. On December 11, as we were on a supply run from our new camp to the Forward Operating Base at Asadabad, about twenty miles away, one of our two Humvees was rocked by an Improvised Explosive Device that detonated underneath it, completely ripping apart the engine compartment, drive train, and front axle. The machine gunner was blown from the turret and sustained mild injuries. I was in the lead truck, which wasn't hit, and my crew was quickly able to secure the IED site as Mike, our medic, began assessing injuries on the parties in the damaged truck. Within ten minutes, other ODA members and the six members of our Afghan Security Force joined the scene, securing the road and keeping onlookers from getting close. Within a relatively short period of time a medevac arrived and took the injured gunner to Bagram Airbase. We had survived an enemy assault with no lives lost. But as I assessed the situation, things didn't look good.

We were on an obviously dangerous road with a small group of fighting men and a vehicle that was damaged beyond repair. The satellite radio had also been damaged, so my communication with Bagram Airbase, where my superiors were located, had to be relayed or echoed through our new A-Camp. The road was flanked by hills and low buildings that might contain the roadside bomber and any number of his friends. And it was 1600 hours on a winter day: the sun was setting. Given this scenario, my priority was clear: Get my men out of there ASAP to avoid further casualties.

But we couldn't leave the damaged truck in its current condition. Even though it was not drivable, it could still prove an asset to a scavenging enemy, who could use its armored plating to reinforce fighting positions. So it had to be destroyed. The only question was the method of destruction. I requested that the medevac escort, an AH-64 Apache gunship, destroy the vehicle with its 30mm cannon or a Hellfire missile. I wanted it to blow the vehicle off the road to avoid collateral damage and to deny the enemy the use of anything we could not strip off it first. From the perspective of a field commander thinking of his men, this was the logical option—in fact, the only option—and so when I radioed command at Bagram to secure approval, I expected the brass to respond with "Roger that."

Amazingly, they did not. My request for destruction by the Apache was denied. And as if that weren't crazy enough, I also heard a "higher" planner's voice issue this order: "We need to retrieve the asset and study it for intel. You and your team will remain and guard it from hostiles." I could hardly believe what I was hearing, and yet as I thought about it afterward, the remote staff officer's order seemed all too typical. It was a perfect illustration of the operational disconnect that can emerge between big-picture planners and commanders on the ground.

THE DISCONNECT

By the time we had medevac'd our personnel and were considering the fate of our destroyed truck, we had already been stationary in that location for over an hour. Since we were a small unit operating in the back yard of the enemy, mobility was the key to our security. The fact that on that day we had been immobilized in a location that the enemy had chosen told me this was ideal terrain for them to mount an attack. The mujahedeen had used that tactic repeatedly against the Russians in the 1980s (Grau 1998). I knew that every minute we remained immobile gave the enemy more time to mass their forces and prepare for an attack on our numerically inferior force. And nightfall, which would normally be to our advantage, would not help us, because half of the Afghan Security Force members who were with us were not issued night vision goggles. Fighting at night without them could invite a friendly fire mishap.

These tactical issues were significant, but for me as a ground commander one other consideration was paramount. It can be stated as a simple axiom: personnel are more important than property. While military tradition may say that "the mission" is paramount—I don't argue with that in principle—it's also true that if you don't take care of your people, there is no mission. On the day of the IED attack, I knew that if we were going to accomplish our mission in the Pech Valley, keeping my men alive was more important than protecting a disabled vehicle. This conclusion reflected a principle that is enshrined in the Special Forces training literature. In a list of the five Special Forces "truths" that constitute a kind of Green Beret philosophy, the first one reads: "Truth 1: Humans are more important than hardware. People—not equipment—make the critical difference. The right people, highly trained and working as a team, will accomplish the mission with the equipment available. On the other hand, the best equipment in the world cannot compensate for a lack of the right people" (United States Special Operations Command, n.d.). I didn't have that wording consciously in mind that December day, but its spirit was an essential part of my attitude.

The attitude, and the spirit, were different back in Bagram headquarters. There, in a compound called Camp Vance, senior officers officially "direct" all the Special Operation missions at the Forward bases. In this HQ are seasoned officers and NCOs that are in the country but not really in the war. They eat three hot meals a day, have showers every day, and have ironed uniforms. There are no beards, no village elders, and no fighters, friendly or hostile, to deal with on a daily basis. Life at such a base, even in war-torn Afghanistan, doesn't differ very much from life at Fort Bragg, North Carolina. Yet it was these fairly isolated individuals manning the radios at Camp Vance that had the authority to respond to my request for vehicle destruction. They may very well have been decent and intelligent people. But their perspective was so divorced from mine that disconnect was built in to the situation.

At the time I requested permission to destroy the vehicle with the AH-64, I assumed it would be approved. When it wasn't, there was a flurry of infuriating messages between our side and Bagram. I was sharing what I was seeing, and Bagram was giving instructions as if they could not comprehend what was being said. I got the impression that the senior officers felt they understood the situation better than I did. Yet the "higher" guidance I was receiving made no sense. And the sense it made to Bagram was of a "strategic" nature. The "intel" they might get from the "asset" would help refine war planning. No matter that getting that intel might cost soldiers' lives and compromise our ability to accomplish our larger mission in the Pech.

As I assessed our situation and weighed the benefits of guarding the vehicle so someone could analyze the blast damage versus doing what my instinct, training, and common sense were telling me to do, I had to make a decision. If we left, I would be putting my career at risk by disregarding an order from a senior officer. If we stayed in that untenable location, I risked losing some of my team. Not only would I take the blame for that but, along with grieving family members, I would have to live with the results of my decision. Although I was junior to the Bagram staffers, including my commanding officer Colonel Walter Herd, I was the one on the ground with the stewardship of the mission. It was my men's lives on the line and my decision.

In the end, although I knew it was professionally risky, in human terms it was an easy decision to make. I had the team strip the dead vehicle of radios, tires, and anything else of worth. Our engineer Jason rigged it with explosives. We moved a few straggling onlookers off to safety, gave the truck a wide berth ourselves, and set off the charges. Within minutes the Humvee was a wreckage of smoldering metal. As darkness fell, we packed everyone into the remaining truck and returned to camp. I felt confident and unconflicted about the decision, but I figured I hadn't heard the last of the incident.

I was right. The men of ODA 936 and the Afghans who worked with us were relieved to return to our A-Camp in one piece. We had come out on top of a nasty situation. But that euphoric feeling was dashed a few days later when it became clear that the senior officers at Camp Vance were not pleased. They interpreted my action as insubordination—as stipulated in UCMJ Article 90. Technically, since my disobedience had occurred "in time of war," I could have faced execution for protecting my men. Nobody at Bagram was so stupid as to invoke that idea, though for months after the fact I was under threat of punitive action. During that time, my fate was in the hands of Colonel Herd, who had selected me as field commander in the first place but whose feathers had been ruffled by my second-guessing his decision.

Given the situation, Herd could have chosen to reward or to punish. He could have rewarded my initiative and supported my decision to protect men in his command; this might actually have earned him some credit for empowering a field commander. Or he could interpret my decision as reckless, as a threat to "discipline," and pursue a punishment designed to deter any other junior officers from making similarly bold, unsanctioned decisions in the future. The colonel decided to punish, and for a time he actually contemplated dragging me into a court-martial. Eventually he opted for a punishment that targeted my pocketbook, issuing a formal demand that I "pay for the truck." This was of course ludicrous, since an armored Humvee at the time cost a quarter of a million dollars. But it was a distracting morale suck all the same, and it didn't improve my opinion of the colonel's common sense.

The issue hung on for months until a *60 Minutes* reporter, Lara Logan, in the course of doing a story about our ODA, started asking the brass embarrassing questions. Seeing the PR downside of disciplining me, the senior officers let the matter drop. The wisdom of my "disobedience" had thus been vindicated not by strategic reconsiderations but by the fear of bad press.

LESSONS LEARNED

There are two major lessons to be learned from the "blown truck" disconnect and its ultimate resolution. The first is that despite official pronouncements that military personnel are members of a unified team, there is a critical and long-standing distinction between field and staff personnel—between, to use Army slang, the "grunts at the front" and the folks who provide rear-area support. Among field personnel, you often sense an "us versus them" mentality that has probably been felt by frontline fighters since the dawn of warfare. That mentality has long been an element of US military life and was particularly pronounced during World War I.

Theoretically, this divide shouldn't exist, because at one time many staff and senior officers and NCOs were junior officers and soldiers on the front lines. As they gained experience, they were relegated to "big picture" oversight or staff positions well behind the front lines, but they carried with them the experience that got them the "promotion." In an ideal world, therefore, military field personnel would be trusted and given the same confidence that the senior officers expected when they were in that position. Likewise, the field personnel would respect the staffers' experience and appreciate the guidance they could offer to the field.

In reality this relationship is rarely the case. There is an animosity from the field personnel towards the staffers that are disconnected from the reality on the ground and distanced from the battle. The field personnel imagine a more comfortable life for the staffers and resent being told what to do by those in the "rear." This contrast leads to an attitude that those in the field are "us" and those that are not sharing the hardships, and do not understand the realities of war, are "them," a disconnect that creates communication static between frontline and rear echelons and can therefore inhibit the troops from accomplishing their aims. This factor was clearly in play during our troubled exchange with Camp Vance.

The second lesson is that while respect for the hierarchy has a valid rationale, in certain cases ignoring the chain of command is the only way for a commander to perform his first duty, which is to protect the integrity of the mission by protecting his or her troops. This truth is best realized, perhaps only realized, in battle. I found this out in Afghanistan by violating a legal order that I knew was wrong. It was this decision that actually made me a leader in the eyes of my men. They trusted me after that incident because I had their back. They knew they meant more to me than any amount of hardware.

What I learned that December day was that while blowing the truck was insubordination in the eyes of the colonel, the staffers, and the UCMJ, to the men I led it was a courageous and commonsense decision. I resented armchair quarterbacks telling me to do something stupid with the men over whom I had a stewardship, and so I made a decision that I knew was only mine to make. When my team saw that, it had an immeasurable positive impact on my ability to lead. The confidence that the troops allotted me from that time forth contributed much to our successful operations in the Pech Valley (Fry 2016).

The impact went far beyond my ODA. So rare is "insubordination" of this type that my "rash" decision acquired a legendary aura. Not long after we returned to camp after the attack, the story of the captain who blew up his own truck went viral on the OEF grapevine. On three separate occasions when I was at Camp Vance, stewing over the possibility of being court-martialed, I was greeted by NCOs who had heard the story and wanted to know if I was "that Captain." When I nodded yes, I got a crisp, respectful salute and a heartfelt thanks. My support of men in the ranks had earned their support. I was flattered by that, and I think back on it with pleasure. But there's also a sense of sadness that accompanies this memory. I think sometimes of the irony that my support of the troops also lends support to the damaging old tradition that within the big team of the service, it's still us versus them.

WORKS CITED

Fry, Ronald, with Tad Tuleja. 2016. *Hammerhead Six: How Green Berets Waged an Unconventional War against the Taliban to Win in Afghanistan's Deadly Pech Valley.* New York: Hachette Books.

Grau, Lester W. 1998. *The Bear Went over the Mountain: Soviet Combat Tactics in Afghanistan.* London: Routledge.

Uniform Code of Military Justice. Articles 90–92, US Code, Title 10, Subtitle A, Part II, Chapter 47.

United States Special Operations Command. n.d. "SOF Truths." http://www.socom.mil /about/sof-truths.

Part III
Questioning the Patriotic Crusade

6

(De)composing the "Machine of Decomposition"

Creative Insubordination in E.E. Cummings's The Enormous Room

Matthew David Perry

THE AMERICAN POET E.E. CUMMINGS was known for idiosyncratic poetry that challenged conventional linguistic structures and traditional forms. He experimented with capitalization, syntax, punctuation, and spelling to produce a unique poetic expression that won him a broad audience by the time of his death in 1962. His experimental style, long considered a hallmark of American modernism, emerged not merely from his personal creativity but from a particular experience in the service during World War I. As a Red Cross ambulance driver in France in 1917, Cummings encountered government censorship firsthand in his letters home, and later, suspected of sedition for letters he helped a friend to write, he was detained in a French military prison for three months. He used that experience as the basis for his first prose work, *The Enormous Room* (1922), a retrospective account of his service and imprisonment. In this chapter I will show how, in that account, Cummings uses a linguistic strategy of creative insubordination as a form of protest against a suppressive wartime climate.

"SUBVERSIVE" LETTERS

Cummings's military experience was as a volunteer in the Norton-Harjes Red Cross Ambulance Corps, an organization whose membership included such other literary figures as Robert W. Service, John Dos Passos, and Ernest Hemingway. He enlisted in the corps officially on April 17, 1917, just eleven days after the United States entered the conflict, mainly as a way of avoiding conscription—or, as Richard Kennedy put it, because of a "desire to govern his own destiny" and because he was "pacifist by inclination and this

DOI: 10.7330/9781607329527.c006

was noncombatant duty" (1980, 136–137). But Cummings quickly became disillusioned with his endeavor. He voiced his displeasure with his service in many letters home, openly disparaging the military effort. He referred to his section chief as "much worse" than a "despicable . . . tight-fisted, pull-for-special-privilege, turd," and he criticized another chief's assistant as having "a complete lack of education plus a perfect absence of inherent intelligence" (Cummings 1969, 27–28). Of a third superior, Cummings writes in French that he has one "eye blocked by a monocle" and that he talks "without moving his mouth" (1969, 26). The impression is that of a blind robot only capable of uttering speech that is not his.

Cummings's early letters are openly critical of the war effort and of military personnel. In one letter to his parents, he openly criticizes the US government, and especially the military. As an inexperienced volunteer, he writes,

> The amazing vulgarity of the whole deal—I mean La Croix Rouge, Voluntier Cummings—keeps one from jubilations on one's successful Escape from conscription, which, says wireless, has magnificently sailed through the "congress" of the Land of the "Free" and the Home of the "Brave." Tra-la, tra-la. All the beef-slobbering, soup-guzzling, khaki-breasted muckers on board will, I trust, someday be congressmen—or senators! (1969, 19)

Cummings's early correspondence is laced with this type of criticism. Identifying both the Red Cross and his own participation in it as "vulgar," he intensifies his criticism by a liberal use of sardonic quotation marks that take aim at patriotic clichés about freedom and bravery, even as they suggest an unsavory alliance between his fellow soldiers—the "khaki-breasted muckers"—and the American government.

Despite reprimands from authorities, as well as the threat of punishment from government censors both abroad and at home, his criticisms continued, though they became increasingly veiled. After learning that his early letters home had been censored, he admits, "I'm at a loss to know what to say, inasmuch as M. le Censor has seen fit to withhold my past effusions." But he adds, "I shall, accordingly, do my best to say nothing at all, trusting that you will understand" (1969, 28). He seems to back away from his criticisms, but the phrase "trusting that you will understand" suggests duplicity, which reverberates throughout many of his letters. In one letter to his father, for example, Cummings describes hiding in pajamas from German artillery, as "the sole piece of 'service' I have seen" (1969, 31). The quotation marks around "service" seem to call into question not only his own behavior but the whole concept of appropriate military service.

In other letters to his mother, he relies on repetition and underlining to convey irony as well: "Please, please, PLEASE don't get the idea that I am <u>ever</u> in danger . . . or that I <u>ever</u> carry wounded, or that I am <u>ever</u> anything but grateful for" being "incapable of escape" from wartime experience (1969, 32). Elsewhere, he reveals his location to his mother as "a place hardly germane to my malcontent nature" and as quiet enough to study Charles Dickens's "little Nell." Thus in the very act of attempting to assuage his mother's anxiety, he circumvents military regulations by revealing, or at least hinting at, his location within the war zone (1969, 33).

In effect, to disguise information in his letters that censors would ordinarily find objectionable, Cummings withdraws from official language. Instead, he employs double entendre, slang, foreign language, variant spacing and punctuation, and obscure literary allusions. His communiqués signify what Jeffrey Walsh would later identify as "code-making," a "manipulating of language registers" in order to convey an alternative message (1976, 35). All of these characteristics, inspired by his wartime situation, would become central elements in an idiolect that he would refine and develop later in his poetry.

As ingenious as Cummings's linguistic disguises may have been, they were not successful in keeping him out of trouble. On September 23, 1917, only five weeks into his service, the young ambulance driver was arrested by French military authorities on suspicion of sedition. The "evidence" against him was that he had helped another soldier, William Slater Brown, write letters that contained "subversive" language that the government wanted suppressed. He is accused of having "written to friends in America and to his family very bad letters" (Cummings [1922] 1978, 12–13). Cummings claims to know nothing of these "very bad letters"; however, he does admit to knowing of a letter written by a French friend to the under-secretary of state in French Aviation requesting that the Americans be permitted to enlist in the Lafayette Esquadrille. Apparently at this point, despite his disdain for the authorities, Cummings retained affection for the Allied cause.

The two Americans are interrogated by French officials about their letter writing, their political sentiments, and their supposed pacifism. Then Cummings's inquisitor asks a direct question: "Est-ce que vous détestez les boches?" (Do you hate the Germans?).

"To walk out of the room a free man," Cummings writes in *The Enormous Room*, "I had merely to say yes" ([1922] 1978, 14). But he will not give the official this satisfaction. Instead of the simple exculpatory "Yes," he offers a deliberately ambiguous answer: "Non. J'aime beaucoup les français" (No. I like the French very much). After some additional verbal fencing in which

Cummings in effect casts doubt on official government reports of German atrocities, he and his friend are arrested on suspicion of spying and sent to a French military prison, the Dépôt de Triage at La Ferté Macé, in Normandy.

There is linguistic irony to this outcome. Whereas war opponents in the United States are being imprisoned under the 1917 and 1918 Espionage and Sedition Acts for both spoken and written criticism of the war, support of Germany, and espousal of radical political ideologies, Cummings is imprisoned for what he does not write and what he will not say. Although he admits that he and his accomplices directed the French serviceman to write the letter in question at his "urgent request," Cummings does not actually write the letter himself (Cummings [1922] 1978, 13). Additionally, his answers to his inquisitors' questions are not explicitly treasonous, and his response that he loves the French when asked if he hates the Germans is not a defense of Germany, but only an insufficiently strong condemnation. He is imprisoned, in effect, for not saying enough—that is, for not paying proper respect to the official line. He discovers that in wartime, failing to wave the flag with sufficient exuberance may easily be construed as trampling upon it.

THE DÉPÔT: THE MACHINE OF DECOMPOSITION

The Dépôt de Triage at La Ferté Macé was a French seminary that was closed in 1906; it was reopened during World War I and converted into a makeshift prison, as Kennedy points out, for people "who were suspected of espionage or whose presence was generally undesirable during time of war" (1980, 148–149). The "undesirables" were a miscellany of multinational, multilingual prisoners held not because they were necessarily guilty of espionage, but because they could not prove they were properly aligned with the French national interests that supported the war effort.

The absurdity of his "trial" notwithstanding, Cummings certainly fit into this category. It might even be argued that his sly answer to the question about hating Germans was not just a defiance of his interrogators' authority over language. In a way it was a strategy for leaving the front. The Dépôt de Triage was a kind of vacation retreat for soldiers, those on leave from battle, and those shirking their duties at the front. It existed partly because "the Armies of the Allies were continually retreating" from city to city, causing refugees to be housed there (Cummings [1922] 1978, 60). As a grim refuge—literal and figurative—within but away from the war, it was therefore a fitting home for a disillusioned ambulance driver. Cummings was sent there as punishment, yet the prison served him as a tactical "retreat," an oppositional position from which he was able to mount a criticism of war and the language of war to assert his own values.

The prisoners at La Ferté Macé were more a ragtag collection of lower-class unfortunates than real criminals, and Cummings refers to them using pet names reflective of their situations and characteristics. Some were refugees from surrounding towns overrun by the military; some were immigrants who could neither speak French nor understand French wartime regulations; some were illiterate, disabled, indigent, or even developmentally disabled (Kennedy 1980). Most were jailed for absurd reasons, on legal technicalities that at best only violated tenuous notions of French officialdom and at worst had no basis in law whatsoever.

In *The Enormous Room*—the title refers to the prison's huge central room—Cummings emphasizes the ridiculous nature of the crimes for which the inmates were imprisoned. The prisoner called Mexique was detained for asking a policeman, "What time is it?" in broken French ([1922] 1978, 132); The Zulu, a Polish farmer, was arrested for the inability to speak French and having a box that contained "extraordinary souvenirs" from all over the world (88, 174–175); Jean Le Nègre was arrested and held for "wearing an English officer's uniform" (200); Surplice was arrested for playing music for poor, working-class "soot-people" (196); and the School Master was arrested for telling "children that there are such monstrous things as peace and good will" (86). Such acts hardly seem criminal, much less overtly seditious—certainly no more seditious than writing a letter asking for transfer to the Lafayette Esquadrille (Kennedy 1980).

Once detained in the Dépôt de Triage, Cummings likens the French-government personnel who operate the prison to a bureaucratic and satanic regime, referring to them as cogs in "the machine of decomposition" ([1922] 1978, 108). With the prison representing the repressive culture under which writers of the era lived and wrote, Cummings depicts its staff as a microcosm of the French and American governments at war, and he consistently evokes images of torment, death, and decay as the demonic overseers mistreat their detainees. By starving the inmates with a *pain sec* diet, putting them in solitary confinement in a tiny *cabinot*, or actually suffocating those who make too much noise, the staff ensures that the Dépôt de Triage is a place of physical cruelty. And as a hellish and oppressive wartime mechanism, its function is to "decompose" or, in Erving Goffman's terms, to "mortify" the individuality of the inmates (1961, 46).

The "machine of decomposition," however, also suggests a process that reverses writing, undoes speech, and disorganizes thought. It thus calls attention to a crisis of representation that affects not only the inner workings of the Dépôt de Triage, where characters' use of words significantly alters their realities, but also the wider society, affected by wartime governments' suppression of language. *The Enormous Room* makes clear that the political climate under which Cummings wrote was suppressive in that it made words themselves dangerous. The words one used could, and often did, subject one to imprisonment, and this inevitably altered the way Americans during the war years used language. Since words could imprison, all Americans, but especially those in the military and the literati, faced a language crisis. They were forced to ask themselves how one could voice a dissenting—or even a critical—view without risking legal punishment.

Upon his release from the Dépôt de Triage on December 19, 1917, Cummings returned to the United States, was drafted into the Army, and was posted to Camp Devens in Massachusetts until his discharge in January 1919. He began working on *The Enormous Room* at the behest of his father. As he did so, he became increasingly aware that the repression he had experienced in prison was matched by a wider government infringement on individual civil rights. He had witnessed the US government not only disrupting peaceful meetings involving trade unions and Socialists, but also interrupting periodical publishing that voiced dissenting political views (Kennedy 1980). He also saw the government use the Espionage Act of 1917 and the Sedition Act of 1918 to fine and imprison US citizens based on tenuous or nonexistent evidence of sedition and espionage (Kohn 1994). In this environment Cummings saw the censorship he experienced during his military service applied to the civilian populace at large for the purpose of silencing political dissidents.

In *The Enormous Room*, Cummings attempted to subvert this governmental suppression of the written and spoken word. Producing a text that critiqued governmental suppression of language without violating the newly enacted laws, however, was a difficult undertaking, one that would require new artistic maneuvers. Cummings's response to this challenge was to fight fire with fire. To combat the "machine of decomposition," he engaged in a type of (de)composition of his own. In his creative hands, *The Enormous Room* becomes more than a straightforward exposé of government abuse. It does indeed condemn the suppressive governmental authorities propagating justifications for the war. But it does so by abandoning usual associations in language and replacing them with unusual referents. Cummings reorganized thought, refashioned speech, and reworked writing to offer covert as well as overt criticism of the suppressive government of his era.

A DUAL CRITIQUE

That Cummings implicates American politics from the outset is clear. Critics have often viewed the book's political content as an oblique reference that merely reinforces its larger antiwar themes. In fact *The Enormous Room* offers an explicitly pointed indictment of two governments' war policy. Richard Kennedy argues that Cummings's book is "laced through with denunciations, both direct and ironic" against the French government, revealing a broad "personal theme of hostility to authority, which extends itself to being antigovernment" (1994, 47). That statement is true, but it doesn't go far enough, for implicit in Cummings's book are political underpinnings that specifically target not just France, and not just the Dépôt de Triage, but also the US government's suppressive control of language.

Letters from Cummings's father that introduced the first edition, which provide an overview of his son's imprisonment, also suggest the political underpinnings of this legal travesty. Summarizing the situation in which his son finds himself in France and detailing the communiqués he has received concerning him, the father pleads with President Wilson to ease their family's suffering. His letters are tantamount to a reprimand of the government, intimating that it is neither a "self-respecting Government" nor properly patriotic (Edward Cummings [1922] 1978, xxv). The father's attitude is clear: the United States government is too focused "on the heart of the world" to be concerned with its upright citizens (xxiii). Throughout the letters, however, Cummings's father is careful not to critique the US war effort outright—even expressing enthusiasm for France, stating that the United States shares France's "cause of civilization" (xxv).

Building on his father's letters, Cummings himself engages in political satire in the first paragraph of the prison memoir, as he mocks Woodrow Wilson at the start of the "I Begin a Pilgrimage" chapter ([1922] 1978, 3). Cummings's initial critique of President Wilson's rhetoric carries with it a sense that Wilson's control over language is impractical if not reprehensible. In mimicking "Our Great President," Cummings describes the relationship between him, Brown, and their commanding officer, saying,

> the lively satisfaction which we might be suspected of having derived
> from the accomplishment of a task so important in the saving of civiliza-
> tion from the clutches of Prussian tyranny was in some degree inhibited,
> unhappily, by a complete absence of cordial relations between the man
> whom fate had placed over us and ourselves. (3)

Here Cummings uses the formal language of statesmen, complete with one of the Wilson administration's grandest self-justifications: that the war was necessary for "the saving of civilization." In the next sentence, though, he immediately undercuts Wilson's manner of speaking, casually stating, "Or, to use the vulgar American idiom, B and I and Mr. A. didn't get on well" (3). On the first page of the book, then, we get a small but telling contrast between a duplicitously "elevated" style and plain English, which hits at the way in which politicians such as Wilson practiced their own form of decomposition.

On the one hand, Cummings points out the obvious: Wilson's rhetoric of elevated diction, multiple clauses and qualifiers, and overall wordiness is as impractical as it is ineffective. On the other, he suggests something much broader in scope: by targeting the figurehead of an American government who has constrained the speech of the American populace at large to save civilization, Cummings suggests that the control Wilson possesses over language on a national scale is also immoral.

Cummings denounces such "civilization" via a satirical jab later in the book when he witnesses the near suffocation of an incorrigible female prisoner, Lena, after a sixteen-day solitary confinement in the *cabinot*. Seeing that, Cummings realizes that the Allied government's "meaning of civilization" is less than civil. And he identifies sarcastically that the government has paid him "the ultimate compliment," because he is unworthy of carrying out such cruelty to "carry forward the banner of progress" ([1922] 1978, 122).

That Cummings sees the French and the Americans as dual agents of decomposition becomes evident at key points in the text. The first occurs when he likens the Dépôt de Triage to Fort Leavenworth, a main US military prison at the time. After criticizing the manner in which French government officials ascertain guilt, rhetorically questioning who was "eligible" to be confined at La Ferté, he concludes that it was "anyone whom the police could find in the lovely country of France (a) who was not guilty of treason (b) who could not prove that he was not guilty of treason" ([1922] 1978, 83). Then, he reasons,

> By treason I refer to any little annoying habits of independent thought or action which en temps de guerre are put in a hole and covered over, with the somewhat naïve idea that from their cadavers violets will grow whereof the perfume will delight all good men and true and make such worthy citizens forget their sorrows. Fort Leavenworth, for instance, emanates even now a perfume which is utterly delightful to certain Americans. Just how many La Fertés boasted . . . God Himself knows. At least, in that Republic, amnesty has been proclaimed, or so I hear. (83–84)

The Dépôt de Triage at La Ferté Macé and Fort Leavenworth, here, are one and the same: holes filled and "covered over," where those in authority put people who have "little annoying habits of independent thought." Both house people convicted of dissentious speech, implying that the two countries share the same policies regarding those who are critical thinkers in times of war. Cummings reinforces this connection in describing the crime of the prisoner known as the Machine-Fixer:

> After all, it is highly improbable that this poor socialist suffered more at the hands of the great and good French government than did many a C.O. at the hands of the great and good American government; or—since all great governments are per se good and vice versa—than did many a man in general who was cursed with a talent for thinking during the warlike moments recently passed; during that is to say an epoch when the g. and g. nations demanded of their respective peoples the exact antithesis to thinking; said antithesis being vulgarly called Belief. (101)

Cummings's language indicates not only that the French and American governments are the same but also that each nation's governing bodies suppress thought—and by extension language—and demand blind trust, "Belief," instead of thought.

Writing at home after his release from prison in December 1917 and his discharge from the Army in January 1919, Cummings can safely denounce the French and tactically criticize the United States through them. He recodes the French government so that it becomes a referent for the US government. And Cummings is both direct and ironic in his negative characterization of the French government. His characters, for example, describe the French government directly as an entity that possesses "unskillful wisdom," is "not very clever," and is incapable of "mercy" in the manner it conducts its operations. In other illustrations the government is characterized ironically as "the considerate French government," "the utterly and incomparably moral French government," "the Almighty French Government in its Almighty Wisdom," and the "excellent French government" whose "Wise Men" are "right . . . as always." Overall, Cummings portrays "le gouvernement français" as a slimy bureaucracy, a "sly and beaming polyp," ensnaring people in its "tentacles": it is a stealthy animal that slowly ensnares its prey ([1922] 1978, 166, 103, 167, 140, 166, 94, 34, 215, 88, 217).

Cummings provides multiple instances in which the French government displays incompetence, if not insanity. In one such instance, the prisoner One Eyed Dav-heed retells a story he heard in a barbershop, saying,

> My brother, said the barber, told me a fine story a few days ago. He was
> flying over the lines, and was surprised, one day, to observe that the French
> guns were not shooting towards the Jerries but at the French themselves.
> He hurriedly landed, jumped out of the plane, went at once to the general's
> office. He saluted, and cried out, very excited: My general, you are shooting
> at the French! The general looked at him without concern, without mov-
> ing, then he said quite simply: We've begun, we must finish. (131)

Not only do the French authorities demonstrate ineptitude by mistakenly
shooting their own soldiers instead of Germany's, but they also exhibit a
pig-headed unwillingness to correct mistakes, when they refuse to stop after
the general is informed of the error.

The government's actions, ranging from military decisions to sedition
trials to prisoner treatment, result in the conclusion that the government is
a cruel, unjust tyranny. Cummings characterizes them as follows: "These
grand gentlemen who couldn't care less if people DIE of hunger, you know
each one believes he's The Good Lord HIM-Self. And Mr. John, you know,
they are all . . . They. Are. Just. SCUM!" (103). And, later, they have "no
hearts . . . they are not simply unjust, they are cruel, savez-vous? Men are
not like these; they are not men, they are Name of God I don't know what,
they are worse than animals; and they pretend to Justice" (226). The French
government authorities, as portrayed in *The Enormous Room*, are clearly arro-
gant, unjust, blasphemous totalitarians—but so are the American government authorities.

SILENCE AS SUBVERSIVE PROTEST

In exposing the absurdity of language suppression, Cummings shows that
in criminalizing dissentious speech and requiring only prowar positions, the
authorities run the risk of elevating innocuous speech to the level of dissent. That this action may lead to ridiculous outcomes he shows in the case
of the prisoner he calls Emile the Bum, who has been apprehended because
he "insulted two potatoes" ([1922] 1978, 87). Cummings provides the following "justification" for Emile's arrest:

> Gendarmes are sensitive in peculiar ways; they do not stand for any
> misleading information upon the probable destiny of the price of
> potatoes—since it is their duty and their privilege to resent all that is
> seditious to The Government, and since The Government includes
> the Minister of Agriculture (or something), and since the Minister of
> Something includes, of course, potatoes, and that means that no one is at
> liberty to in any way (however slightly or insinuatingly) insult a potato. (87)

Although the actual text, as Cummings writes it, sounds eerily logical, the basic justification for why insulting potatoes is treasonous remains absurd. His hyperbolic satire gives justification for almost any speech being dissentious.

In analyzing the case of another prisoner, Cummings shows how the suppressive system can criminalize even utterances that are barely comprehensible. He depicts the man in the Orange Cap as a quiet, shy, little Austrian who is unable to speak intelligibly and must communicate through inarticulate moans such as "GOO" and "WOO" (87–88). Questioning why this man had been detained at all, Cummings writes, "I still don't see how the gouvernement français decided to need him at La Ferté, unless—ah! that's it . . . he was really a super-intelligent crook . . . and all the apparent idiocy of the little man with the Orange Cap was a skillfully executed bluff" (88). The evidence for the man in the Orange Cap's possessing this intelligence lies in his moans:

> Yes, now I remember, I asked him in French if it wasn't a fine day (because, as always, it was raining, and he and I alone had dared to promenade together) and he looked me straight in the eyes, and said WOO, and smiled shyly. That would seem to corroborate the theory that he was a master mind, for (obviously) the letters W, O, O, stand for Wilhelm, Ober, Olles, which again is Austrian for Down With Yale. Yes, yes. Le gouvernement français was right, as always. (88)

The absurd reasoning shows Cummings at his satirical best, as he purports to be able to decipher inarticulate groans and provide a rationale for the Austrian's imprisonment that is better than the obvious one of his nationality. And his literary wit shows to good effect. "Wilhelm Ober Olles" pokes fun at both the German Kaiser Wilhelm and the German national anthem "Deutschland uber Alles," while the fake translation "Down with Yale" lets this Harvard graduate take a swipe at a traditional rival. The overriding point, however, is not humorous: in a regime that criminalizes speech, making any noise at all can endanger the speaker.

Given this situation, Cummings focuses his attention on what is left: silence. Silence, as Kennedy suggests, can be rightly seen as a product of the poet's "Romantic outlook" that "gives value to feeling over thinking, respects the natural life rather than the civilized life," or "admires untutored ignorance more than education" (1994, 48). It might also be seen as the condition that Cummings reverts to "when the linguistic symbol fails . . . as a means for identifying the essence of humanity" (Olsen 1992, 84). Cummings positions expressive silence as an ironic tactical maneuver to subvert and to critique language restriction. It is the one virtue that will serve him well not just at La Ferté Macé but also back home, when he returns to the ironically named Celestial City of New York.

Since silence is seen as a mark of dissent and therefore as a virtue, Cummings bolsters his critique of language suppression by classifying nearly all of the characters arrested in his text, at one time or another, as silent or quiet. On the way to La Ferté Macé, he encounters the silent "divine 'deserter'" ([1922] 1978, 25). A prisoner called Danish Jan is virtually unable to speak (71). The Silent Man about whom no one knows a thing possesses a "brilliant quietness" (71). Pete the Shadow thinks and acts with "the same quietness and firmness" despite solitary confinement (130). And the Wanderer is always quietly and silently speaking and moving (162–164). Cummings even depicts the entirety of La Ferté Macé itself as possessing "the ponderous ferocity of silence" (55). Given that all but three or four of the detainees are illiterate, mute, developmentally disabled, or uneducated further exposes the absurdity of making particular speech illegal, for it categorizes these atypical noncommunicators as criminal when they are mostly unable to engage in the traditional modes of communication. Cummings implies that all those arrested for such crimes of silence are mistakenly detained.

Silences, ultimately for Cummings, are dissentious withdrawals from language compelled both by the government authorities and by the multiple languages of the Dépôt de Triage. It is in this sense, not only the literal one, that the main room of the prison becomes "enormous." It contains not only representatives of multiple Western nations who do not share a common language, but also numerous silent war dissidents. What results is reliance upon other forms of communication, expressive silences that transcend and subvert "official" language. Those other forms of communication are best embodied in the prisoner he calls The Zulu, the man who is a force rather than a mere person, who can only be described as the verb "IS." The Zulu speaks and questions in "silences," in "unutterable communication." Being unable to fully characterize this enigma, Cummings envies him, desiring "one-third command over the written word" that The Zulu possesses over the unspoken. Despite The Zulu's illiteracy and silence, or perhaps because of it, language could not match his "directness accuracy and speed" of communication (176–177). Clearly, ironic and expressive silence is Cummings's answer to and indictment of language restriction.

Many scholars have noted that Cummings creatively altered language registers, contextual referents, and traditional signs to produce poetry that was artistically unique and distinctively modernist. His work also reveals a political sensibility that reflects this same "creatively insubordinate" approach to language. In this chapter I have emphasized this political strain, showing how in Cummings's first prose work, *The Enormous Room*, he produced an account of his imprisonment that, in turning official "decomposition" back on itself, called attention to a wartime linguistic crisis and critiqued official suppression of political language. Because at the time it was dangerous to offer open criticism of the American government, Cummings mounted his attack in a satiric and often comic vein, replacing overt dissent with indirection and cunning. The result, by this military ambulance driver turned political prisoner, was an ironic work that tactically subverts regular language associations and marks a withdrawal from the official language of critique that, in its very withdrawal, makes that critique more powerful.

WORKS CITED

Cummings, E.E. 1969 *The Selected Letters of E.E. Cummings*. Edited by F. W. Dupree and George Stade. New York: Harcourt, Brace and World Inc.

Cummings, E.E. (1922) 1978. *The Enormous Room*. New York: Boni and Liveright Inc.

Cummings, Edward. (1922) 1978. "Introduction to the First Edition (1922) to E.E. Cummings, *The Enormous Room*." In *The Enormous Room*, xxi–xxvi. New York: Boni and Liveright.

Goffman, Erving. 1961. *Asylums: Essays on the Social Situation of Mental Patients and Other Inmates*. New York: Doubleday.

Kennedy, Richard S. 1980. *Dreams in the Mirror: A Biography of E. E. Cummings*. New York: Liveright.

Kennedy, Richard S. 1994. *E.E. Cummings Revisited*. New York: Macmillan.

Kohn, Stephen M. 1994. *American Political Prisoners: Prosecutions under the Espionage and Sedition Acts*. Westport: Praeger.

Olsen, Taimi. 1992. "Language and Silence in *The Enormous Room* (1922)." *Spring: The Journal of the E.E. Cummings Society* 1 (1): 77–86.

Walsh, Jeffrey. 1976. "The Painful Process of Unthinking: E. E. Cummings' Social Vision in *The Enormous Room*." In *The First World War in Fiction: A Collection of Critical Essays*, edited by Holger Klein, 32-42. London: Macmillan.

7

Café Colonels and Whizz-Bangs

Tad Tuleja

MOST OF THE SONGS THAT ARE COMMONLY ASSOCIATED with World War I fall into two categories. In one category are the patriotic anthems—often used as recruiting tools—such as the British "Let's Put the Kibosh on the Kaiser," the German "Watch on the Rhine," and George M. Cohan's "Over There." In the United States alone, of the nearly 90,000 songs copyrighted during the war years, more than a third fell into this flag-waving category (Vogel 1995, 45). In the second category are sentimental ballads such as "The Long Long Trail," "It's a Long Way to Tipperary," and the German lounge standard "Lily Marlene." Many of these commercial songs were popular with soldiers. The earliest catalog of songs sung by British soldiers, *Tommy's Tunes*, contains numerous hymns and music hall favorites. Its compiler—Royal Flying Corps officer F. T. Nettleingham—recalls his mates' best-loved songs being the tearjerkers "Annie Laurie" and "Home Sweet Home" (Nettleingham 1917, 7).

But the musical tastes of World War I soldiers were not confined to the uplifting and comforting products of professional songsmiths. Running alongside—or one might say underneath—this public musical expression was the private and less salubrious expression of occupational folksong. In this chapter I will look at one small slice of this underground repertoire: English-language songs popular with soldiers that expressed a critical rather than positive attitude toward the war. I'll focus on a small but well-known body of songs that depicted soldiers' superiors—sergeants, colonels, generals—as cowardly or inept. Songs with this theme appear frequently in the anthologies by Brian Murdoch (1990) and Max Arthur (2008). While acknowledging the utility of these retrospective volumes, I will draw mostly on collections made by individuals for whom the Great War was a living memory (Brophy and Partridge [1930] 1965; Cary 1934, 1935; Nettleingham 1917; Niles, Moore, and Wallgren 1929).

DOI: 10.7330/9781607329527.c007

"FAR, FAR FROM WIPERS"

The most transparent of the negative songs described the many miseries of life at the front. Often these songs acquired their bite by parodying sentimental favorites from back home. "My Little Wet Home in the Trench," for example, adopted the tune of the music hall ballad "My Little Grey Home in the West," while the darkly humorous "Bombed Last Night" was a takeoff on another music hall number, "Drunk Last Night and Drunk the Night Before." "When Very Lights Are Shining" (Very lights were flares used to illuminate No Man's Land) borrowed the tune of "When Irish Eyes Are Smiling." The lullaby "Hush, Here Comes the Dream Man" evoked the macabre riposte "Hush, Here Comes a Whizz Bang," a whizz-bang being a German shell. And the well-known hymn "Holy, Holy, Holy" generated a spoof with verses that began "grousing, grousing, grousing," "raining, raining, raining," and "marching, marching, marching."

Close in sentiment to these "grousing at death's door" songs were songs that spoke of home with wistful desperation. One popular example, which Arthur (2008, 72) credits to the Canadian officer Gitz Rice, was "I Want to Go Home." The *Tommy's Tunes* version (Nettleingham 1917, 58) notes the soldiers' anxiety about Germans (Allemands) and about the large caliber shells known as Jack Johnsons—a reference to the long-reigning heavyweight boxing champion.

> I want to go home, I want to go home
> I don't want to go to the trenches no more
> Where there are shells and Jack Johnsons galore
> I want to go home where the Allemand can't get at me
> Oh my, I don't want to die, I want to go home

Another example was a parody of "What a Friend We Have in Jesus," which had been adapted during the American Civil War as "When This Lousy War Is Over" and which became, in Tommy's voice, "When This Bloody War Is Over." Nettleingham (1917, 21) gives a slightly sanitized version, substituting "ruddy" for "bloody."

> When this ruddy war is over O how happy I shall be
> When this ruddy war is over and we come back from Germany
> No more blooming kit inspection, no more church parade for me
> When this ruddy war is over you can have your RFC

A poignant example of this genre was "Far, Far from Wipers I Long to Be," set to the tune of a ballad called "Sing Me to Sleep." The Belgian town of

Ypres, commonly mispronounced as *Yeeprez* or *Wipers*, was the site of one of the war's most terrible campaigns, resulting in hundreds of thousands of casualties. The parody begins with the same four words as the original but is quickly highjacked by reality, referencing the flares over No Man's Land and likening the Boche's (German) lullaby to a song of death (Nettleingham 1917, 24):

Sing me to sleep where Very lights fall
Let me forget the war and all
I've got the wind up, that's what they say
God strafe 'em like hell till break of day
I feel so weary, warworn and sad
I don't like this war—it makes me feel bad
Dark is my dugout, cold are my feet
Waiting for Boches to put me to sleep
Far far from Wipers I long to be
Where German snipers can't snipe at me
Take me to Egypt or Salonika
Where I can hear of the Boche from afar

Another version of this grimly popular song, cited by Arthur (2008, 70), has the soldier waiting not for Boches but for the artillery shells whose whistling sound gave them the slang term "whizz-bangs." In their classic study of World War I song and slang, John Brophy and Eric Partridge ([1930] 1965, 204) explained why soldiers so feared them: "Owing to the short range and low trajectory, whizz-bangs arrived as soon, if not sooner, than anyone heard them."

Some songs, reflecting a more general cynicism, adopted a tone of humorous self-deprecation. The most popular example was "Fred Karno's Army." Karno was a music hall performer prone to slapstick and studied fecklessness, so to own membership in his army was to suggest the humorous futility of the war effort. The tune was adapted from the hymn "The Church's One Foundation," and military units creatively varied the lyrics to ridicule their own incompetence or that of others. In one verse recorded in *Tommy's Tunes* (Nettleingham 1917, 42), the humorously stigmatized unit was the Royal Engineers (RE):

We are Fred Karno's Army, a jolly fine lot are we
Fred Karno is our Captain, Charlie Chaplin our O.C.
And when we get to Berlin, the Kaiser he will say:
Hoch! Hoch! Mein Gott! What a bloody find lot
Are the 2–4th R.E. T.

A similar slap at the idea of noble purpose was embedded in the inanely repetitive lyrics of "We're Here Because We're Here." Sung to the tune of "Auld Lang Syne," the refrain "We're here because we're here because we're here because we're here" became a sardonic comment on the sense of an ending that, to soldiers on the Western Front, must have seemed a constant invitation, a constant rebuke. Nodding slyly to Tennyson's "Charge of the Light Brigade," Nettleingham calls this parody "The Reason Why." It was sung, he notes, "and so on, until exhausted" (1917, 27).

"IF YOU WANT TO KNOW WHERE THE PRIVATES ARE"

Cynicism also informed songs that questioned the way the war was being managed by those in command. In these songs—and in occasional verses from songs with other themes—we hear a drumbeat of resentment at the privileges of rank, at injustices endured at the hands of superiors, and at officers and NCOs who are seen as unfair, incompetent, cowardly, or all three.

Not all superiors are tarred with the same brush. Brophy and Partridge observe that the greatest animus was directed toward colonels—"the supreme authority the private soldier knew"—and sergeants, who were "close at hand." "Officers generally escaped satire," they write, "not that the private failed to recognize that they had a much more comfortable time than he, but because they belonged to the excessively privileged class, the barons, so to speak, of the anachronistic feudal system in which the private soldier was serf, scullion and load-carrier" ([1930] 1965, 19).

The qualification "generally" is well advised, for there are, even in Brophy and Partridge's own collection, some quite tart examples of antiofficer sentiment. In addition, while the authors are certainly right that the sergeant is a frequent target of satire, that satire is often couched in terms not of anger or rebelliousness, but rather of a grumbling resignation to the realities of the situation, in which NCOs—sergeants, sergeant-majors, "top kicks"—even as they were seen as the enforcers of discipline, also faced the same muck and shrapnel as their subordinates. When sergeants are attacked, therefore, it is rarely because they are seen as removed from the private's own world but, rather because, in that world, they are responsible for enforcing its privations and so come symbolically to embody them.

"Never Mind," for example, was a sentimental tune from 1913 (Murdoch 1990, 93). In a popular trench parody, it complains about shelling, gas, and barbed wire, but in the print versions at least it usually begins with a verse about a sergeant's abuse of authority. Here is the opening of a version cited by Nettleingham (1917, 28):

If the Sergeant's pinched your rum, never mind
If the Sergeant's on the bum, never mind
If he collars all your fags and you've nothing on but rags
It's his affair not yours so never mind

Not surprisingly, this song is often indexed under the alternate title "If the Sergeant Steals Your Rum." The habitually inebriated NCO makes his appearance in other songs as well. In one we find him "lying on the canteen floor," in another "mentioned in dispatches for drinking the privates' rum." At one level this is merely slapstick: an evocation of the comic boozer who is a staple of music hall caricature. But given the importance of the rum ration in British military life, there's a serious bite to it as well: an NCO who can be seen, however humorously, as stealing his men's allotment of alcohol is shown as selfishly subverting an ancestral right. There is a gravity to such an offense that humor barely mitigates.

But stealing rum is a minor offense compared to what many of Tommy's tunes see as the sins of the officer class. In a song variously entitled "Grasshopper" or "Leapfrog," the target is military ambition. It was sung to the tune of "John Brown's Body." This is the version given in *Tommy's Tunes* (Nettleingham 1917, 54).

One grasshopper jumped right over another grasshopper's back
And another grasshopper jumped right over the other grasshopper's back
A third grasshopper jumped right over the two grasshoppers' back
Whilst a fourth grasshopper jumped over all the other grasshoppers' backs
We were only playing leapfrog
We were only playing leapfrog
We were only playing leapfrog
Whilst the other grasshopper jumped right over the other grasshopper's back

What's implicit here is that, in their zeal to get ahead, senior staff officers—the brass hats, the red tabs, the swagger sticks—are remote from the carnage and indifferent to the suffering of their men. That conviction animates so many of the songs that it seems to be a central "folk idea" of the soldiers' worldview (Dundes 1971).

Some of the antiofficer songs followed a "chain" structure, with each verse devoted to the purportedly typical experience of a different rank or position. Such songs often (not always) began at the bottom, with the privates, and worked their way up, with appropriate satire, to the general staff. A mild example was an adaptation of the nursery rhyme "Old King Cole," where every private "had a great thirst," every sergeant "a loud voice," every adjutant "a pair of fine spurs," every major "a big swear," and every general "two red tabs" (Nettleingham 1917: 32–35). A more acerbic example was "If You Want to Know Where the Privates Are." Here is the first verse of a version recorded by veterans John Jacob Niles and Douglas Moore (1929, 59–61) in their invaluable collection *Songs My Mother Never Taught Me*:

If you want to know where the privates are, I'll tell you where they are,
I'll tell you where they are, yes I'll tell you where they are
If you want to know where the privates are, I'll tell you where they are
Up to their ears in mud
I saw them, I saw them, up to their ears in mud
If you want to know where the privates are, I'll tell you where they are
Up to their ears in mud

In subsequent verses of this version, we hear that the captains are "drinking the Privates' rum" and that the generals are "back in gay Paree." Variants of the song, which was popular with American as well as British troops, tell us that the "quarterbloke" is "miles and miles and miles behind the line," that it's the sergeant major "boozing up the private's rum," and that the commanding officer is "down in the deep dugout" (Brophy and Partridge [1930] 1965, 61–62).

Some versions of "If You Want to Know Where the Privates Are" end with a stanza in which the "old battalion"—that is, the company of common soldiers—is "hanging on the old barbed wire." That chilling image elicited alternate titles: "Hanging on the Old Barbed Wire" (Arthur 2008, 68) and simply "The Old Barbed Wire" (Brophy and Partridge [1930] 1965, 61). Although Niles and Douglas avoid this macabre detail, the contrast between officers and men that the song evokes is deftly shown in "Wally" Wallgren's illustrations for their volume (see figures 7.1 and 7.2). "There is a lot more truth in this song," they comment, "than one is likely to suspect, official reports of Army Operations to the contrary notwithstanding" (Niles and Moore 1929: 59).

We also hear antiofficer attacks in "Mademoiselle from Armentieres," the "Hinky Dinky" song that Niles and Moore (1929, 22) call "undoubtedly the folk song of the war." They give about forty verses of the song, while its most diligent student, Melbert Cary, compiled hundreds. The song's structure is well known from its signature verse, given here in Cary's sheet music version (1935, xlvii–xlix):

Mademoiselle from Armentieres, parlez vous
Mademoiselle from Armentieres, parlez vous
Mademoiselle from Armentieres,

Figure 7.1. "If you want to know where the privates are." Drawing by "Wally" Wallgren in John J. Niles and Douglas Moore, *The Songs My Mother Never Taught Me* (The Macaulay Company, 1929). Harry Ransom Center, University of Texas at Austin.

> She hasn't been kissed in forty years
> Hinky dinky parlez vous

In many of the verses of this song—more popular with doughboys than with the British—the name of a French location (e.g., Armentieres) antici-pates a clever, not infrequently bawdy, rhyme. "Mademoiselle from Villet le

Figure 7.2. "If you want'a know where the officers are." Drawing by "Wally" Wallgren in John J. Niles and Douglas Moore, *The Songs My Mother Never Taught Me* (The Macaulay Company, 1929). Harry Ransom Center, University of Texas at Austin.

Duc," for example, sets up an obvious profanity, while "Mademoiselle from St. Nazaire" leads to the less obvious "Couche avec moi pour pomme de terre?" (Will you sleep with me for a potato?) Indeed, the bulk of Cary's repertoire reflected on the erotic appeal of French girls, often in language so coarse that the compiler felt obliged to supply a preface warning the reader that the verses—and Alban Butler's racy illustrations to his 1935 volume—might not appeal to everyone's taste.

A subtheme to the erotic play complicates the picture. Liaisons between soldiers and French women occurred, for the most part, far behind the front lines, that is, in areas secure from whizz-bangs. These were areas that the trench soldier was sometimes allowed to visit. But precisely because these places were safe, they acquired in the soldiers' worldview a mixed reputation. "Gay Paree" took on an aura of undeserved pleasure, of ill-gotten release from the common travail. Those who frequented such places, temporarily relieved from the horrors of battle, may have been envied, but they were also, to judge from the songs, seen as shirkers who could not stick it out at the front. In several "Hinky Dinky" verses, we hear reference to characters who, while Bert the Tommy or Johnny the Doughboy is repairing parapets and dodging mortars, are sampling wine and women out of harm's way. I will call this archetypal shirker the Café Colonel. He is an early prototype of the character that American soldiers today call the "REMF," or "rear echelon mother-fucker" (see Levy 2012).

The image of those who pass down orders but do no fighting themselves is a frequent leitmotif in the "Hinky Dinky" corpus, and one section of Cary's book (1935, 47–53), from which I am quoting below, is devoted to verses grousing about "The Officers." Sometimes these higher-ups—identifiable by their distinctive headgear—are condemned en masse:

> The brass hats have a hell of a time
> Twenty miles behind the line

Other verses single out individuals, or at least individual ranks, beginning with the officer closest to the men:

> The Captain's gone to gay Paree
> We know he's on an awful spree

Occasionally the target is the military police who, by virtue of their authority, may be seen as surrogates for unfair officers:

> The damned MPs behind the line
> Screwing the women and drinking the wine

Other verses snap at the highest and most remote of superiors, the generals:

> Oh General ——won the war
> Back in Chaumont, engaged in . . . amorous pleasantries

The General made a front-line tour
'Twas after the armistice, to be sure

Occasionally the boulevardiers and café colonels get their comeuppance, as the high-life in gay Paree delivers poetic justice in the form of venereal disease:

Oh the Sergeant went to gay Paree
And came back with crabs and gonorrhee

The General slept with Mademoiselle
And now he's giving the doctor hell

Finally, in a verse that combines suspicion of French women with resentment at the privileges of rank, an officer "falls" not in battle but in amorous and presumably contagious contact:

X marks the spot where our Captain fell
He tried to out-hug the Mademoiselle

All of these lyrics seem direct enough, but also a bit velvet-gloved. For a more venomous take on superiors, we may turn to a song that Niles and Moore (1929, 221–223) say "explains itself—and how!" "What Do the Colonels and Generals Do" condemns those in authority for keeping their own hands clean—and their persons safe—while men in the line performed a "dirty little job for Jesus." The song opens with a broad, nationalist perspective:

Colonel said that Kaiser William surely was a pest
Dirty little job for Jesus
Said I ought to lay the Kaiser's hips to rest
Dirty little job for Jesus
Oh what do the Generals and Colonels do
I'll tell you, I'll tell you
Figger out just how the privates ought to do
The dirty little job for Jesus

"I'll tell you, I'll tell you" echoes the more widely known "If You Want to Know Where the Privates Are," and as in that song there's a stated divide between those who direct the war and those who fight it. The refrain "dirty little job for Jesus," however, introduces a poignant complication, as the work of the warrior is identified both as morally problematic and as permissible—the privates are killing other privates in Jesus's name.

The Great War was widely endorsed as a spiritual enterprise, but I don't see the ambiguity of this verse as theological, or even conventionally

Christian. The tone suggests either an outrage against hypocrisy or (which I think is more likely) a decent person's confusion about performing a service that he knows from experience to be heartrendingly brutal but that those on high—whether speaking from a headquarters or a pulpit—have told him is laudable. The song's second verse suggests that, faced with this dilemma, the soldier wants to flee, indeed, that he imagines his escape:

> Now when I run away they said I was afraid to die
> Dirty little job for Jesus
> I said the only reason why I ran was 'cause I couldn't fly
> Dirty little job for Jesus

Here in fantasy the soldier evades both the brutality of the war and his own conflicted complicity, as the officers, in the refrain, continue their work of "figgering out" how the privates can continue to fight.

And of course to die. The song's final verse reflects somberly on this reality, condemning not only religious support for the war but also its supposed democratic impulse—and, once again, the different levels of investment and of sacrifice that the war is exacting from officers and from men.

> Fifty thousand privates died for democracy
> Dirty little job for Jesus
> Twenty major generals got the DSC
> Another dirty little job for Jesus

The DSC was the Distinguished Service Cross, a medal established by the American President Woodrow Wilson in 1918 to honor conspicuous bravery in battle. It was awarded to slightly more than 6,000 Americans who served in World War I, most of them US Army. In suggesting that the DSC was a "brass hat" commendation, the verse echoes a trope that appears frequently in these songs: the idea that the senior officers were given undue credit—in the form of medals such as the DSC and the French Croix de Guerre—for the sacrifices that were made by their men. We encounter the characterization, for example, in two verses of "Mademoiselle from Armentieres" (Cary 1934, 371):

> The General won the Croix de Guerre
> But the son of a bitch wasn't even there
>
> Oh, the CO wants a Croix de Guerre
> For sitting around in an office chair.

It appears also in the final verse of "Oh, It's Drive the General's Car, My Boy," where the "back area tin hat generals" spend most of their time posturing in a Paris café (Niles and Moore 1929, 109–113).

> Oh, they hang around the Crillon and 'tis there they do their stuff
> Then click their heels together and they spread a mighty bluff
> But they've never seen the trenches nor the bloody enemy
> But they'll get more credit for the war than either you or me

CLASS DISTINCTIONS

If we were to judge troop morale simply on the basis of the "café colonel" repertoire, we might conclude that on the whole, the British soldier in World War I harbored fierce resentment at his superiors and felt himself a victim of their abuse and neglect. That was certainly my sense of things when I first heard these songs. They seemed obviously driven by class antagonism—the sardonic and righteous anger of working-class blokes who obeyed their superiors under duress and saw their brass hat commanders as feckless martinets.

That there were class distinctions at play in the trenches is beyond dispute. British officers as a rule had a public-school (that is, what Americans would call a private-school) education, and while there they absorbed, as a matter of course, a sense of entitlement. Infantry Captain Graham Greenwell, reflecting on his upward trajectory as a public-school boy—first as fag (errand runner for a senior student), then as house prefect, finally as school prefect—believed that this experience had fitted him for command. "I think it was Mrs. Sydney Webb," he mused, "who said, 'There are people in England who are born to give orders and there are people who are born to take them.' It's true, isn't it?" (qtd. Arthur 2002, 148). It was a rumination typical of that social class from which, in Lord Kitchener's "New Army," the higher ranks were drawn.

And rank had its privileges. Some, like higher pay and better lodgings, were the presumably "pragmatic" perks one expects in a hierarchy. Montague Cleeve, a lieutenant with the Royal Garrison Artillery, invited to dinner by a brigadier commander, recalled the event with a mixture of awe and shame:

> There was a terrible din from the machine-guns and shells bursting all
> around us, but he insisted on having an old-fashioned mess dinner at 7
> o'clock promptly. And we sat at a large table in his dugout, and the wine
> was brought round in decanters. This was a bit of a contrast to trench life.
> (qtd. in Arthur 2002, 136)

Similarly, at a time when privates' diet consisted of bully beef, Lieutenant Edwin Vaughan's diary describes one officers' dinner in which, he writes, "we sent up several of our servants to assist . . . and the champagne flowed very freely" and another that consisted of seven courses but that—alas!— lacked mayonnaise (Vaughan 1988, 108–111).

Other class markers were symbolic and petty. Paul Fussell makes much of these in discussing the "wide, indeed gaping distinction between officers and men."

> In London an officer was forbidden to carry a parcel or ride a bus, and even in mufti—dark suit, white collar, bowler, stick—he looked identifiably different from the men. When a ten-minute break was signaled on the march officers invariably fell out to the left side of the road, Other Ranks to the right. (1977, 82)

Inane as this particular form of segregation may seem, some officers saw it as critical to discipline. When Vaughan's platoon, halted in a narrow defile, falls out on both sides of the road, he is upbraided and reported to his CO by an outraged brigadier (1988, 111).

The few consolations of life in the trenches were also demarcated by rank. The traditional rum ration of the Royal Navy, for example, was part of the daily allotment for men on the line, while their officers had access to—and the means to acquire—such tonier drinks as whiskey and brandy. Whiskey became such a comfort for Second Lieutenant Edwin Vaughan that his family feared the war had made him an alcoholic (Cowley 1981, xvi). Access to another soldiers' comfort—prostitution—was also segregated. While French brothels in general may have been open to all with the requisite *sou*, the officially sanctioned ones were identified as Blue Lights for officers and Red Lights for "other ranks" (Fussell 1977, 270).

Siegfried Sassoon mentions an additional privilege of rank that must have been seen as particularly galling. If an officer succumbed to "funk," if he "crumpled up" under the pressures of the war, Sassoon's superior simply "sent him home as useless, with a confidential report." "But if a man became a dud in the ranks, he just remained where he was until he was killed or wounded. Delicate discrimination about private soldiers wasn't possible" (1930, 44). Sassoon writes this disapprovingly, and yet it is this very unwritten policy of coddling officers over their men that removed him from harm's way later in the war, as his eloquent condemnation of the war got him sent to a military hospital, where he was treated for shell shock.

STUBBORN FACTS

There's no question, then, that the socioeconomic rigidity of Edwardian England carried over into the trenches. It might seem to follow that the disdain for authority that one hears in the songs reflected class resentment at patrician privilege. This reading seemed obvious to me when I first heard the "café colonel" songs. It took some deeper listening, and some parallel reading, to realize that, seduced by my own social bias, I had been reading the Great War through the same lens that Richard Attenborough and his colleagues brought to their 1969 antiwar farce *Oh, What a Lovely War.* This film used some of the same songs I've mentioned to condemn militarism (at the height of the Vietnam War) and the British class system of which Attenborough himself was a product. But this class-based, quasi-Marxist reading leaves some stubborn facts unexplained.

Facts, for example, like the actual social relations on the Western front. To judge from the normative trench ballad, privates did the war's dirty work and were sacrificed in droves; sergeants stole their rum; COs hid out in fortified bunkers; and senior officers—the café colonels and tin-hat generals—lounged in bistros and brothels far from the action until they were given the rewards—DSCs, for example—that should have been given to the soldiers. But does that vivid picture capture reality?

To answer that question systematically, we would have to compare the picture suggested by the "café colonel" repertoire with other contemporary evidence such as memoirs, trench newspapers, letters, and other songs, that is, sources in which officers appear as competent or courageous. To test the specific conceit that officers both avoided battle and were disproportionately rewarded for their service, we could turn to regimental casualty lists and see what percentage of each rank was killed or wounded and what percentage received a DSC or similar commendation. I must leave to more patient souls the number crunching that such research would require and provide here merely a general impression based on the writings of British soldiers such as Sassoon and Vaughan.

The consensus of these sources is that the antagonism suggested by the "café colonel" songs was more a rhetorical caricature than a snapshot of reality and that with regard to the hazards of battle in particular, officers suffered at least as much as the men. In fact, Cambridge historian J. M. Winter, noting the preponderance of middle-class men among British enlistees, argues that especially at the outset, "officer casualty rates were significantly higher than casualty rates among the men in the ranks," perhaps twice as high (Winter 1989, 121, 147). In terms of gross numbers, of course, the men paid far greater prices, but as they outnumbered the brass by many orders of magnitude, that is to be expected. I do not have data from these sources about the distribution of medals.

We might also investigate the degree to which the songs, whether "accurate" or not, expressed soldiers' dominant attitudes toward their commands. Here again comparative analysis of vernacular sources is in order, and those sources provide mixed evidence. Winter, for example, notes in a trench newspaper a humorous definition of a "dud" as an officer who "draws a big salary and explodes for no reason. These are plentiful away from the fighting areas" (1989, 137). However, he also points to evidence that "many privates felt a bond of shared experience with officers with whom they served in the trenches, and whom they followed whatever the dangers" (147).

Max Arthur's collection of the war's "forgotten voices" reveals that this sense of comradeship could be reciprocal; a lieutenant offered a post at Brigade Headquarters recalls, "It was very tempting but I didn't want to go. There was something about the relationship with the men that one didn't want to break. One would somehow have felt rather a traitor to them, so I refused it and stayed with them" (qtd. in Arthur 2002, 200; cf. Vaughan 1988, 53, 196). You hear the same sense of military noblesse oblige throughout Sassoon's *Memoirs of an Infantry Officer* and in his famous "Declaration," condemning the war not as a conscientious objector but as "a soldier who believes he is acting on behalf of soldiers" (1930, 288). Sassoon stands out because of his later celebrity, but he was certainly not alone in feeling fellowship with his men.

Indeed, many British soldiers seemed to have regarded at least some of their superiors—Sassoon again is a notable example—with respect, admiration, even in some cases a kind of worshipful awe. We actually do get this picture from certain "lost voices of the Great War." (Arthur 2002). If you look for evidence of relationships between men and officers, you find a great variety, and one that tends generally toward a recognition of common struggle, common humanity. For every instance of a soldier disgusted by the privileges of rank, there's an instance of genuine admiration. It's only by selective viewing of the evidence that you can find the class animosity that I originally suspected was universal.

Further complicating the picture, we have some puzzling facts about Tommy's behavior—specifically, about his readiness to follow the orders of those allegedly despised superiors. We know, for example, that in the four terrible years between the guns of August and the 1918 Armistice, there is no record of a single British mutiny, as there were in other armies (Winter 1989, 158–159). In addition, the rates of court-martial for desertion or cowardice are bewilderingly low: in the entire conflict, barely 3,000 British soldiers were tried for these crimes, and only 346 of them were executed. Niall Ferguson notes correctly that this was a "minute percentage" of the total enlistment: 5.7 million (1999, 346–347).

And finally, there is the gruesome evidence of many battles in which, on command, soldiers walked steadily into No Man's Land to the sound of German machine guns scything their ranks. On dawn on the first day of the Somme offensive, for example, the advancing British infantry numbered 100,000. By nightfall one in five of them were gone—and similar losses mounted on the Somme for the next four months (Keegan 1999, 299). F. Scott Fitzgerald's character Dick Diver, in speaking of that offensive, writes, "The land here cost twenty lives a foot that summer" ([1934] 1962, 56). It sounds like poetic hyperbole, but if you do the math, you find he was eerily precise. I suggest that this kind of disciplined dedication to mission, this suicidal willingness to follow the plans of tin hat generals, is not the product of a force that despises its commanders.

EMBRACING VICTIMIZATION

And yet the songs are there. Given the more nuanced battlefield picture I've laid out here, how do we explain that? If resentment at command was not, as the songs suggest, a universal attitude, how do we explain the popularity of a song cycle that so pungently celebrates it? In short, why did World War I soldiers sing these songs?

Given their literal content, that is, their texts, it seems natural to consider them as laments or cries of outrage: these would be the logical responses of injured parties to situations that they see as victimizing them. Given the absence of overt resistance to that victimization, though, this "direct" reading of the evidence becomes problematic. What might resolve the contradiction between the resentment expressed in the songs and the dutifully "soldierly" behavior of the singers?

While acknowledging the obvious—that the songs are narratives about victimization—we might begin by considering what we mean by that term. In everyday parlance, to be a victim is to have an undesirable identity—what Erving Goffman (1986) called a "stigmatized" identity. But, as I have suggested elsewhere (Tuleja 2012), victimhood can also have psychological value. It can reduce complex events to neat, linear scenarios of right versus wrong, where the messy collusion of social interaction becomes a simple collision of Us versus Them.

In World War I, millions of young men who in August 1914 had been turning a lathe or driving a lorry found themselves only months later in the midst of a nightmare. By January 1915, the high hopes for a rapid end to the conflict had been laid to rest in the scarlet banks of the Marne, and an entire generation of optimistic Edwardians entered what would become four years of whizz-bangs, shrapnel, mutilated bodies, mustard gas, and shell shock. I want to suggest that, in this environment, when soldiers sang about their victimization, they may have been doing so in a spirit not of complaint but of ironic celebration. Singing about whizz-bangs and café colonels was a way of taking collective ownership of their powerless status—and thus of making their very victimization a badge of honor.

In his study of "Jody calls"—the cadence chants first used in the US Army during World War II—Richard Allen Burns (2012) notes that the adulterous "Jody" antihero of the chants allowed soldiers not simply to vent their frustrations at this backdoor victimizer but also to acknowledge their own complicity in his assault on fidelity. I wonder if the victimizers in these World War I songs served a similar function for the soldiers who sang them.

In ridiculing the boozing sergeant, the craven captain, and the whoring general, might the beleaguered privates not be simultaneously relishing their own victimhood and acknowledging that if given the opportunity, they would be just as quick as their superiors to become the victimizers? Might not the subtext of these "complaint" songs be that, brass hats or no, we're all in this together and bound for hell. And might not the only way to confront that existential monstrosity be to celebrate it in a voice of exuberant fatalism? In this sense the songs, as Brophy and Partridge put it, "poked fun at the soldier's own desire for peace and rest, and so prevented it from overwhelming his will to go on doing his duty. They were not symptoms of defeatism, but strong bulwarks against it" ([1930] 1965, 18).

Of course we don't know what these songs sounded like as they came from Tommy's throat, and perhaps "celebration" goes too far. But listen again to Sassoon, who commanded an infantry platoon through the hell of the Somme. On the way to that nightmare, he reflects on what he sees as a disjunction between the horrors his men have already seen and their seemingly placid demeanor on a reprieve between battles.

> It was queer how the men seemed to take their victimization for granted. In and out; in and out; singing and whistling, the column swayed in front of me, much the same length as usual, for we'd had less than a hundred casualties up at Bazentin. But it was a case of every man for himself, and the corporate effect was optimistic and untroubled. (1930, 120)

"Less than a hundred casualties." "Optimistic and untroubled." How does one reconcile those two phrases? How does one explain why soldiers should be singing and whistling *anything* as they trudge toward an encounter with guns where "a tragic slaughter was inevitable" (1930, 71)? "Therapy" and "celebration" may point us toward an answer, though not one that correlates easily with resentment of officers. The answer itself, perhaps, will remain as elusive for us as it was on that awful day in 1916 when 20,000 singing Tommies met their deaths on the Somme.

WORKS CITED

Arthur, Max, ed. 2002. *Forgotten Voices of the Great War.* Guilford: The Lyons Press.

Arthur, Max, ed. 2008. *When This Bloody War Is Over: Soldiers' Songs of the First World War.* London: Piatkus Books.

Brophy, John, and Eric Partridge. [1930] 1965. *The Long Trail: What the British Soldier Sang and Said in the Great War of 1914–18.* London: Andre Deutsch.

Burns, Richard A. 2012. "Where Is Jody Now?" In *Warrior Ways*, edited by Eric A. Eliason and Tad Tuleja, 79–98. Logan: Utah State University Press.

Cary, Melbert B., Jr. 1934. "Mademoiselle from Armentieres." *Journal of American Folklore* (47) 186: 369–376.

Cary, Melbert B., Jr. 1935. *Mademoiselle from Armentieres* Vol. 2. Illustrated by Alban B. Butler, Jr. New York: Privately printed, Press of the Woolly Whale.

Cowley, Robert. 1988. "Introduction." In *Some Desperate Glory: The World War I Diary of a British Officer, 1917*, by Edwin Campion Vaughan. New York: Henry Holt.

Dundes, Alan. 1971. "Folk Ideas as Units of Worldview." *Journal of American Folklore* (84) 331 (January–March): 93-103.

Ferguson, Niall. 1999. *The Pity of War: Explaining World War I.* New York: Basic Books.

Fitzgerald, F. Scott. [1934] 1962. *Tender Is the Night.* New York: Charles Scribner's Sons.

Fussell, Paul. 1977. *The Great War and Modern Memory.* London: Oxford University Press.

Goffman, Erving. 1986. *Stigma: Notes on the Management of Spoiled Identity.* New York: Touchstone.

Keegan, John. 1999. *The First World War.* New York: Alfred Knopf.

Levy, Elinor. 2012. "Upper Echelons and Boots on the Ground." In *Warrior Ways*, edited by Eric A. Eliason and Tad Tuleja, 99–115. Logan: Utah State University Press.

Murdoch, Brian. 1990. *Fighting Songs and Warring Words: Popular Lyrics of Two World Wars.* London: Routledge.

Nettleingham, Frederick Thomas. 1917. *Tommy's Tunes.* London: Erskine MacDonald.

Niles, John J., Douglas S. Moore, and A. A. Wallgren, ed. 1929. *The Songs My Mother Never Taught Me.* New York: Macaulay.

Oh, What a Lovely War. (1969) 2006. DVD. Directed by Richard Attenborough. Paramount.

Sassoon, Siegfried. 1930. *Memoirs of an Infantry Officer.* New York: Coward, McCann.

Tuleja, Tad. 2012. "The Grievance Tale: On the Utility of 'Mere Folklore.'" Panel presentation, American Folklore Society annual meeting, October 25. New Orleans.

Vaughan, Edwin Campion. 1988. *Some Desperate Glory: The World War I Diary of a British Officer, 1917.* New York: Henry Holt.

Vogel, Frederick G. 1995. *World War I Songs.* Jefferson, NC: McFarland and Co.

Winter, J. M. 1989. *The Experience of World War I.* New York: Oxford University Press.

8

The Wild Deserters of No Man's Land
A Ghoulish Legend of the Great War

James I. Deutsch

TWO YEARS AFTER THE END OF WORLD WAR I, a decorated officer who
had served with the British cavalry recalled a horrific and mysterious scene
from the war. It was early 1918 on the marshes of the Somme in northern
France, the site of some of the bloodiest battles of the war. Lieutenant-
Colonel Ardern Arthur Hulme Beaman and members of his cavalry squadron were trailing thirty German prisoners of war who had escaped into
"that devastated land." Beaman writes:

> We saw a man in German uniform come to the edge [of a copse of trees],
> and look around. We formed line and galloped around the copse, thrilling
> with excitement and delight at the prospect of having so soon rounded
> up our quarry. The copse was not more than fifty yards square. The man
> vanished inside. For an hour we searched every inch of it, the dug-outs
> with which it was honeycombed and all the open country around. But no
> sign of a German did we see. Greatly puzzled we rode away . . . As we
> advanced, the country became more and more difficult . . . Soon we got
> into the old front system of the Somme, the wildest part of it that I had
> ever seen . . . The armies of France had swept over it and on, leaving it
> behind them, and it was still as they had left it. Here and there were hid-
> eously disemboweled factories and machinery, all overgrown with grass.
> Food, stores, ammunition and unburied dead, still lay plentifully around.
> At Fresnes, on the borders of this horrid desolation, we met a Salvage
> Company at work. They told us that we were the first people they had seen
> since they had been there, and they laughed at our mission. That warren
> of trenches and dug-outs extended for untold miles, and we might as well
> look for a needle in a haystack. They warned us, if we insisted on going
> further in, not to let any men go singly, but only in strong parties, as the
> Golgotha was peopled with wild men, British, French, Australian, German

DOI: 10.7330/9781607329527.c008

deserters, who lived there underground, like ghouls among the mouldering dead, and who came out at nights to plunder and to kill. (1920, 186–87)

Beaman's account appears to be the earliest published version of a legend that I am calling "The Wild Deserters of No Man's Land." In his prize-winning study *The Great War and Modern Memory*, the literary scholar and World War II veteran Paul Fussell praised it as the "finest legend of the war, the most brilliant in literary invention and execution as well as the richest in symbolic suggestion" (1975, 123). In this chapter I trace the literary afterlife of this gruesome tale and then, returning to Fussell, provide some observations about its symbolic richness.

Like all legends, "The Wild Deserters of No Man's Land" has several variants, but the basic kernel warns of fierce deserters from nearly all sides (Australian, Austrian, British, Canadian, French, German, and Italian—but not from the United States) who were living underground, deep beneath the No Man's Land that separated the front lines of the opposing armies in the First World War. According to some versions of the legend, they were living in caves and grottoes; other versions suggest that they had dug deeper into the abandoned trenches and dugouts that once had contained troops. In some versions of the legend, the deserters have turned to scavenging corpses for clothing and food; and, in at least one version, the deserters have become ghoulish beasts, vampiric creatures emerging from underground only at night to feast upon the bodies of those killed or wounded in combat.

The First World War is a particularly fertile field for disturbing legends because it marks a profound shift in the nature of warfare, distinguishing it from all previous episodes of combat. "Many wars have been fought in modern times," literary historian Alfredo Bonadeo has noted, "but never before World War I did so many nations meet on the battlefield, never before were the resources of the combatants so fully engaged, and never before was human life destroyed on such a vast scale" (1989, vii). This new mode of warfare made an indelible impact on the combatants, particularly in the way it transformed the identities and expressive cultures of those who survived. Accordingly, it was known at the time not by what we call it today, World War I, which "defines the event as merely the first in a series of global apocalypses," but rather as the Great War, "the war of wars" (S. Gilbert and Gubar 1989, 259).

The area of the Somme, where Lieutenant-Colonel Beaman learned of "ghouls among the mouldering dead," epitomized the utter madness of the Great War. On July 1, 1916, the Battle of the Somme's first day, Great Britain

Figure 8.1. No Man's Land. Print by Lucien Jonas, 1927. Library of Congress Prints and Photographs Division. Accessed at http://www.loc.gov/pictures/resource/pga.03885/

suffered 57,470 casualties, including 19,240 killed. By November 19, 1916, "when it ended in the snow and fog of winter, more than 300,000 British, Commonwealth, French and German soldiers had been killed, and twice that number wounded" (M. Gilbert 2006, xvii). If World War I was the war to end all wars, then the Somme was "the battle to end all battles" (xix).

One of the elements that made the Battle of the Somme so costly, and that also makes it conducive to the wild deserters legend, is its "'tangled desert' of No Man's Land" (Brown 1996, 66; see figures 8.1 and 8.2). No Man's Land was a terrifying place that held the greatest danger for combatants. Literary historian Fran Brearton pictures it as containing "men drowning in shell-holes already filled with decaying flesh; wounded men, beyond help from behind the wire, dying over a number of days, their cries audible, and often unbearable to those in the trenches; sappers buried alive beneath its surface" (2000, 253). The poet Wilfred Owen described No Man's Land as "like the face of the moon chaotic, crater-ridden, uninhabitable, awful, the abode of madness" (qtd. in Brearton 2000, 253). For historian Eric J. Leed, No Man's Land marked the boundary "between the known and the unknown, the familiar and the uncanny. The experience of war was an

Figure 8.2. No Man's Land—Once a Forest in "Flanders Fields." Photograph by F. J. Lamphere, 1919. Library of Congress Prints and Photographs Division. Accessed at http://www.loc.gov/pictures/item/2006677392

experience of marginality, and the 'change of character' undergone by the combatant could adequately be summarized as marginalization" (1979, 15). This made No Man's Land fitting terrain for the appearance of liminal figures such as the wild deserters.

According to the *Oxford English Dictionary*, the term comes from the Middle English *Nomanneslond*, circa 1350, which was "a piece of ground outside the north wall of London, formerly used as a place of execution." It took on a military connotation as early as 1864 to describe "the terrain between two opposing (usually entrenched) armies." It became especially prevalent during the First World War, with the Germans using a cognate equivalent, *Niemandsland*, and the French adapting the English term, *le no man's land*. The term—both literally and metaphorically—seems perfectly suited to describe the places haunted by these "ghouls among the mouldering dead," who were no longer fully human, and thus "no man." Moreover, the fact that the legend of wild deserters is most often associated with the No Man's Land of the Somme is probably also not accidental. According to a report from Private Clifford Carter (Tenth Battalion, East Yorkshire Regiment, Ninety-second Brigade, Thirty-first Division), there was "an underground passage running under No Man's Land," which offered temporary shelter from German shells (Hart 2008, 79).

There were also more than enough deserters from the Battle of the Somme to provide additional plausibility for the legend. Reliable numbers are difficult to obtain, in part because it is not easy to differentiate between desertion and missing in action, but one source estimates that between 1914 and 1918 there were 10.26 deserters for every 1,000 men in the British Army (Corns and Hughes-Wilson 2005, 216). Given that some 7 million served in the Army, this would mean—extrapolating at least from this single source—that 70,000 men deserted over the course of the war. One other indicator is that 3,080 men in the British Army were sentenced to death between August 4, 1914, and March 31, 1920—largely for military offenses, including desertion (Putkowski and Sykes 1989, 8). Of these, 321 (or 10.4 percent of those receiving the death sentence) were executed—including 268 for the crime of desertion (Putkowski and Sykes 1989, 16). Of those who were executed for desertion, approximately 60 were deserters from the Battle of the Somme (M. Gilbert 2006, 248–49). This figure might suggest that there were hundreds of other deserters at the Somme who were sentenced to death but not executed. What cannot be determined is how many deserters from the Somme were never captured, much less sentenced or executed—and thus possibly living underground in the liminality of No Man's Land.

Lending additional plausibility to the legend is the stature of Ardern Beaman (1886–1950) and his firsthand description in *The Squadroon*—a book that critic H. M. Tomlinson highly recommended "to those who were not there [in the war], but who wish to hear a true word or two" (1922, 179). Beaman graduated from the elite Rugby School (founded in 1567) and joined the South Wales Borderers in 1905 after attending the Royal Military Academy at Sandhurst. He served in the First Lancers of the Indian Army and took part in several military operations there before serving in France during 1917 and 1918, for which he received both the Croix de Guerre and the Distinguished Service Order. Following the war, Beaman married the daughter of a baronet and served in a number of honorary positions, including high sheriff of Gloucestershire in 1948 ("Lieut.-Col. A.A.H. Beaman" 1950, 6). His purpose in writing his first-person memoir, as indicated in his foreword, was "to paint in plain and faithful colours the life and sentiments of that small body of young officers and other ranks which goes to make up a Squadron of Cavalry in the field" (Beaman 1920, xii). But there is certainly nothing plain about Beaman's description of the ghoulish deserters "who came out at nights to plunder and to kill."

Beaman's observations are made even more vivid by the report from one of the officers for the salvage company in Fresnes, who tells Beaman that at night, "mingled with the snarling of carrion dogs, they often heard inhuman cries and rifle shots coming from that awful wilderness, as though the bestial denizens were fighting among themselves" (Beaman 1920, 187–188). No one from the salvage company had "ever ventured beyond the confines of their camp after the sun had set." One time "they had put out, as a trap, a basket containing food, tobacco, and a bottle of whisky. But the following morning they found the bait untouched, and a note in the basket, 'Nothing doing!'" (188). Beaman doesn't explain how the contents of the basket may have "trapped" the deserters, but their two-word response indicates their familiarity with British slang for "No way." It also invests them with a certain wiliness that is in keeping with their depiction as antisocial and cunning.

No other telling of the legend—at least in print—is as horrifying as Beaman's. The next published version comes ten years later in a 1930 novel, *Behind the Lines*, (or *The Strange Case of Gunner Rawley*, its title in the United States). Written by Walter Frederick Morris, the novel reinforces the horror, madness, and chaos of the war at a time when such novelistic sentiments were very much in vogue. For instance, Erich Maria Remarque's novel *Im Westen nichts Neues* (*All Quiet on the Western Front*) was first published in January 1929, and Ernest Hemingway's *A Farewell to Arms* appeared in September 1929. Morris was born 1892 in Norwich and educated at St. Catharine's College of Cambridge University. He served as a battalion commander during World War I and subsequently wrote seven novels between 1929 and 1939, several with wartime settings. The first of those, *Bretherton* (1929), was termed "a masterpiece of First World War fiction" and "an authentic account of conditions at the Front" (Valentine 2011).

The central protagonist in Morris's *Behind the Lines* is Peter Rawley, a second lieutenant, who deserts his Royal Field Artillery unit after killing his company commander. Somewhere on the battlefields of France, Rawley meets up with Alf, another deserter, who leads him underground into the type of hidden, secretive landscape imagined by Beaman:

> Beyond the flattened village the ground sloped upwards and was covered with coarse grass and pitted with weed-grown shell holes. Alf led the way, and occasionally gave warning of a tangle of rusty wire or of an old half-filled trench that had to be jumped. He halted finally and said: "Here we are, mate." But there was nothing to be seen . . . Alf bent down and his dark form was instantly swallowed up. A moment later his voice came muffled from below Rawley's feet. "Come on; it's about a six-foot drop." . . . Rawley squeezed through the hole, feet first. He found himself in a low and narrow tunnel, revetted with rotting timbers and half-blocked with

falls of earth . . . Then down several steps to a curtain of dirty sacking
which Alf pulled aside. "Ere we are, maite [*sic*], 'ome sweet 'ome." Rawley
followed him past the curtain and found himself in a medium-sized dugout . . . Against the post stood a rough table on which at the moment
rested a dirty piece of newspaper, an empty bully-beef tin with jagged
rusty edges, and much candle grease . . . above were a number of stained
photographs of actresses, torn from illustrated papers. The whole place
was indescribably dirty and had a musty, earthy, garlicky smell, like the lair
of a wild beast . . . "Where do you draw your rations?" asked Rawley . . .
"Scrounge it,['] [Alf] answered, . . . [']We live like perishin' fightin' cocks
sometimes, I give you my word . . . There's several of us livin' round 'ere in
these old trenches, mostly working in pairs. But I never took to any of 'em
and kept on me own." (Morris 1930, 140–41, 143, 145)

Learning from Alf, Rawley becomes a denizen of this underworld, scavenging through a network of abandoned trenches, appearing "to be the only
living things in the landscape" "On [their] expeditions they seldom saw a
soul. Occasionally in the distance Rawley saw one of the other outcasts
moving furtively across country to disappear presently into some burrow.
They were like rats that appear for a few moments in search of scraps and
then go to earth again" (Morris 1930, 148, 150).

Later Rawley and Alf encounter a group of German deserters living in
similar fashion. Morris's detailed description reinforces not only the details
of the legend, but also the ways in which the "Wild Deserters of No Man's
Land" were the antithesis of military order, discipline, and camaraderie.

There were about thirty of them all told, and although they had all been
soldiers and most of them wore some article of military clothing or equipment, a casual glance would not have revealed that fact. Thick plasterings
of dried mud covered them from head to foot, and it was only on looking closer that one perceived such incongruities as a stained and tattered
tunic above a muddy pair of civilian trousers or an old corduroy peasant
jacket above an almost unrecognizable pair of military riding breeches.
All were dirty and unshaven, and there were beards varying from short,
black wiry stubble to dirty tangled growths several inches in length. Two
or three wore civilian greatcoats that had once been black, and with the
torn, mudstained skirts flapping about their legs and their untidy beards
hanging down over the ravelled upturned collars they looked like outcasts
from a ghetto. Some wore sandbags tied with string about their legs; others had made a hole for their heads in brown army blankets and fastened
them round their waists with wire or rope. One man wore a coat of stained
ground sheets laced together . . . Several men carried rifles, and one or two
had dirty web equipment buckled over civilian jackets and overcoats. And

two men wore muddy field grey with faded red numbers on the shoulder-straps. These, Rawley learnt, were Germans who had been hiding in the devastated area with their former enemies ever since they had found themselves on the wrong side of the Line during one of the Somme battles of 1916. The men stood about in groups of two or three, and what little conversation there was, was carried on in subdued tones. Each group kept to itself and displayed no desire for the companionship of another group. They eyed one another suspiciously and even hostilely. Evidently there was no camaraderie of common distress among this collection of outcasts. It was each man for himself. (Morris 1930, 187–88)

Nothing could be further from the notion of "One for All and All for One," the type of military cohesion found in sources from Alexandre Dumas's *Three Musketeers* (1844) to popular songs from World War I ("One for All and All for One" 1918a and 1918b). These deserters, each marching to his own different drummer, constitute visually and emotionally a rebuke to the ideal of military comradeship.

One of the most vivid accounts of the legend comes in 1948 with *Laughter in the Next Room*, volume four of the five-volume autobiography of Sir Osbert Sitwell (1892–1969), fifth baronet, a captain in the British Army, and younger brother of the poet Dame Edith Sitwell. Like Beaman and Morris before him, Sitwell cites no sources for his version of "The Wild Deserters." However, perhaps in keeping with the idea of a United Nations, which was organized in 1945, just a few years earlier, he emphasizes the universal nature of the band: "For four long years . . . the sole internationalism—if it existed—had been that of deserters from all the warring nations, French, Italian, German, Austrian, Australian, English, Canadian" (Sitwell 1948: 8). Perhaps to reflect Sitwell's nobility and wealth, as well as his frequent visits to Italy, he draws parallels between the deserters and Neapolitan *lazzaroni*, described in one source as "a mixture of paupers, indigent unskilled workers, and mendicants who scraped a living through begging" (Deasy 2008, 16). According to Sitwell,

Outlawed, these men lived—at least, they *lived*—in caves and grottoes under certain parts of the front line. Cowardly but desperate as the *lazzaroni* of the old Kingdom of Naples, or the bands of beggars and coney catchers of Tudor times, recognizing no right, and no rules save of their own making, they would issue forth, it was said, from their secret lairs, after each of the interminable checkmate battles, to rob the dying of their few possessions—treasures such as boots or iron rations—and leave them dead. Were these bearded figures, shambling in rags and patched uniforms, and pale with a cellar dampness that at first put men off their guard, so that they were unprepared for their ferocity—were they a myth created by suffering among the wounded, as a result of pain, privation, and exposure, or did they exist? . . . It is difficult to tell. At any rate, the story was widely believed among the troops; who maintained that the General Staff could find no way of dealing with these bandits until the war was over, and that in the end they had to be gassed. (1948, 8–9)

Sitwell's final point adds a new dimension to the legend, that of a massive conspiracy engineered by the General Staff to make the problem disappear by secretly gassing the deserters and then presumably covering up the evidence. This description brings to mind the most atrocious war crimes committed by dictators in the late nineteenth and early twentieth centuries. It attributes to the British high command culpability in the use of the war's most fearsome weapon. And it suggests that the legend, "widely believed among the troops," may have evoked in common soldiers a class resentment that saw in the deserters' outlaw status a dangerously seductive freedom from rules.

A more recent fictional account—and one that demonstrates the durability of the legend—comes from Reginald Hill (1936–2012), author of some fifty novels, many of them police procedurals. In his preface to *No Man's Land* (1985), Hill explains the genesis of the novel:

Though I acknowledge a tremendous debt to all those historians and memoirists whose books brought me into at times unbearably close contact with the Great War, nowhere did I come across any concern with my central theme, the fate of those men who, for whatever reason, walked away from the War, and didn't get caught. Paul Fussell in *The Great War and Modern Memory* (OUP 1975) refers briefly to the legend of a wild gang of deserters living in the waste land of the old Somme battlefield, but the truth behind the legend, the real story of what became of these men both during and after the war, must still be locked in individual minds and family tradition. I would be fascinated to hear from anyone who can turn the key. (1985, iii)

Unfortunately, Hill's novel does very little itself in turning keys to understand the legend. The author seems to have used Fussell's book purely as inspiration to speculate on what these deserters may have looked like. As described early in the novel, "They were a wild-looking gang, in dirty ragged clothing and with unkempt hair and unshaven faces. They were also very well armed" (Hill 1985, 13). An inspector is pursuing these deserters and "guessed what his superiors and the General Staff refused to acknowledge: just how vast a population of deserters had taken refuge in the Desolation and elsewhere . . . They came swarming out of nowhere, out of the bowels of the earth" (114–15). Hill's novel thus reinforces and perpetuates the legend, even though it seems based entirely on Hill's imagination and what he has read from other sources.

The literary treatments of "The Wild Deserters of No Man's Land"— from *The Squadroon* and *Behind the Lines* (both published within fifteen years of the war's end) to *Laughter in the Next Room* and *No Man's Land* (both published after thirty years or more had elapsed)—are remarkably consistent. They all portray a thoroughly dehumanized environment that serves as a horrific home for men who have been thoroughly dehumanized and marginalized themselves. In sharing a legend like this, soldiers could establish bonds across the national lines that divided them and at the same time demonstrate their own humanity, in contrast to the wild ghouls who had lost theirs.

The legend might also express a type of wish fulfilment, in which soldiers imagine a world free from military discipline and regimentation, where they exist purely on their basic need to survive, on their own terms—obeying, as Sitwell says, "no rules save of their own making." As Fussell observes, the legend "offers a virtual mirror image, and a highly sardonic one, of real, orderly trench life, in which, for example, night was the time for 'work.' . . . It embodies in objectified dramatic images the universal fantasy—the Huckleberry Finn daydream—of flagrant disobedience to authority" (Fussell 1975, 124). That this fantasy gained such currency among the Great War's soldiers suggests, perhaps, that their emotional commitment to the "war of wars" may at times have been complicated by resentment and doubt. Indeed, if the authorities promoting the war represented its insanity—ordering thousands to their death for temporary possession of territory that might flip to the other side the next week—the legendary wild deserters might offer a rare instance of sanity. These erstwhile soldiers who had abandoned their national allegiances could demonstrate (in Sitwell's words) "the sole internationalism" of the war.

A variant of Sitwell's internationalist reading was offered in 2006 by former Roman Catholic priest James Carroll, in a newspaper column written on the ninetieth anniversary of the Battle of the Somme. According to Carroll, these deserters, numbering in the dozens, "perhaps hundreds," had "organized themselves into a kind of third force—not fighters any more, but mere survivors, at home in the caverns . . . Human beings caring for one another, no matter what uniform they were wearing" (2006, n.p.). In his reading, rather than coming out at night to kill or plunder, the deserters "came out of their underground warrens to minister to the wounded left behind in no man's land after the daily charge. They were angels, the soldiers told one another ahead of each assault, who would take care of those who fell" (n.p.).

Intrigued by Carroll's revisionist take on the legend, I e-mailed him, asking if he could provide a source for his unusual reading. He replied, "Alas, I have moved several times since 2006, and my files are far from complete. I do not have access to my research notes for the columns I published then" (August 20, 2017). The frustrating answer leaves Carroll's humanizing twist on the tale, perhaps, as just another version of wish fulfillment—one person's desire to salvage a shred of humanity from the unspeakable awfulness of the war.

Whether its protagonists are seen as beastly ghouls or as heroic angels, the Wild Deserters legend remains, as Fussell claimed, extremely rich in symbolic value. It expresses a powerful antagonism toward authority and regimentation, featuring individuals who are nominally part of the military—still wearing their uniforms, according to the descriptions of Beaman, Morris, and Sitwell—but decidedly outside of any military units or operations. As renegades from authority, the wild deserters invite comparison with older European legendary figures such as the medieval Wild Man, the vampire, and the social bandit. Yet at its heart, this legend is anchored in its own dreadful historical moment. As an emblem of enforced bestiality, it continues to represent the madness, chaos, and senseless horror that have become associated with our indelible memories of the Great War more than 100 years after it began.

WORKS CITED

Beaman, Ardern. 1920. *The Squadroon*. London: John Lane.

Bonadeo, Alfredo. 1989. *Mark of the Beast: Death and Degradation in the Literature of the Great War*. Lexington: University Press of Kentucky.

Brearton, Fran. 2000. *The Great War in Irish Poetry: W.B. Yeats to Michael Longley*. New York: Oxford University Press.

Brown, Malcolm. 1996. *The Imperial War Museum Book of the Somme*. London: Sidgwick and Jackson.

Carroll, James. 2006. "Angels of War." *International Herald Tribune*, July 10, 2006.

Corns, Cathryn, and John Hughes-Wilson. 2005. *Blindfold and Alone: British Military Executions in the Great War*. London: Cassell.

Deasy, Martin. 2008. "Local Color: Donizetti's *Il furioso* in Naples." *19th-Century Music* 32 (Summer): 3–25.

Fussell, Paul. 1975. *The Great War and Modern Memory*. New York: Oxford University Press.

Gilbert, Martin. 2006. *The Somme: Heroism and Horror in the First World War*. New York: Henry Holt.

Gilbert, Sandra M., and Susan Gubar. 1989. *No Man's Land: The Place of the Women Writer in the Twentieth Century*. Vol. 2, *Sexchanges*. New Haven, CT: Yale University Press.

Hart, Peter. 2008. *The Somme: The Darkest Hour on the Western Front*. New York: Pegasus Books.

Hill, Reginald. 1985. *No Man's Land*. New York: St. Martin's Press.

Leed, Eric J. 1979. *No Man's Land: Combat and Identity in World War I*. Cambridge: Cambridge University Press.

"Lieut.-Col. A.A.H. Beaman." 1950. Obituary. *Times*, August 28, 1950, 6.

Morris, Walter Frederick. 1930. *Behind the Lines*. London: Geoffrey Bles.

"One for All and All for One." 1918a. Lyrics by Neville Fleeson, music by Albert Von Tilzer. New York: New York Art Music.

"One for All and All for One (World Democracy)." 1918b. Lyrics and music by Charles H. Hope. Providence, RI: Charles H. Hope.

Putkowski, Julian, and Julian Sykes. 1989. *Shot at Dawn*. South Yorkshire: Wharncliffe Publishing.

Sitwell, Osbert. 1948. *Laughter in the Next Room*. Boston: Little, Brown and Co.

Tomlinson, H. M. 1922. *Waiting for Daylight*. New York: Alfred A. Knopf.

Valentine, Mark. 2011. "W.F. Morris—Bretherton." *Wormwoodiana*, December 3, 2011. http://wormwoodiana.blogspot.com/2011/12/wf-morris-bretherton.html.

Part IV
Messing with the Narrative

9

Breaking Ranks
Initiative and Heroism in a Vietnam Firefight

Richard Allen Burns

IN MY FOUR YEARS IN THE US MARINE CORPS (1969–1973), I often heard the phrase "Ours is not to reason why; ours is but to do or die." The expression echoes the famous line in "The Charge of the Light Brigade," Alfred Lord Tennyson's poetic tribute to the British cavalry at the Battle of Balaclava. But the sentiment applies well to soldiers in general and especially to combat Marines, such as the Vietnam veterans I interviewed in the preparation of this chapter. For combat infantry, the saying underscores the importance of following orders without hesitation, even at the risk of your own death. As a motivational adage, it is meant both to instill camaraderie and to shape the behavior of a fighting unit. Under fire you do not disobey a direct order, because lives depend on the efficient carrying out of commands. This is the very heart of military discipline.

But unit discipline is only one facet of the Marines' core values. Marines are also encouraged to take initiative when necessary, to face danger bravely, and in a sense to disregard their own safety if doing so can protect the safety of others. In other words, they are taught to respond as courageous individuals, not just as interlocking parts of an efficient machine. Sometimes—and ideally—the value of individual courage is in sync with the value of efficient common effort. But sometimes it's not. Sometimes, the only way to further that common effort is to "break ranks," that is, to display a "disobedient" behavior that protects the group.

In this chapter, I explore the complications that can arise when the values of unit discipline and individual courage are at variance with each other. Such was the case on an August day in 1969, when a nineteen-year-old Marine named Bruce Wayne Carter lost his life in a firefight near the Demilitarized Zone (DMZ) in South Vietnam. What happened that

DOI: 10.7330/9781607329527.c009

137

day earned Carter a posthumous Medal of Honor, the highest award our military bestows on its warriors. But, as my interviews with Carter's surviving squad mates make clear, there is more to be said about the manner of his death than the military or the government acknowledged in the MOH citation.

That citation, however, is the official story. It is the version of Carter's death that the government endorsed as fact and that it presented as such both to Carter's grieving family and to the public at large. I'll give the full text here, as a vivid example of a "master narrative" that, with Tennysonian reverence, celebrates the core military value of self-sacrifice.

A HERO'S DEATH: THE OFFICIAL STORY

Carter's death came during the engagement Operation Idaho Canyon, in which his unit—the Second Battalion, Third Marines, of the Third Marine Division—had for several weeks been fighting North Vietnamese Army (NVA) forces in Quang Tri Province. At the beginning of the operation, the action had been generally small in scale and short in duration, consisting of encounters with NVA reconnaissance teams of two to three men. However, by late July, NVA soldiers were launching more daring, stronger attacks against the Third Marines. Just northwest of a combat base, the Second Battalion focused on an area known as Mutter's Ridge, where Hotel Company (Carter's unit) and other companies were to establish a primary field base and then send out squad-size patrols and five-man fire teams, ensuring maximum coverage of the area to be searched. By early August, as the Marines were encountering an ever-increasing number of fresh, energetic NVA troops, a Third Marine Division regulation directed all companies to move toward the DMZ at least 1,000 meters per day, an order that was resented by exhausted Marines in the field.

It was in this troubled situation, with the Marines caught between an increasingly aggressive enemy and an impatient rear echelon, that Carter returned from a field hospital to Hotel Company after recovering from a bout of malaria. He was killed on August 7, 1969, just days after his return to the field and not quite four months since landing in Vietnam. Two years later, Vice President Spiro T. Agnew, acting on behalf of President Nixon, presented the posthumous Medal of Honor to Carter's mother. The accompanying citation, which praised him for "conspicuous gallantry and intrepidity at the risk of his life above and beyond the call of duty," described his death as follows:

Private First Class Carter's unit was maneuvering against the enemy during Operation Idaho Canyon and came under a heavy volume of fire from a numerically superior hostile force. The lead element soon became separated from the main body of the squad by a brush fire. Private First Class Carter and his fellow Marines were pinned down by vicious crossfire when, with complete disregard for his safety, he stood in full view of the North Vietnamese Army soldiers to deliver a devastating volume of fire at their positions. The accuracy and aggressiveness of his attack caused several enemy casualties and forced the remainder of the soldiers to retreat from the immediate area. Shouting directions to the Marines around him, Private First Class Carter then commenced leading them from the path of the rapidly approaching brush fire when he observed a hostile grenade land between him and his companions. Fully aware of the probable consequences of his action but determined to protect the men following him, he unhesitatingly threw himself over the grenade, absorbing the full effects of its detonation with his body. Private First Class Carter's indomitable courage, inspiring initiative, and selfless devotion to duty upheld the highest traditions of the Marine Corps and the United States Naval Service. He gallantly gave his life in the service of his country. (Home of Heroes website [www.homeofheroes.com], Medal of Honor Recipients, Vietnam War)

Before turning to what Carter's fellow Marines have to say about this citation, let me make some observations about the text itself. First, we should notice how closely it hews to a conventional rhetoric of "heroes under fire" and particularly to that of doomed heroes under fire. I do not mean this disrespectfully, nor do I mean to deny that this may be a good description of what happened. But when we hear phrases such as "numerically superior hostile force," "vicious crossfire," "complete disregard for his safety," and "devastating volume of fire," we should suspect a certain amount of dramatization.

Such dramatization is a conventional, even predictable, element of military citations. In certain circumstances, though, it can not only embellish but distort the events being celebrated. This circumstance was evident, for example, in General Stanley McChrystal's approval of a posthumous Silver Star for Army Ranger Pat Tillman, who was killed by friendly fire in Afghanistan in 2004. Although McChrystal eventually acknowledged that he—and the Army—had misrepresented the incident, his initial medal citation mentioned boilerplate heroics: Tillman had fallen, he wrote, to "devastating enemy fire." That is the conventional explanation: what one wants to believe.

Similarly, the writer of Bruce Carter's citation, who did not witness the young Marine's death, presents a picture of that event that fulfills heroic expectations. A version of what historian John Keegan calls the emotional "battle piece" (1976, 36–46), it is a celebratory rather than elegiac passage, meant to inspire us rather than to invite our mourning. This quality doesn't discredit the message, but it should make us wonder how much of the scene reflects eyewitness accounts and how much of it reflects the stereotypes of cinematic last stands.

A second thing to notice is that the military values celebrated here are not those of unit discipline or efficiency. Here a single hero, acting on his own, accomplishes something—the repulsion of a hostile force—that his unit apparently could not accomplish collectively. When Carter stands up, exposing himself to enemy fire, he's not following an order but breaking ranks. In doing so, moreover, he is assuming a responsibility of command ("shouting directions," "leading" his men) that is far beyond the authority of a private first class. That he throws himself on a grenade only reinforces the idea that he is in charge, "protecting" his men. What the citation honors is individual heroism, not the dutiful attention to discipline that Carter learned at Parris Island. There's obviously a tension here between conflicting sets of values.

CONFLICTING VALUES, CONFLICTING ACCOUNTS

That tension came to my mind many times as I interviewed some of the men who had survived that day—Marines in Carter's unit who had been in Quang Tri and who had their own memories of that fateful firefight. As these veterans shared the details with me, I found that even though each of them remembered the incident a little differently, they all agreed that the official version of Carter's death was incorrect in some details.

RUDY'S STORY

One of the first Hotel Company veterans I spoke to was Rudy Underwood, whom I met while shopping in a local Lowes a couple of years ago. Noticing each other's Marine Corps caps, we soon got to talking about the Corps, about where and when we had served, and—inevitably, given our ages—about Vietnam. It turned out Underwood had joined the Marines and begun Basic Training at the Marine Corps Recruit Depot in San Diego in January 1968. His tour in Vietnam, which included deployment in Operation Idaho Canyon, had begun the following January and ended just shy of one year later. It was Rudy—known in Vietnam as "Underdog"—who first told me about Bruce Carter and who told me that Carter's nickname had been "Batman"—a logical enough tag, given his middle name Wayne.

To Rudy Underwood, the polished words in the MOH citation did not ring true. He first saw them, he told me, sometime in the 1990s. By that time, he had been suffering from PTSD for twenty years and unable to leave behind him the memory of that day. This is what he told me about first reading the citation.

> I think I've had it [PTSD] for a long time, and there's a lot of things that have transpired, and it all came to a head when I came home. I got on the Internet and saw my old unit, and I looked it up there and recognized a recipient for a Congressional Medal of Honor. And I thought, "What the hell?!" So I got to reading this article. I got to reading about the former Vice President Spiro Agnew's citation that he wrote for my friend that got killed in Vietnam, Bruce Carter. And I read the citation about him, where he was a PFC and he was on this patrol, and to protect the entire patrol he jumped on this grenade and took the full concussion of the grenade, and then there was a fire, and he was scorched in the fire, and this, that and the other. And it talked about how Bruce was yelling out orders and instructions to everybody else. Hell, he was a PFC! A PFC don't give orders! And he was on a patrol all right, we were doing a perimeter sweep, just four of us. But he didn't jump on a grenade to protect his squad. (Rudy "Underdog" Underwood, personal interviews, 2016–2018, Jonesboro, Arkansas).

As Rudy's comments show, the differences between his and the government's version of events are small but significant. The citation doesn't mention Carter being "scorched" by the fire, though that point sticks in Rudy's mind as a gruesome detail. He takes exception to the idea that a private first class would be giving orders to anyone else. And, most significant, he rejects the trump card in this hero story: the picture of Carter throwing himself on a grenade. In Rudy's memory, Carter died from a single gunshot wound. The grenade was mere invention, an exaggerating detail.

Crazy Horse's Story

In summer 2018, I had a phone conversation with another Hotel Company veteran, Lawrence Singleton of Modesto, California. In Vietnam he had been known as "Crazy Horse." I had seen an online post in which he dismissed the accuracy of the MOH citation: "It is not all true, the way he died in the *official report* is not all true. I know, I was there that day." He signed it with his service number and his two names: Larry B. Singleton and Crazy Horse. When I e-mailed him asking for details, he basically corroborated Rudy's account: Carter had been killed not by a grenade but by a single NVA bullet. But that wasn't all that he had to say.

The MOH citation was likely based on an after-incident report written up in the field, so I asked Larry who had written up the report. He wasn't sure. But he said that if it was a lieutenant, the lieutenant either got it wrong or "was not totally informed." His recollection of this uninformed officer wasn't flattering.

> Let's go back to that morning. The whole Second Battalion linked up. The captain of First Platoon of H Company Second Battalion Third Marine in Idaho Canyon was only supposed to rest. After an hour, the captain ordered our lieutenant (a ninety-day wonder who had received little combat training) on patrol. For a couple of hours, he kept making excuses that he wasn't ready. The captain of Hotel Company threatened to court-martial the lieutenant for disobeying his orders. The lieutenant was afraid of us, we believed. (Lawrence Singleton ["Crazy Horse"], telephone interviews by author, June 20–22, 2018)

Larry recalled that the lieutenant—a FNG or "fucking new guy"— feared that his own troops might "frag" him or that the NVA might kill him. He also thought that the lieutenant might have assigned him as a radioman to Bravo Squad because he knew such an assignment would probably draw fire and get *him* killed. He realized that there was no way to prove these speculations, but he still considered them important as indications of the company's poor morale at a time when they were exhausted and (in his view) incompetently led. These speculations also show that the internal dynamics of Carter's unit were more complicated and less gung-ho than the picture painted by the MOH citation.

MIKE'S STORY

A third Marine I interviewed, a Louisiana veteran named Mike Cantrell, also cast doubt on the accuracy of the citation. On the day of the firefight, as the leader of a machine gun team from Bravo squad, Mike was leading a patrol of about five Marines down a hill when they nearly walked into an NVA ambush. One of the team, whom Cantrell remembers only as Bob, saw Carter standing up and yelled for him to get down. Instead, Carter remained on his feet and aimed his "blooper" (an M79 grenade launcher) toward a rock where a fellow grunt had seen an NVA soldier. As he swung the firearm in that direction, another NVA on the other side of the rock shot him under his right arm, and the bullet entered his lung.

That shot coming from an unexpected direction may have inspired the citation language "vicious crossfire," when in fact, according to Cantrell,

Carter had stepped into a kill zone that was covered by just two enemy soldiers—hardly a "numerically superior hostile force" but still enough to get him killed. In any event, Cantrell's assessment of the situation was that Carter, courageous though he may have been, died mainly because he acted foolishly. An M79 delivers only one round at a time and to advance on an enemy position with only that protection was reckless at best. In addition, Cantrell told me, he yelled to Carter moments before he was hit, "Get the fuck out of here! They've booby-trapped the place!" But Carter ignored him.

So, in Mike Cantrell's memory, Carter didn't deliver "a devastating amount of fire," he didn't force the NVA to retreat, he didn't shout directions to his squad, and he didn't jump on a grenade. There *was* a grenade, he said. It was a homemade "chicom" (Chinese Communist) grenade, whose shape gave it the nickname "potato masher," and it started the brushfire mentioned in the citation. When Carter fell, Cantrell carried the body some distance away from where he had been hit—an action that earned him a Bronze Star—but the fire forced him and the rest of the squad to leave the body there until the fire had played out and they could retrieve it. They found it badly burned—a detail that the citation does not mention—though Cantrell was confident that the fire had not killed him. "He was dead before he hit the ground," he told me grimly (Mike Cantrell, telephone interviews by author, June 19–22, 2018).

PRIMARY EVIDENCE: GRUB'S JOURNAL

The most detailed recollection of Bruce Carter's death I encountered came from a Marine who considered him a good friend and who kept a diary of events during Operation Idaho Canyon. It was Larry Singleton who put me on to him. "If anybody can tell you what went down that day," he told me, "it's Grub McLaughlin."

"Grub" was the in-country handle of Kevin McLaughlin, who in Vietnam carried a radio and an antitank weapon but whose unofficial role was that of "tunnel rat." At five feet, three inches tall, he was better suited than most of his fellow grunts to draw the hazardous duty of searching the tunnels that served as hiding places for enemy forces. He was also a sharp observer and a thoughtful writer, and the "battlefield journal" he kept during his time in the jungle offers vivid descriptions of what Marines went through in what Grub himself described as a "hopeless quagmire." "Unlike other wars," he wrote about being in Vietnam in 1969, "where American soldiers fought to win, we were simply trying to keep each other alive and to get back home in one piece."

I got in touch with McLaughlin in July 2018 at Crazy Horse's urging, and he was kind enough to let me quote the sections of his journal that covered Idaho Canyon and Bruce Carter's death. In the excerpts that follow, the short italicized entries are McLaughlin's original in-country comments. The commentaries after these entries are annotations that he added only a few years ago. The entire text of his journal—field notes plus annotations—was deposited on July 8, 2014, in the USMC Archives in Quantico, Virginia. I've condensed some of the annotations in the interest of space, but added nothing: everything that follows in this section is seen through McLaughlin's eyes.

8/5/69
humped towards ridge. Everyone is pissed off at the world.

I was wet, exhausted, and covered with bug bites after being awake all night . . . Just before I crashed, Bruce Carter snickered, "It ain't no doubt Grub, the Third Marine Division is going home." It was the last thing he ever said to me. "Dream on Batman," I muttered while wrapping myself into a damp, ragged poncho liner before crawling under some jungle debris before drifting off to sleep with my loaded rifle close to my side.

8/6/69
Set up on hill near ridge. Echo got into some action.

We were in a killing zone! . . . Other than sounds of Echo Company in a firefight nearby, and an occasional stray bullet zinging over our heads, things were uneventful. For some reason, the NVA, who were everywhere, had spared us for the moment. Maybe they had something special planned. The emotional torment anticipating combat was almost as bad as the confrontation.

We had a lot of new guys. This made things more dangerous, because they tended to panic. Sometimes they started yelling or firing at shadows if they heard the slightest noise. Sometimes they freaked out and ran like crazed idiots. Until they were "battle hardened," they were a serious liability. We all went through it, so we understood, but sometimes these guys were scary.

My watch was somewhere around midnight until 3:30 A.M. As I sat looking into the inky blackness, I felt like I was in some kind of cosmic waiting room made especially for me. A vexatious feeling consumed me. Bleak silence, other than biting mosquitoes that never let up, made things even more dismal! At a time like this, while feeling impending doom, I didn't think I'd be among the living much longer, so I did a spiritual inventory, as I pondered where I would spend eternity.

8/7/69

Echo, Fox, plus Hotel all saw action. Fighting all over the ridge. Bravo went on an ambush and got hit. Bruce (Batman) Carter died. God bless his soul. A good dude. Got pinned down by gooks. Sticky and Ski saved my neck with the machine gun. Carried Bruce's body up hills. Fire all over the place. Battles all around us. Bou Cou NVA. Fox Co. got hit real bad, so did Echo. Approx. 15 died.

I don't know exactly how many were killed in my battalion, but this was one of my worst days in Vietnam.

Bravo squad came upon an area where there were scattered pieces of NVA items in elephant grass that looked like it had been slept on recently. Larry "Crazy Horse" Singleton pleaded with his squad to fall back to a safer position. He had well honed instincts after eleven months in a combat zone. At one point he refused to go any further, but under threat of disciplinary measures, he reluctantly moved on with his squad.

Bruce "Batman" Carter perhaps had the same premonition that a bloodbath was imminent if they didn't fall back. Suddenly he darted ahead, despite orders to rejoin his squad. Well in front of the rest, he approached a large rock formation. The NVA suddenly opened up with heavy small arms fire and grenades. Bruce quickly became a casualty.

Obviously, in a known danger zone, nobody dashed ahead of their unit unless they have a good reason, which in this case, it was to draw fire away from the rest of the squad. Bruce knew his squad wasn't going to fall back, so he did what felt he had to do to prevent a massacre.

The survivors became separated, as an inferno spread through the surrounding elephant grass. Michael Cantrell, a fire team leader, directed them out of a smoky fire into a defensive position. He was later awarded a Bronze Star for his leadership and gallantry. Michael was one of the most respected and liked Marines in our company, He reminded me of a "southern gentleman."

We heard the rifle fire and explosions from a nearby hill. Squad leader Tom O'Donnell asked for volunteers to establish an OP (observation post) to monitor the area, because there was a possibility the enemy was planning another ambush. Our mission was for Bravo to join with another squad and then return to the ambush scene to retrieve Bruce's body. I already had a radio on my back so volunteered.

While creeping up the side of a nearby hill, I approached a small bomb crater and wondered if the NVA were near. To be sure, I flipped my M16 into automatic and then randomly fired into the heavy jungle undergrowth. Within seconds, heavy AK47 rifle fire came from about 100 yards away. Bullets zinged all around me as I made myself an integral part of the lowest point of what now seemed to be a shrinking bomb crater. My squad was observing from a nearby hill and opened fire, led by two buddies with their M60 machine guns. There is no doubt they saved my life . . . It was the closest I came to getting killed in Vietnam.

A reinforced Bravo squad retrieved Bruce's body. They then made their way to my position before returning to our main camp. Upon their arrival, I helped Navy Corpsman Lou Salamon and another Marine carry him. His remains had burns, several holes, and shrapnel wounds; his face, which I avoided looking at, was smudged with muddy ashes and blood. When we reached our camp, we put him on the ground. Lou covered him with a poncho. I sometimes think about how Lou had carried Bruce from the ambush site to my position, then all the way to our base camp.

The weather deteriorated with pounding monsoon rain and heavy fog. There was no chance that a chopper could land and evacuate Bruce. Meanwhile, if we were attacked, we would have had neither air support nor artillery protection other than illumination rounds fired from a nearby base named The Rockpile. Everyone was mentally and physically worn out. Food supplies were low and water was foul. We sat emotionally and physically drained, with wooden, manikin like thousand mile stares. An attack was imminent.

I sat near in my foxhole that silent and empty night in the thick, gray, dismal fog. Bruce laid fifty feet away, now a piece of mortally extinct human debris, waiting to be dumped into a body bag. In this world he was a hero, in the next, hopefully a saint. I should have felt terrible about another friend getting killed but was incapable of any genuine feelings. When I think back about this paralyzing numbness, I realize that it was my mind getting a temporary rest on an emotional life raft in order to prevent a total meltdown. Emotions were still there, but not like those of normal people. There is a saying among combat veterans: "For those who have experienced it, no explanation is necessary; for those who haven't, none is possible."

Many of us were capable of picking up the scent of an enemy force from miles away. We had become just like any other wild animal. Endless months of living in the jungle had transformed many of us into almost feral creatures while relying on primitive instincts for survival.

After the ambush, when Bravo squad retreated, Larry "Crazy Horse" Singleton rammed his rifle into a new guy's face, ready to blow him away because he panicked and ran as they were pulling back. A couple of buddies tore him away to avoid a murder. In a recent conversation, Larry told me that at this point in his tour he was close to "totally losing it."

When I reflect on those days, I think we were half mad, but it felt normal at the time. We were what a present day psychiatrist might call "war normal."

8/8/69

Took Bruce's body away. Things look very bad.

The sky cleared enough for a chopper to pick up Bruce's remains. Then it was work as usual. We went on a long patrol but saw no action, although we heard sporadic gunfire and artillery blasts all around us. When we returned from our patrol, an NCO or an officer (I don't remember) told me that I was being considered for a citation.

I looked at him and asked, "What does Batman get?"

"A Purple Heart."

"That's all?" I asked incredulously.

I wasn't being disrespectful to those who earned them, but for him to only receive a Purple Heart didn't seem right. I was furious and told him I wanted nothing to do with any citation. I hated the Marine Corps that day. By this time in my tour, I felt that our efforts here were a tragic waste of lives in a war that most people back home didn't give a damn about!

When I returned home, I tossed my journal away and forgot about it for many years. I never discussed my experiences. After forty years, out of curiosity, I did some research about the Vietnam War. It was only then that I learned that on September 7th, 1971, PFC Bruce W. Carter was posthumously awarded the Medal of Honor by then Vice President Spiro Agnew.

I don't really know what Bruce was thinking when he darted off into a jungle full of enemy soldiers. Someday I'll ask him.

A MISSING ELEMENT: "WAR NORMAL"

McLaughlin's account, more detailed than the other Marines' recollections and than the citation, is distinguished by an acknowledgment of emotion that is absent, as a rule, from "battle piece" writing. Carter's MOH award depicts a valiant soldier leading a charge against overwhelming odds: the mood is unbridled courage and determined effort. McLaughlin, on the other hand, shows us a war zone in which this kind of "Semper Fi" bravery must struggle with the less admirable emotions of fear, panic, exhaustion, and "paralyzing numbness." In the Vietnam he remembers, young men sleep with their rifles sensing "impending doom." If like Larry Singleton they have "well honed instincts," they know that pulling back is sometimes the better part of valor. And they fight not to win a war that nobody gives a damn about, but just to keep each other alive, one day at a time. McLaughlin shows us something that the MOH citation doesn't even try to show us: a world in which being "half mad" passes for normal.

In that world, rushing the enemy with a grenade launcher might pass for normal too. McLaughlin suggests that Carter did that to protect the squad, to "draw fire" and thus "prevent a massacre." In this generous reading, Carter's death becomes a sacrifice, the moral equivalent to jumping on a grenade. But McLaughlin also says he doesn't know for sure what his friend Batman was thinking when he "darted off" toward an enemy position. There's no way anyone can know that, but we might gather some clues from other US Marines who lived in the "war normal" world and who, like Carter, broke cover to expose themselves to enemy fire.

One of these Marines was Karl Marlantes, author of the 2009 novel *Matterhorn*, set in Quang Tri Province, and of the memoir *What It Is Like to Go to War*. In the memoir's chapter entitled "Heroism," Marlantes describes how, in a firefight, he dragged a wounded Marine down a hill, away from a kill zone, and back to safety. He knew the danger, and before starting up the hill he was "split three ways." He wanted to rescue his guy; he wanted to listen to his staff sergeant and stay safe. "Then there was the third part. I wanted a medal" (2011, 162–163).

With those mixed emotions he goes up the hill and gets the wounded man down. The man dies, but Marlantes gets his first of several medals, a Bronze Star. He receives that too with mixed emotions. He felt it wasn't enough to do heroic things; he had to be recognized for them so that when he went home, others would know that in Vietnam he had done something extraordinary. At the same time, he knew that he received his medals not only for brave acts "but also, in part, because the kids liked me and they spent time writing better eyewitness accounts than they would have written if they hadn't liked me" (2011, 169). Was wanting a medal part of Bruce Carter's motivation? It's possible. He told McLaughlin he thought their unit was going home. Maybe before he left, he wanted recognition. Maybe he wanted, as Marlantes says, to "feel special."

Another possibility is suggested by Philip Caputo. A few days before Christmas in 1965, Caputo, then a Marine lieutenant, led a platoon a few miles west of Danang to clear Viet Cong out of a village called Hoi-Vuc. In his 1977 memoir *A Rumor of War*, Caputo wrote that as his platoon succeeded in clearing the village in the face of machine guns and small arms fire,

> I felt a drunken elation. Not only the sudden release from danger made me feel it, but the thrill of having seen the platoon perform perfectly under heavy fire and under my command . . . And perhaps that is why some officers make careers of the infantry, why they endure the petty regulations, the discomforts and degradations, the dull years of peacetime duty in dreary posts: just to experience a single moment when a group of soldiers under your command and in the extreme stress of combat do exactly what you want them to do, as if they are extensions of yourself. ([1977] 1990, 254)

Clearly, this recollection invokes the type of behavior that Marines instill in their recruits during boot camp and advanced training: the coordinated observance of a good leader's orders that leads to what I have earlier described as efficiency and that ideally (as in this case) brings mission success. In the scenario Caputo describes here, no one breaks ranks. "The platoon was one thing," (253), with everyone functioning seamlessly together. But that's not the end of the description. Once the village is cleared, Caputo continues,

> I could not come down from the high produced by the action. The firefight was over, except for a few desultory exchanges, but I did not want it to be over. So, when a sniper opened up from a tree line beyond the village, I did something slightly mad. Ordering the platoon to train their rifles on the tree line, I walked up and down the clearing, trying to draw the sniper's fire. (254)

He continues this "slightly mad" behavior for several minutes, all the while taunting the unseen sniper. "C'mon, Charlie, hit me, you son of a bitch," he yells. "HO CHI MINH SUCKS. FUCK COMMUNISM. HIT ME, CHARLIE" (254). The sniper "declines his offer," but Caputo remembers that moment of exposing himself to danger as an adrenalin high and a "delirium of violence." As World War II infantryman J. Glenn Gray notes in his classic study *The Warriors*, such exhilaration is common among soldiers who have experienced the "thrill" of battle; he even calls it one of the appeals of war. Could the allure of such a sensation have played a part in Carter's "darting" into the jungle? It seems likely.

Caputo's action, in which concern for one's safety drops away, suggests he may have been experiencing the "ecstasy of power" that psychiatrist Jonathan Shay calls the "berserk" state. In his study of combat trauma *Achilles in Vietnam*, Shay describes the characteristics of this state, based both on his reading of the *Iliad* and on his extensive interviews with Vietnam veterans (2003, 77–99). A couple of the characteristics call to mind comments that McLaughlin makes about himself and his Hotel Company squad mates.

A temporarily berserk warrior, according to Shay, can feel himself less like a human than an animal: "beastlike" is the term he applies to this trait. McLaughlin notes that in that summer of 1969, the men had become "just like any other wild animal." They had become "almost feral creatures . . . relying on primitive instincts for survival." Another berserker trait is coldness, indifference—exactly what McLaughlin himself feels following the loss of his friend. "I should have felt terrible about another friend getting killed," he writes, "but was incapable of any genuine feelings." He retreated into numbness to save himself from a "total meltdown." It's possible that

Carter also experienced these feelings. It's also possible that at the moment he stood to face the enemy, he was experiencing other berserker emotions, such as recklessness, the absence of fear, and a feeling of invulnerability. Or perhaps, like Crazy Horse facing a panicky buddy, he became momentarily "enraged" (another berserker trait) and simply "lost it."

There's no clear consensus among the Marines I interviewed about what impelled Carter to do what he did. But a couple of things seem beyond dispute. It's clear first that, when Carter "darted" off, he was violating one soldierly value (coordinated discipline) in the service of a conflicting value (individual initiative). It's clear too that in "breaking ranks" to expose himself to enemy fire, he achieved a posthumous notoriety that he probably would not have achieved if he had followed Mike Cantrell's orders and kept his head down. The men who survived that firefight have differing views on the wisdom of his fateful decision. But all of them agree that at a time when morale was low, the nineteen-year-old grunt demonstrated an inspiring form of courage. Not one of them doubts that he deserved the recognition he received.

WORKS CITED

Caputo, Philip. (1977) 1990. *A Rumor of War.* New York: Ballantine Books.

Gray, J. Glenn. 1959. *The Warriors: Reflections on Men in Battle.* New York: Harcourt, Brace and Company.

Keegan, John. 1976. *The Face of Battle.* New York: Penguin Books.

Marlantes, Karl. 2011. *What It Is Like to Go to War.* New York: Atlantic Monthly Press.

McLaughlin, Kevin ("Grub"). "Excerpts from my Vietnam Battlefield Journal: Operation Idaho Canyon." Kevin McLaughlin Collection. COLL/5641, Archives Branch, Marine Corps History Division, Quantico, VA.

Shay, Jonathan. 1994. *Achilles in Vietnam: Combat Trauma and the Undoing of Character.* New York: Scribner.

10

Challenging the Male Hierarchy
Women Warriors in Iraq and Afghanistan

Catherine Calloway

ACCORDING TO THE US DEPARTMENT OF VETERAN AFFAIRS, in the first decade and a half following the attacks of September 11, 2001, 700,000 women served in the American military, including in Operation Iraqi Freedom and Operation Enduring Freedom, with 161 of these women ending up as casualties (Department of Veteran Affairs 2017). As Helen Benedict noted in her study *The Lonely Soldier*, "More American women have fought and died in Iraq than in any war since World War II," and the number of them who had died there by 2008 was "more than in the Korean, Vietnam, first Gulf, and Afghanistan wars combined" (2009, 3).

These sobering figures, reminding us that Iraq was a costly battle zone for women, may also obscure the fact that by the time America declared a War on Terror, American women had been present in combat areas for many decades. As far back as the Civil War, ingenious and intrepid women such as Sarah Wakeman (1994) dressed as men in order to serve in the ranks as "patriots in disguise" (Hall 1993). And of course many unsung female nurses—Clara Barton's silent sisters—served at or near the front lines in that conflict, as they have in every conflict since. These women's stories, told in books such as Evelyn Monahan and Rosemary Neidel-Greenlee's *And If I Perish: Frontline U.S. Army Nurses in World War II* (2003) and Lynda Van Devanter's *Home before Morning: The Story of an Army Nurse in Vietnam* (1983), show that women have served honorably at the front in every US engagement for a century and a half.

However, despite this evidence of military service, despite the fact that women have been and still are sacrificing their lives for their country, and despite the fact that women are now officially allowed in combat zones, the question of whether females "belong" in combat is far from a settled issue

DOI: 10.7330/9781607329527.c010

within the ranks themselves. The official line may be that women soldiers can perform any roles they are physically capable of performing, but the on-the-ground reality is often different, as capable women confront a masculinist mindset that sees combat as an exclusively male preserve and that sees female soldiers as a threat to that tradition. Whatever the Pentagon's official line may be, for some male soldiers the truth of combat is still expressed by men such as Martin Van Creveld, one of the most vocal opponents of what he called the feminization of the military.

In his study *Men, Women and War,* Van Creveld contended that the place of women "neither does nor should include war and combat" (2001, 7); the idea that women should fight wars he called "the great illusion" (9). He wrote that in the first Gulf War, for example, veterans believed that "the presence of women caused some problems of unit readiness, cohesion and morale" and that "women's performance, while creditable, was rated somewhat lower than that of men" (203). In fact, Creveld argued, "military women are often absolutely detested by the male majority" (234), and men are less likely to want to serve in the military if they must serve alongside women (220–221). Both the lowering of fitness standards and the decline in enlistments after Vietnam, he argued, were the results of the military coddling the so-called weaker sex.

Van Creveld represented the traditional view of warfare as a man's game. A well-known feminist response to that view was made forcefully by Cynthia Enloe, who met Van Creveld's attack on the feminized military by condemning the militarization of women's lives. In her first major book, *Does Khaki Become You?,* she observed that even though women have been on the front lines for years, "women *as women* must be denied access to 'the front,' to 'combat' so that men can claim a uniqueness and superiority that will justify their dominant position in the social order" (1983, 15). "Women may serve the military, but they can never be permitted to *be* the military. They must remain 'camp followers,'" that is, marginalized women who are permitted to provide temporary services to the troops so long as they do not impede their progress (2). If women were to be permitted "into the essential core of the military," Enloe wrote, it "would throw into confusion *all* men's certainty about their male identity and thus about their claim to privilege in the social order" (15).

Enloe wrote that in 1983, before the public battles of the Clinton years over whether women should be permitted to take combat roles. Two decades later, with women increasingly visible in such roles, male reluctance to accept this fact was still inhibiting the integration of women soldiers. Two scholars writing from the perspective of "liberal feminism" pointed out that even though women were understood to possess "the 'masculine' qualities of aggression and toughness deemed necessary to confront the violence and horror of war," gender integration was still being met with a "fierce intransigence" driven by "the very masculinity of military culture" (Zeigler and Gunderson 2005, vi, 5). A few years later, in a book on the "private war of women serving in Iraq," Benedict suggested that masculinist bias against women comrades had actually intensified as their enlistment numbers increased. The reasons for this were, she said, grounded in traditional stereotypes about gender and identity:

> [As] the visibility of women combat soldiers is increasing in Iraq, so, it seems, is the hostility of their male comrades against them . . . War always fosters an increase in the sexual violence of soldiers. Many men resent women for usurping the masculine role of warrior. And the military is still permeated with stereotypes of women as weak, passive sex objects who have no business fighting and cannot be relied upon in battle. (Benedict 2009, 5)

It is partly because of this hostility that the stories of women warriors in the American armed forces have been relatively underreported in the general media. I say underreported rather than unwritten because in fact there is an extensive body of writing by female combat soldiers that documents their experiences in Iraq and Afghanistan—dozens of their accounts have been published (see appendix 10.A for a sampling of these books). But few of them have made the splash that Jessica Lynch's *I Am a Soldier Too* made in 2003, and none have commanded the movie audiences earned by macho chronicles such as Marcus Luttrell's *Lone Survivor* and Sebastian Junger's *War.* New York Times writer Cara Hoffman may perhaps be forgiven for claiming that "stories about female veterans are nearly absent from our culture" (2014, A23), for those stories, while hardly "absent," do tend to be marginalized and overshadowed by male hero tales.

In this chapter I bring the stories of two female combat veterans out of the margins. Kayla Williams, who served as an interpreter in the US Army in Iraq in 2003, wrote about her deployment in *Love My Rifle More than You* (2005) and her difficult homecoming in *Plenty of Time When We Get Home* (2014). Mary Jennings Hegar, an Air National Guard helicopter pilot, served three tours in Afghanistan, was wounded there on a 2009 medevac mission, and returned home to fight the military's Ground Combat Exclusion Policy. She tells her story in the ironically titled memoir *Shoot Like a Girl* (2017).

Both of these women's experiences belie the fiction that the realm of war belongs only to men. Both of them show strong women fighting bravely and capably alongside men, even as the masculinist culture of the United States services continues to marginalize and sexualize warrior women. Both of them show these women continuing the fight for respect on the home front as they become military activists, calling attention to the sexist attitudes of commanders and fellow soldiers and working to improve veterans' benefits for all.

IDEALS VS. REALITY

Neither Williams nor Hegar enlisted in the military with the idea of marching to a different drummer. Williams joined the Army mainly for financial reasons: for a five-year enlistment, the service offered her a $15,000 signing bonus plus $50,000 for graduate school. But she also wanted to "prove a former boyfriend wrong"—to show this abusive would-be Marine that she had what it took to "make it in the military" (2005, 40). Her goal was to become a cryptologic linguist and an interpreter. She thought that her chances of going to war were unlikely.

Later, though, despite coming to believe that the war in Iraq was wrong, Williams also felt a sense of duty and loyalty to the military. While she needed foot surgery that might have enabled her to miss the war entirely, she chose to delay the surgery so that she could deploy with her unit in February 2003. "We would go to war because that was the way it worked. We had signed a contract. We had given our word" (2005, 61). Williams idealistically hoped that she could do some good in her war. "That was what kept me going," she writes, "hoping I could make a difference; hoping I could provide good intelligence that saved even one life" (2005, 70).

Once in country, Williams worked toward fulfilling that hope by utilizing the Arabic the Army had taught her and serving as a translator for ground troops. But—contrary to the conventional image of women soldiers as protected "support" troops—she was also "danger close" to hostile action. In reflecting on her battle zone experience, she is eager to debunk the idea that "girls don't do combat zones." "That's bullshit," she writes.

> We are Marines. We are Military Police. We are there as support to the infantry in almost every way you might imagine. We even act in support roles for the Special Forces. We carry weapons—and we use them. We may kick down doors when an Iraqi village gets cleared. We do crowd control. We are also often the soldiers who negotiate with the locals—nearly one third of Military Intelligence (MI), where I work, is female. (2005, 16)

Mary Jennings Hegar—friends call her "MJ"—joined the Air Force because she had wanted to be a fighter pilot since she was a child. Her stepfather, who had served with the Marines in Vietnam, had taught her "that the warrior spirit wasn't only for men" (2017, 15), and she spent years working to attain her goal in a male-dominated culture. This work included overcoming feeling betrayed by a mentor who, after encouraging her throughout high school, had given her a negative recommendation for an ROTC scholarship because he believed that the military was "no place for a woman." He was the "first of many people," she wrote, who "believed they had to protect me (and protect our nation's military) from harm by denying me the opportunity to serve" (2017, 21).

While she loved to fly, Hegar didn't join the military just "to fulfill [her] dreams"; "I was here to serve my country" and "to save people's lives" (2017, 105). She was willing to work hard and to take risks to achieve those goals. As a University of Texas college student and a member of an ROTC organization called the Arnold Air Society, she was already focused on her pilot's dream. The thought that this might entail participating in a war didn't disturb her:

> It was 1995, and although the wars in Afghanistan and Iraq were many years ahead, I was always mentally preparing for the eventuality that we'd be involved in another conflict. I knew that I wanted to be a pilot, and the most important thing to me was to live my life in a way that ensured I'd serve with honor. I wanted to make my parents proud of me, to save the person beside me if I could, and to make some sort of lasting impact on the world. (2017, 24)

Once in the service, the two women's idealism soon ran into reality, as they discovered that much of American culture's traditional gendering—including the coarsening of men and the objectification of women—was if anything more intense in the military than in civilian life. A female soldier had to be tough, Williams writes, "not just for the enemy, for battle, or for death" but because she would be "spend[ing] months awash in a sea of nervy, hyped-up guys who, when they're not thinking about getting killed, are thinking about getting laid" (2005, 13). In Iraq, she asserts, a woman soldier had only two choices: to be a bitch (professional or reserved) or a slut (chatty or friendly). There is a sexual dynamic to being deployed, and Williams notes that it was both intimidating to be one of only a few women in a unit of five hundred soldiers and tempting to play the role of "Queen for a Year" (2005, 18).

SEXUALIZATION AND ISOLATION

Despite the fact that Williams eschewed relationships that required emotional involvement and that she kept a professional distance from the male soldiers, she was frequently sexually propositioned. One married soldier told her, " 'I'd love to break the back axle of that Humvee on you. If you get my drift . . . We see you girls in your T-shirts. We can see your boobs. You know we're watching'" (2005, 72). On at least two occasions she received unwanted physical contact. One drunken soldier grabbed her and roughly squeezed her breasts and another opened his pants, pulled her toward him, and tried to force her to sexually gratify him. She endured remarks such as "Show us your tits, bitch!" (2005, 22). "Guys stared and stared and stared," she notes. "Sometimes it felt like I was some fucking zoo animal . . . It was like a separate bloodless war within the larger deadly one" (2005, 22).

While Hegar did not experience the rape jokes and crude sexual remarks from fellow soldiers that Williams did, she did endure the harassment of gendered roles and attitudes throughout her military service. Her "career field . . . was highly-male dominated," she notes, "and filled with people who treated [her] as if [she] didn't belong" (2017, 47–48). She wanted to be on the flight line, "in the middle of the action, learning and being challenged every day" (49). Yet when she first reported to one new commander, he looked her over and said, "Lieutenant, the first time your time of the month gets in the way of doing your job, you're fired. Now get out of my office" (2017, 51). On another occasion, her Group Commander rejected her request for pilot training because she was married: "How's that going to work with both of you as pilots?" he asks. "Who's going to watch your kids? What if you both get deployed? If he's going to be successful in the Air Force, he'll need a strong support system at home. Don't you want to be a good wife to him?" (2017, 69).

During an assignment at Whiteman Air Force Base in Missouri, where she supervised the maintenance of bombers, Hegar endured an actual sexual assault—a result of what she calls the military's "predator culture" (2017, 286). While undergoing a flight physical, she was crudely groped by a flight surgeon who would not accept a military ob-gyn doctor's exam results and insisted on examining Hegar himself. "What followed was in no way a gynecological exam," writes Hegar. The doctor "aggressively and painfully conducted his 'exam,' as if he was trying to embarrass me, to hurt me, to put me in my place, to assert his control" (2017, 75). While the physician immediately regretted his behavior and reported himself, he was not disciplined for the assault. Military commanders gave Hegar the option of pressing charges against him but assured her that if she did not, they would "be sure to 'handle it'" (2017, 77). Later, when both Hegar and the offending physician were nominated for officer-of-the-year awards, Hegar realized that he had been honored, protected, and rewarded "for his so-called honesty" (2017, 80). Realizing that "the general culture of the Air Force" had permitted this outrage, she left that service to join the Air National Guard.

While Hegar had more opportunities in the Guard, where she could not only fly but deliver air support in "real-world missions" (2017, 85), she realized that her options as a woman were still limited. One captain, who continually marked her lower than he should have on her training record, told her that women shouldn't be pilots and that she belonged with her husband. He was "never admonished" (2017, 111) for his discriminatory behavior. Then, when she was deployed to Afghanistan, one member of her crew, Richard, told her "straight to [her] face that he didn't want [her] on the crew." It's "nothing personal," he added. "It's just that women can't hold their own in an evasion scenario" (2017, 145).

Later Richard stole her ammunition and spread a rumor that she had lost it "out by the fence" during a sexual encounter (2017, 159). The sleazy lie didn't bother Hegar as much as "the fact that Richard and the others didn't see [her] as a strong, competent, well-trained pilot who deserved his respect" (2017, 160). "Just because my anatomy was different from his," Hegar comments, "he had to objectify and sexualize me. He had to paint me in a role subservient to him and his fellow men, and what was worse, they [her fellow pilots] had gone along with it" (2017, 160).

Faced with these types of incidents, both Williams and Hegar tended to feel more and more isolated. In summer 2003, struggling to shake the image of watching a man die, Williams had to endure her fellow soldiers telling rape jokes and one of them calling her a whore ("because I wouldn't fuck him"). The pressure got to her. She "began to experience intrusive images" (2005, 212) of the man dying, and she started to feel "utterly powerless to make a difference here" (2005, 213).

> I cried every day, and felt like I couldn't handle it anymore. The shit was too overwhelming . . . And I felt this powerful desire to be even thinner and thinner. Until I could simply slip away. Disappear . . . It was around this time that I contemplated offing myself. It could all be over in a moment. It would be too easy. (2005, 214–215)

Hegar had a similar reaction not long after Richard created the "out by the fence" rumor. She realized that for some of the men in her unit, her competence as a fellow flyer threatened their identity. "About half of the guys were really awesome," she writes, "but that other half, the ones who defined their masculinity by the job they did, were obviously threatened by the fact that I was just as good at my job as they were" (2017, 1600). Faced with that realization, she writes,

> I found myself spending more and more time alone. It was an entirely self-imposed isolation. I withdrew from the people around me, no longer knowing who my real friends were. I would have taken a bullet for any one of those guys, but many of them apparently didn't feel the same way. They just wanted me to disappear. (160–161)

This reaction of self-isolation is, according to Benedict, not an uncommon one for women in combat zones. In a book appropriately called *The Lonely Soldier*, she makes this sobering observation:

> Even as they increase in numbers, women soldiers are painfully alone . . . they often serve in a platoon with few or other women, or none at all. This isolation, along with the military's traditional and deep-seated hostility toward women, can cause problems that many female soldiers find as hard to cope with as war itself: degradation and sexual persecution by their comrades, and loneliness instead of the camaraderie that every soldier depends on for comfort and survival. (2009, 3)

HOMECOMING AND ACTIVISM

Returning from Iraq in February 2004, Williams felt out of place in a civilian environment and experienced problems adjusting to a stateside culture. While she had some issues with the way that the military system worked, in Iraq she had still been dedicated to fighting the war and "had developed a deep commitment to [her] fellow soldiers" (2005, 231). She knew, though, that "there was no connection between the war in Iraq and 9/11" (2005, 193), and that fact made it difficult for her to rationalize her time in a combat zone: "It was a year of my life," she writes, "And what the fuck for? What was it all about? Not having an answer for that makes it hard. Makes it feel dirty . . . The fact that the war was based on lies destroys some of the sense of purpose for me. It degrades some of the goodness of our efforts" (2005, 282–283).

Williams was challenged not only by her misgivings about the war but also by the lack of medical and social resources available to her husband-to-be, Brian McGough, who suffered a traumatic brain injury in Iraq from an IED. When Brian was discharged from Walter Reed Hospital, he was merely returned to Fort Campbell, Kentucky, and told to stay off base and at home. Not only did he not receive the additional surgeries he needed; he also received no occupational or physical therapy. He was eventually assigned eight case managers for different physical and social needs, but all operated in isolation from the others.

To make matters worse, no one asked Williams herself how she was doing or suggested a support group for her. "I couldn't stand being treated as 'just a wife' and not the veteran I was," she writes. "Going from soldier to civilian and from sergeant to spouse was humiliating" (2014, 96). When Brian finally retired from the military, he received a disability rating of only 30 percent and was given access to few resources. Without a housing and food allowance, the couple ended up on unemployment. Williams writes that the Army's shabby treatment of her husband and other veterans was a source of "the deepest disillusionment" (2014, 287).

Hegar served three tours in Afghanistan, was wounded in combat, and received a Purple Heart and the Distinguished Flying Cross with Valor, which had previously only been given to one other woman. Like Williams, when she returned home she had difficulty adjusting. It bothered her that not everyone her team had rescued on medevac missions could be saved. Then she failed her physical fitness test due to an old knee injury and was grounded. When she realized that there was a ground job that she was qualified for, that of a special tactics officer, she planned to continue serving her country. In that role she could "forward deploy with ground forces, calling in their airstrikes and ensuring there was no miscommunication that could result in friendly losses or civilian casualties" (2017, 272). To her surprise, she was excluded from applying for the position. "The job was not open to women," she notes, "because there was an antiquated policy on the books called the Ground Combat Exclusion Policy, which was intended to keep women out of combat" (2017, 272).

To someone who had just left a combat zone with two decorations, this was unacceptable. So, when she was asked by the American Civil Liberties Union to be a plaintiff in a lawsuit challenging the Ground Combat Exclusion Policy, Hegar readily agreed. The suit, *Hegar, et al. v. Panetta*, was filed on November 27, 2012, against the then secretary of defense, Leon Panetta, in the hope of reversing a 1994 civilian-issued order that originated because women were being allowed in combat cockpits. Convinced that the discriminatory order was "not good for the military," Hegar later reflected,

> Women are needed on the front lines for a variety of reasons, and that's the bottom line. Either they are the best person for that particular job (say, a unit's top marksman) or they have to do a job only a woman can do (e.g., patting down female attendees at the fragile council meetings with local

warlords). Whatever the reason, women were needed on the front lines, and commanders were constantly having to tap-dance to get them out there. (2017, 281)

The purpose of the lawsuit was "to untie the hands of the commanders in order to allow them to select and train the best teams for the job at hand without regard to gender" (282). On January 23, 2013, Panetta signed an order reversing the exclusion policy and allowing women to serve in ground combat. With that reversal, Hegar writes, "women all over the country had thousands of jobs open to them that, for years, they had been barred from even considering" (284).

Williams and her husband have made their own contributions as advocates for veterans. In 2007, they became involved with VoteVets, an organization "that was dedicated to getting veterans of Iraq and Afghanistan engaged in politics and elected to public office" (2014, 164). There they found a sense of community with other veterans as well as a meaningful way to contribute to their country. They realized that their problems after the war resulted from "normal reactions to abnormal events" rather than from faults of their own and that they "had fallen through gaping holes in the safety net that should have been there to ease [their] readjustment and reintegration" (165). Williams served on the boards of directors and committees for nonprofit organizations, including Grace after Fire and the VA Advisory Committee on Women Veterans, and she testified on Capitol Hill.

After campaigning for Barack Obama during the 2008 presidential campaign, Williams was honored with other veterans from Iraq and Afghanistan at the Democratic National Convention. This recognition was a powerful experience for them and helped rejuvenate their sense of American patriotism. "After years of feeling alienated from my own country," Williams states, "I finally felt as if we were coming home" (2014, 186). She ends her second memoir, *Plenty of Time When We Get Home*, with an appendix of resources for veterans, family members, and others who may interact with veterans. "All of us, as citizens," she notes, "have an obligation to ensure that services are in place for those who need them" (240).

In addition to winning the American Civil Liberties lawsuit, Hegar also helped to found the Combat Integration Initiative, an organization housed in Washington, DC, that, along with Women in International Security, "work[ed] to ensure that our nation's leaders didn't take a step backward and that our military leaders were required to order full integration with no exceptions" (2017, 285). She spoke around the country, collaborating with others and working to keep military jobs of all types open to women.

In June of 2013, she helped to organize a "Storm the Hill day," on which women involved in the Combat Integration Initiative made their case to both congressional houses' Armed Services Committees. Hegar herself argued during that meeting for "reversing the predator *culture* that currently exists" in the US military (2017, 286).

CHANGING A CULTURE

Such initiatives do not change a culture overnight. Pentagon directives may ban gender discrimination as an official policy, but they do not erase the history of masculine dominance or eliminate the conventional mindsets of either predatory sexism or "protective" paternalism. Upon their return to civilian life, both Williams and Hegar—warriors who had served with dignity as the equals of men—were reminded that not only at the front but on Main Street as well, there was still plenty of support for the ancient narrative that war is an endeavor suitable only for men.

When Williams went out to dinner or to bars with other veterans, for example, only the men were recognized for their service. She had been in an area where insurgents had hit supply routes so often that it was "frequently the non-infantry soldiers like us—with fewer up-armored vehicles—who end[ed] up getting hit and engaging in combat," yet she still had to constantly debunk the notion that "girls don't do combat zones" (2005, 16). Even though the women veterans "showed the same military ID cards," they "were overlooked" (2014, 37). Civilians "didn't understand," Williams writes, "didn't think about the fact that women were in the Army too, didn't think of us at war . . . We were invisible" (2014, 37). To add insult to injury, even fellow veterans who knew that Williams had been in Iraq often took it for granted that she had been a "fobbit," someone who spent her tour on a Forward Operating Base and never ventured outside of the compound.

Hegar experienced an even more jarring recognition that, despite her combat medals, the fact that she was a women still made her, in the eyes of some, not a "real" warrior. In 2013, *Foreign Policy* magazine honored her as a Leading Global Thinker for her work on behalf of her sisters in uniform. At a celebratory dinner, a former US ambassador and Marine Corps veteran informed her—one of the honorees—that women had no place in combat. "'Little lady,' he said, 'why can't you just leave the fightin' to the men who are so good at it? I mean, what could you possibly have to contribute?'" (2017, 288).

The irony of that comment is as striking as its ignorance. If its sentiment was confined to representatives of the old guard such as the former ambassador, it might be dismissed as the relic of a fading patriarchy. But, as women soldiers such as Kayla Williams and MJ Hegar know all too well, such traditional views are still alive and well in the military—and of course in civilian society as well. That is why they are eager to tell their stories, and to have those stories serve as a counternarrative to the ancient fiction that war "belongs" to men.

There is a proprietary element to that traditional understanding, which the bravery of women warriors uncomfortably disrupts. Hence the resistance of old soldiers like the ambassador. But history, as Hegar writes, "will do what it always does." She ends her memoir on an optimistic note, arguing that as women continue to fight for inclusion in the "boy's club," history will force societal change and prove the old story wrong. It remains to be seen whether her optimism is justified. Clearly, though, by disrupting the dominant narrative about gender expectations, today's women warriors are raising serious challenges to a military culture that has privileged male dominance—and excused sexual assault—for thousands of years.

Appendix 10.A

Accounts of Women Warriors from Iraq and Afghanistan

Blair, Jane. 2011. *Hesitation Kills: A Female Marine Officer's Combat Experience in Iraq.* Lanham, MD: Rowman and Littlefield.

Bowden, Lisa, and Shannon Cain. 2008. *Powder: Writing by Women in Ranks, from Vietnam to Iraq.* Tucson: Kore Press.

Bragg, Rick. 2004. *I Am a Soldier, Too: The Jessica Lynch Story.* New York: Vintage.

Browder, Laura, and Saschia Pflaeging. 2010. *When Janey Comes Marching Home: Portraits of Women Combat Veterans.* Chapel Hill: University of North Carolina Press.

Conroy, Paul. 2013. *Under the Wire: Marie Colvin's Final Assignment.* New York: Weinstein Books.

Gentile, Carmen. 2018. *Blindsided by the Taliban: A Journalist's Story of War, Trauma, Love, and Loss.* New York: Skyhorse Publishing.

Germano, Kate, and Kelly Kennedy. 2018. *Fight Like a Girl: The Truth behind How Female Marines Are Trained.* Amherst, NY: Prometheus Books.

Goodell, Jess, and John Hearn. 2011. *Shade It Black: Death and After in Iraq.* Philadelphia: Casemate Publishers.

Hikiji, Miyoko. 2013. *All I Could Be: My Story as a Woman Warrior in Iraq.* Palisades, NY: History Publishing Company.

Holmstedt, Kirsten. 2007. *Band of Sisters: American Women at War in Iraq.* Mechanicsburg, PA: Stackpole Books.

Holmstedt, Kirsten. 2011. *The Girls Come Marching Home: Stories of Women Warriors Returning from the War in Iraq.* Mechanicsburg, PA: Stackpole Books.

Johnson, Shoshana. 2010. *I'm Still Standing: From Captive U.S. Soldier to Free Citizen—My Journey Home.* New York: Touchstone Books.

Karpinski, Janis, and Steven Strasser. 2005. *One Woman's Army: The Commanding General of Abu Ghraib Tells Her Story.* New York: Miramax.

Lemmon, Gayle Tzemach. 2015. *Ashley's War: The Untold Story of a Team of Women Soldiers on the Special Ops Battlefield.* New York: HarperCollins.

Monahan, Evelyn, and Rosemary Neidel-Greenlee. 2010. *A Few Good Women: America's Military Women from World War I to the Wars in Iraq and Afghanistan.* New York: Anchor Books.

Morgan, Cynthia I. 2006. *Cindy in Iraq: A Civilian's Year in the War Zone.* New York: Free Press.

Ruff, Cdr. Cheryl Lynn, and Cdr. K. Sue Roper. 2005. *Ruff's War: A Navy Nurse on the Frontline in Iraq.* Annapolis, MD: Naval Institute Press.

Simon, Anna, and Ann Hampton. 2012. *Kimberly's Flight: The Story of Captain Kimberly Hampton, America's First Woman Combat Pilot Killed in Battle.* Havertown, PA: Casemate Publishers.

Skiba, Katherine M. 2005. *Sister in the Band of Brothers: Embedded with the 101st Airborne in Iraq.* Lawrence: University Press of Kansas.

Smith, Amber 2016. *Danger Close: My Epic Journey as a Combat Helicopter Pilot in Iraq and Afghanistan.* New York: Atria.

Spinner, Jackie, and Jenny Spinner. 2006. *Tell Them I Didn't Cry: A Young Journalist's Story of Joy, Loss, and Survival in Iraq.* New York: Simon and Schuster.

Squier Kraft, Heidi. 2012. *Rule Number Two: Lessons I Learned in a Combat Hospital.* New York: Back Bay Books/Little, Brown, and Company.

Thorpe, Helen. 2014. *Soldier Girls: The Battles of Three Women at Home and at War.* New York: Simon and Schuster.

Walters, Joanna Sprtel. 2015. *Girl at Sea: A Story of Courage, Strength, and Growth from One of the First Women to Serve on US Warships.* New York: Skyhorse Publishing.

WORKS CITED

Benedict, Helen. 2009. *The Lonely Soldier: The Private War of Women Serving in Iraq.* Boston: Beacon Press.

Department of Veterans Affairs, 2017. "Women's Veterans Report: The Past, Present, and Future of Women Veterans." *National Center for Veterans Analysis and Statistics.*

Enloe, Cynthia. 1983. *Does Khaki Become You? The Militarisation of Women's Lives.* Boston: South End Press.

Hall, Richard. 1993. *Patriots in Disguise: Women Warriors of the Civil War.* New York: Paragon House.

Hegar, Mary Jennings. 2017. *Shoot like a Girl: One Woman's Dramatic Fight in Afghanistan and on the Home Front.* New York: New American Library.

Hoffman, Cara. 2014. "The Things She Carried." *New York Times,* April 1, A23.

Monahan, Evelyn, and Rosemary Neidel-Greenlee. 2003. *And If I Perish: Frontline U.S. Army Nurses in World War II.* New York: Knopf.

Van Creveld, Martin. 2001. *Men, Women, and War.* London: Cassell and Co.

Van Devanter, Lynda. 1983. *Home before Morning: The Story of an Army Nurse in Vietnam.*
    New York: Beaufort Books.
Wakeman, Sarah. 1994. *An Uncommon Soldier: The Civil War Letters of Sarah Rosetta Wakeman,*
    Alias Pvt. Lyons Wakeman, 153rd Regiment, New York State Volunteers, 1862–1864.
    Pasadena, MD: The Minerva Center.
Williams, Kayla. 2005. *Love My Rifle More than You: Young and Female in the U.S. Army.* New
    York: W. W. Norton.
Williams, Kayla. 2014. *Plenty of Time When We Get Home: Love and Recovery in the Aftermath of*
    War. New York: W. W. Norton.
Zeigler, Sara L., and Gregory G. Gunderson. 2005. *Moving beyond G.I. Jane: Women and the*
    U.S. Military. Lanham, MD: University Press of America.

11

A Good Coffin

The Iraq War Poetry of Gerardo Mena

Ron Ben-Tovim

IN HIS 1975 STUDY OF THE MODERN PRISON COMPLEX, *Discipline and Punish*, Michel Foucault defines the emergence of "discipline" as a principal means by which the modern military develops effective soldiers. Prior to the eighteenth century, he argues, the good soldier was slowly fashioned through a combination of both natural abilities and accumulated battle experiences. He could be "recognized from afar," for

> he bore certain signs: the natural signs of his strength and his courage, the marks, too, of his pride; his body was the blazon of his strength and his valor; and although it is true that he had to learn the profession of arms little by little—generally in actual fighting—movements like marching and attitudes like the bearing of the head belonged for the most part to a bodily rhetoric of honor. (Foucault [1975] 1991, 135)

Quoting a seventeenth-century work on the French militia, Foucault notes that the "natural signs" of a someone suited for the military included "a lively, alert manner, an erect head, a taut stomach, broad shoulders, long arms, strong fingers, a small belly, thick thighs, slender legs and dry feet" (Montgommery 1636, 6–7, cited in Foucault [1975] 1991, 135). In that period, a man's innate abilities led to his being selected as a soldier, and his experience as a warrior honed skills that he already naturally possessed: it brought his existing "heroic" qualities to the fore.

With the rise of large modern armies, though, this focus on natural ability became replaced by "discipline," and the soldier came to be seen as "a trainable entity with a fundamentally clockwork organization" (Smith 2008, 276). No longer a combination of nature and experience, modern soldiers were seen as being shaped by power, as exponents not of individual ability but of the workings of discipline:

DOI: 10.7330/9781607329527.c011

> The soldier has become something that can be made; out of formless clay,
> an inapt body, the machine required can be constructed; posture is gradu-
> ally corrected; a calculated constraint runs slowly through each part of the
> body, mastering it, making it pliable, ready at all times, turning silently into
> the automatism of habit; in short, one has "got rid of the peasant" and
> given him the "the air of the soldier." (Foucault [1975] 1991, 135)

Modern soldiers thus were no longer considered "born" to bravery; they
were now "made men," as pliable as clay. They were the products of "a
policy of coercions that act upon the body, a calculated manipulation of
its elements, its gestures, its behavior" (Foucault [1975] 1991, 138). The
outcome of this manipulation was a body molded according to the needs
of power, in which every gesture was programmed into the soldier until it
became automatic. Soldierly actions became "second nature" and operated
to some extent in opposition to nature. As the product of artifice, the new
soldier was himself artificial, that is, a construct rather than a natural entity.

This process of molding the soldier's body produces a new kind of
human, one who is not only shaped by power but whose very identity is
inseparable from his weapon. "Over the whole surface of contact between
the body and the object it handles, power is introduced, fastening them to
one another" so that the modern soldier becomes fused with the lethal tool
of his trade. Ceasing to be a human being *with* a weapon, he becomes what
Foucault—anticipating the cyborgs of our day—calls "a body-weapon,
body-tool, body-machine complex" ([1975] 1991, 153).

This shift in focus from body-with-weapon to body-weapon complex raises questions about the nature of soldiering. What happens to the
body-weapon complex, for example, when it is faced with the decidedly
unregulated chaos of warfare? What happens when the tool the soldier
has become fails to accomplish its given objective? And how do soldiers
themselves react to this shift? How do people who are supposed to behave
as body-weapon complexes actually behave when they are faced with war's
ability to turn human beings into objects?

In this chapter, I address these questions through a reading of the poetry
of Gerardo Mena, a Marine veteran of Operation Iraqi Freedom and the
author of a collection of war poems entitled *The Shape of Our Faces No Longer
Matters*. While Mena's work makes no direct reference to Foucault, I believe
he reveals a deep consciousness of the body-weapon complex and strives
in much of his poetry to express the painful duality of human being and
weapon. What emerges from his poetry is a double frustration. He shows
us soldiers' inability to revert to a predisciplined human sense of self and
simultaneously a failure to become a reliable nonhuman tool. Faced with

limits on either side, Mena's poetic speakers are, time and again, compelled to accept the mantle of the body-tool complex, but in the form of poetic resistance to the military discipline that has manufactured that complex. I see this resistance is a form of subversion, since the acceptance of a half-human, half-object cyborg nature does not promote either battlefield success or endorsement of military discipline. I will argue that Mena uses poetry to resist the objectification of contemporary soldier-weapons and to create a new object, the poem itself, which performs the moral function of commemorating those lost in war.

SPEAKING WEAPONS

Mena's heightened awareness of objects, especially dangerous objects, is evident in the titles of poems such as "Bayonet," "The Bullet Maker," and "Ode to a Pineapple Grenade." It may be implicit, too, in the title of his book, which offers painful recollections of fallen comrades who, having been turned into objects, no longer have faces. I'll discuss here four of the poems in that collection, beginning with one that recalls a combat incident in which a soldier's transformation into an object takes on a uncharacteristically comic dimension. "Rocket Man" (2014, 30) begins with a brief prose headnote, describing the event that the poet is about to memorialize:

> For Corporal Benavidez, affectionately called "Rocket Man" by the platoon after the explosion on December 9, 2006, launched him from his gun turret on the vehicle, through the air, and safely onto the sand fifty meters away.

This detailed introduction—citing the specific date, time, and place of the protagonist's brush with death—speaks to a function that is central to many of Mena's poems: the act of remembering, precisely, what has happened in war and those to whom it has happened. "Rocket Man" is one of several poems in *The Shape of Our Faces No Longer Matters* that is prefaced by such a localizing headnote, and the book's dedication honors ten of Mena's friends, each one listed with the precise date he was killed in action.

In "Rocket Man," Mena gives us the corporal's exact location prior to his "launch" (the gun turret) as well as the exact distance that he traveled before landing safely. In doing so, I would argue, Mena performs an ethical act, asking us to remember the situation with him and giving us the data we require to do so. The identification of rank (corporal) and a date in the middle of Operation Iraqi Freedom tells us that the poem is about a specific war and reminds us, if we recall anything about that IED-infested arena, that the outcome of most such incidents was anything but comic. As

the speaker remembers and cites these facts, he asks that readers mark and
remember them as well. But then, in the stanzas of the poem proper, we get
a less localized picture (Mena 2014, 30):

> I dreamed that I opened my mouth and slowly
> swallowed an entire rocket.
> When I awoke,
> I was a rocket.
>
> I had rocket guts and rocket blood.
>
> My rocket feet were plastic fins.
> My rocket arms surmounted into steeple.
> My rocket hands held a blast wave
> and smoke.
>
> I screamed into the earth,
> became wind.

The meaning of "rocket" here is clearly different from that in the Elton
John song that the platoon members allude to. In the song, a space traveler rides safely *inside* a rocket-propelled vessel: he is captain of a ship that
he controls. In Mena's poem, Benavidez is transformed into a ballistic
missile—an object whose function is not transport but destruction. In
the dark humor of the poem, we see an articulation of the soldier-weapon
complex, or at least an articulation of the tension between the human and
tool aspects, where the soldier has become an object that he cannot control. Through the first-person narration, we encounter the confusion and
violence that come from being not the operator *of* a rocket but literally a
man-as-rocket.

   This part of the poem should not be read as necessarily an interpretation of Benavidez's own experience. While the title obviously refers to the
nickname given to him following the incident, his experience is not a private
one. In fact it violently exposes the object nature of the soldier-weapon
complex in a more general manner, as soldiers other than Benavidez are
also being hurled through the air, as helpless as objects. Mena's use of the
metric measurement here indicates what type of object is being hurled and
the military context in which this is happening. In that context, the human
body, fashioned to work in unison with an object, turns out to have more in
common with that object than may have been expected. Only partly human
now, it has assumed a hybrid identity, possessing not just mechanical limbs
but even "rocket guts" and "rocket blood."

The poem's last lines tie together these different aspects of the poem into the complete poetic object. The "Rocket-Man" of the speaker ultimately fails as both rocket and man: as a man by the very fact of becoming a rocket, a tool or object, and perhaps also by becoming an instrument of violence, and as a rocket as a result of what could be thought of as an ineffective launch. In other words, the rocket fails to strike a target and instead strikes the ground, turns to air: "I screamed into the earth / became wind." Despite the dual failure of the rocket to perform either function, the transformation into a speaking object ultimately results in a kind of success: the scream denoting the anguish of the soldier-weapon mode of existence and, at the same time, bewailing the loss of lives among soldiers less fortunate than Benavidez. All the while, however, the scream and wind do nothing more or less than imitate the blast effect of any detonating explosive—a scream and a wail, in other words, that still sound like a rocket exploding.

Another expression of the half-dead, half-alive experience of the soldier-weapon entity is the poem "Dreams of Brass" (2014, 46). This poem, like "Rocket Man," investigates the torn-apart consciousness of the soldier-tool:

I dreamed that I opened my mouth and slowly
swallowed brass.
When I awoke,
I was a bullet.

My bullet arms raised high in a V,
My bullet feet stamped with a 5.56,
I spiraled blindly through the air.

I swam into the skin of your chest.
I swam into your muscle and marrow.
I swam into the chambers of your heart.
You were full of knives—questions.

Here, as in "Rocket-Man," the figure standing at the center of the poem is the speaker-weapon—in this case, a 5.56-caliber bullet. And as with "Rocket-Man," we again encounter the disturbing hybrid experience of the soldier-weapon. When the human swallows the lethal object, he becomes by that action out of control: with his "bullet arms" and "bullet feet," he can only spiral "blindly," destined for a target that he himself cannot see; the sense of war's unpredictability is here very strong, while the repetition of that calming word "swam" gives a sardonic undertone to what is being described. "Skin" and "marrow" and "chambers of your heart" suggest a romantic, even an erotic, connection—certainly a fleshy one—while the contact that is about to happen is both mechanical and deadly.

For the outcome in this poem is not the innocuous one of "Rocket Man." Rather than ending in a scream or wind, the bullet here strikes a target identified by the pronoun "you." Upon penetrating its target, the bullet-soldier continues its hybrid action as it reaches the chest and finally the heart of the personalized target. On the surface this sounds like simply a piece of metal impacting a human ("you"). But that knives-questions equation introduces a complexity that goes beyond the fact of killing. What the soldier-bullet ultimately encounters, I would argue, is another soldier-weapon identified as "you." The victim here is the soldier-weapon complex imagined as inhabiting another body: the body "full of knives" and filled with the same type of tensions—the same "questions"—that make behaving as a docile soldier-weapon so troubling to humans.

THOSE LOST TO FORCE

Mena's most complicated exploration of the soldier-tool complex comes in the poem "So I Was a Coffin," which won first prize in a 2010 war poetry contest sponsored by *Winningwriters* magazine. Originally published online in 2010 and accompanied by a video performance scored by Mena himself, the poem performs beautifully that double commemorative-expressive function that I argue the poet's works are meant to fulfill.

The poem describes the death of a fellow soldier in the arms of the speaker, and also addresses the death of the speaker himself and his transformation from a soldier with the identity of a weapon to one speaking through a different object: the poem itself. It illustrates poignantly the double function of Mena's postwar poetry: the expression of a loss of humanity, and the commemoration, the symbolic revival, of those lost to war.

Like "Rocket-Man," "So I Was a Coffin" (2014, 55–56) begins with a dedication that anchors the commemorative aspect of the poem: "For Kyle Powell, died in my arms, November 4, 2006." When compared to the dedication to "Rocket-Man," this dedication bears the evident mark of firsthand experience and intimacy. It recalls not someone else's near-death experience, but Mena's own experience with the death of a friend. This is significant since if part of the shocking encounter with violence is the objectification of the body—the soldier hurled by an explosion, the tissue tearing as the bullet enters the chest—then Kyle's dying in Mena's arms is the very act of a living body becoming an object, of a human being succumbing to what Simone Weil calls "Force."

"Force," Weil writes, "is that *x* that turns anybody that is subjected to it into a thing. Exercised to the limit, it turns man into a thing in the most literal sense: it makes a corpse out of him. Somebody was there, and the next minute there is nobody there at all" (1965, 6). It is Force that hurls Corporal Benavidez into the air, that tears the flesh of the bullet's target, and that in this poem, "exercised to the limit," turns Corporal Kyle Powell into a thing. En route to that pivotal moment of death, "So I Was a Coffin," like the two previous poems, exposes the complications of the soldier-weapon complex as the speaker—here it is not an abstract "voice" but Mena himself—struggles with the challenge of turning himself into a "good" object.

That struggle happens in four phases, each one linked to a different object that is associated with warriors' experience. The first object, a spear, typically evokes more the *Iliad*'s world of chariots and heroes than the modern battlefield of snipers and drones; Mena's metonymic use of the term, one also used to reference forward-positioned battle units, such as in the term "tip of the spear," suggests that his poem is speaking of Iraq, but not only of Iraq. The first section of the poem is as follows:

They said *you are a spear*. So I was a spear.

I walked around Iraq upright and tall, but the wind blew and I began
to lean. I leaned into a man, who leaned into a child, who leaned
into a city. I walked back to them and neatly presented a city of bodies
packaged in rows. They said *no. You are a bad spear.*

In this preliminary section the poem's speaker takes on the duties of the spear, only to prove "too good" at its task, with the quickly escalating chain of violence—from man to city—indicating the arbitrary and out-of-control nature of wartime violence. The unleashing of the soldier-weapon is at first that of the "upright" spear, a reference both to the positioning of the weapon when not engaged in combat and to the "upright" soldier who aims to please and perform well. However, despite these intentions the unleashing of the weapon in battle, even with a diminutive "lean," leads to death. An uncontrollable destructive force breaks out of the "upright" position, leading to a "city of bodies packaged in rows," itself a symbol of the methodical nature of the carnage.

In the poem's second section, the speaker tries to become a flag—an object linked to the soldier as national emblem, in his role as occupier of one nation by another and as a representative of the American people and the American way of life. This does not go well either:

They said *you are a flag.* So I was a flag.

> I climbed to the highest building, in the city that had no bodies, and I smiled
> and waved as hard as I could. I waved too hard and I caught fire and I burned
> down the city, but it had no bodies. They said *no. You are a bad flag.*

The speaker's failure here comes at battle's end, with the flag serving as a sign
both of victory and of patriotism catching fire with seeming overzealousness.
Whether the "city" indicated is one in the war zone or one back home remains
unclear, as the lack of bodies may refer to the embattled city now emptied of
its inhabitants or to an American city that holds only the living and not the
war's dead. Regardless, however, the soldier-flag's failure, as opposed to that
of the soldier-spear, is a national one. The soldier fails not as a warrior, as he
had in the previous stanza, but as a symbol, representing the metonymic role
soldiers play in representing the American military and people and indicating
perhaps his inability to do just that in the murky aftermath of the war in Iraq.

So, both as fighting thing and as national symbol, the poem's speaker
fails to fulfill his function. This might be because the tasks themselves are
presented here as unreasonable, or because, unlike the object identities
taken on in "Dreams of Brass" and "Rocket Man," the identities here are
imposed on him from outside. The speaker is *ordered* to become an object,
and by an impersonal voice known only as "they." Because there is no sense
here of a despised superior or an inept chain of command, we might see
the ordering voice, the "they" of the poem, as the implacable voice of
Foucauldian "discipline," or even as a variant of Weil's Force, that deper-
sonalized mechanism that transforms the human body and human subjec-
tivity into a soldier-weapon complex that can only obey.

While it would be possible to imagine the "they" as the voice of military commanders, I believe, again, the voice it represents seems to come
from outside the strictly military context. It may be the "they," for example,
of civilian society, and the pressure, especially post-9/11, to serve one's
country, or the "they," perhaps, of familial authority figures, encouraging
the soldier to engage with the violence of war. We might also read the
"they" not as an external source of authority but as the speaker's own internal voice. Doing this would turn the conflict between the speaker and those
who would like to see the speaker become a weapon or symbol into a harrowing internal dialogue in which the speaker questions his own responsibility for violence, his attraction to the soldier's life, perhaps to violence, and
his personal culpability during war.

In the first two sections of the poem, we see the soldier-weapon as performing "too well," killing indiscriminately in one case, and exhibiting what

can be read as an overzealous patriotism in the other. One would have to raise the possibility that those who deem the soldier as "bad" in both cases may not be the same people who had ordered him to become a spear or a flag in the first place. We might see hints here of a common scenario during wartime: soldiers being sent to kill by military authorities and damned for those very actions by civilian society. In this sense the soldier's internal struggle would be the introjection of a public debate.

The most moving passages in this poem come in the third section, where Mena, whose actions as soldier-object have led to multiple casualties, attempts to prevent one more casualty by becoming a bandage. In this section the grim promise of the headnote is spelled out, and the soldier-weapon hybrid is broken down by the speaker's failure to save Kyle Powell's life. Kyle's death is the emotional center of the poem, announced in the phrase "died in my arms" and displayed powerfully as Mena tries three times to save his friend until in the end he cannot hear a heartbeat. In using identical language to describe each attempt, Mena highlights his frustration and growing desperation, so that the poem's deadpan tone ultimately cracks under the emotional terror of Kyle's demise:

They said *you are a bandage.* So I was a bandage.

I jumped on Kyle's chest and wrapped my lace arms together around his torso and pressed my head to his ribcage and listened to his heartbeat. Then I was full, so I let go and wrung myself out.

And I jumped on Kyle's chest and wrapped my lace arms together around his torso and pressed my head to his ribcage and listened to his heartbeat. Then I was full, so I let go and wrung myself out.

And I jumped on Kyle's chest and wrapped my lace arms together around his torso and pressed my head to his ribcage but there was no heartbeat. They said *no. You are a bad bandage.*

While whole cities are decimated earlier in the poem, this section focuses on only one life lost, and the inability of the soldier-bandage to fulfill its function. It describes a failure, in other words, both human and mechanical.

From that fact emerges the intimacy of the moment in which the speaker tries so desperately to succeed at his task. That intimacy is boldly on display, as the speaker and Kyle share an ambiguously erotic embrace, Mena wrapping his "lace" arms around Kyle's body as he tries to secure the bandage—or rather himself *as* bandage—to the wounded area. It is this final embrace that breaks the emotional monotony of the poem and that highlights the need to find a way through language, even if by repetition, to depict the physical proximity of "bandage" and "wound."

As Santanu Das writes in her study of soldier writing, the military setting allows for great physical proximity between fighting men, and thus for heightened male intimacy as a daily routine. During World War I, Das writes, "The most immediate and evanescent of human senses, touch could only be preserved in memory and through language. Consequently, there is the urgent need within war writings to remember and re-present these moments" (2006, 114). It is that "immediate and evanescent sense" that Mena is so desperate to hold on to, that he feels as he becomes "full" and must wring himself out, and that he loses, along with the heartbeat, when Kyle dies.

The moment of Kyle's death represents the ultimate moment of failure for the soldier-weapon: the soldier has failed to save the life of his comrade, and the bandage has failed to stop the bleeding, allowing the once warm body to become an object. I would argue that this failure, in literally objectifying Kyle, in transforming him from a semiobject to an ultimate object, serves to objectify the speaker as well. In other words, the event also brings about the death of the speaker, one perhaps similar to other cases of wartime death that do not reduce the body to a literal corpse.

As Jonathan Shay, a leading veterans' therapist, writes, many soldiers return from war having both survived and died: "'I died in Vietnam' is a common utterance of our patients," he writes. "Most viewed themselves as already dead at some point in their combat service, often after a close friend was killed" (1994, 51). The centrality of the moment of Kyle's death, then, reveals the possibility of reading it as the death of the speaker. The process that began with the objectification of a wounded soldier culminated in the complete undoing of the man trying to save him. We see here, perhaps, an example of what Weil calls the "other force," the force that "does not kill just yet" but that calcifies the soul, depriving the living being of a sense of life.

> It will surely kill, it will possibly kill, or perhaps it merely hangs, poised and ready, over the head of the creature it *can* kill, at any moment, which is to say at every moment. In whatever aspect, its effect is the same: It turns a man into a stone. (Weil 1965, 7)

A SPEAKING OBJECT

To counter the impasse and failure of the last moments of Kyle's life, however, it is possible to see the "death" the speaker undergoes in seeing his friend die not as a final bowing to hopelessness but as the beginning of a creative resistance. At the end of the poem, rather than passively accepting his hybrid identity, the speaker makes one more attempt to become a "good" object, and this time the attempt is somberly successful.

> They said *you are a coffin*. So I was.

> I found a man. They said he died bravely, or he will. I encompassed him
> in my finished wood, and I shut my lid around us. As they lowered us
> into the ground he made no sound because he had no eyes
> and could not cry. And as I threw dirt upon us we held our breaths together
> and they said, *yes. You are a good coffin.*

In becoming a good coffin, the speaker performs a double act of creativity. On the one hand, he produces a physical object, a literal coffin, that "encompasses" and honors those who have died, or who will die. But he also produces another type of object, one that allows soldiers to drag themselves out of the silence of the military object by "screaming into the earth," by becoming "wind." At the moment of ultimate failure, of complete dehumanization, a new possibility is put forth. The poem itself becomes a speaking object that expresses the tension at the heart of the soldier-weapon complex as it enables the commemoration of those lost to that tension.

As "So I Was a Coffin" culminates, the calcification of the soldier-weapon complex, the transformation from the human to semihuman to nonhuman, seems to be complete. Force, to return to Weil's concept, has operated on all the individuals Mena's poems mention and remember. Yet through the work of poetry, which has recorded the slow march of soldiers' dehumanization, as well as the dehumanization of the civilian bodies "packaged in rows," we also see the commemoration and burial of those annihilated by Force. In serving as the instrument of Kyle's burial and mourning, the poem restores his humanity through a creative act of speaking from beyond the grave.

Originating in the utter silence of a postwar living death, a taking over of the human by the object or weapon, the poem, finally, breaks through the silence of the dead object to reveal the horror and cost of the soldier-weapon complex. Mena's poems reveal that in his wartime experience, "good" soldier-weapons struggle with a kind of split consciousness. Having encountered the ravages of wartime violence, the newly formed human weapon cannot revert back to its preweapon phase, nor can it completely succumb to the silence of the tool. As a witness to this double impasse, Gerardo Mena creates a series of speaking objects that give voice to the tensions that accompany a divided identity. At the same time, he fulfills an ethical responsibility as old as Homer: the enabling of communal mourning in poems for the dead.

Mena himself is quite conscious that this is his duty. In the dedication to *The Shape of Our Faces No Longer Matters*, he lists his fellow Marines who were lost to Force. "Remember these men," he says. "The burden is heavy." It is a burden not just of sorrow, but of calling them to mind. In his short poem "Memorial Day" (2014, 39), while sipping Scotch, Mena worries that he is starting to forget

> the fading faces
> of my friends that are
> now just granite
> and pitied whispers
> on a single day of the year.

It is to fight against that forgetting that Mena, a combat veteran, commits himself to poetry. So that the shape of his friends' lost faces may once again matter, he fashions the speaking objects that keep their memory alive.

ACKNOWLEDGMENT

The poems cited in this chapter appeared in Gerardo Mena's 2014 collection *The Shape of Our Faces No Longer Matters*. I am grateful to the publisher, Southeast Missouri State University Press, for permission to reprint them here.

WORKS CITED

Das, Santanu. 2006. *Touch and Intimacy of First World War Literature*. Cambridge: Cambridge University Press.

Foucault, Michel. (1975) 1991. *Discipline and Punish: The Birth of the Prison*. Translated by Alan Sheridan. New York: Vintage Books.

Mena, Gerardo. 2014. *The Shape of Our Faces No Longer Matters*. Cape Girardeau: Southeast Missouri State University Press.

Montgommery, J. de. 1636. *La milice francaise*. In *Discipline and Punish: The Birth of the Prison*. By Michel Foucault. Translated by Alan Sheridan. N.p. New York: Vintage Books.

Shay, Jonathan. 1994. *Achilles in Vietnam: Combat Trauma and the Undoing of Character*. New York: Scribner.

Smith, Philip. 2008. "Meaning and Military Power: Moving on from Foucault." *Journal of Power* 1 (3): 276.

Weil, Simone. 1965. "The Iliad, or the Poem of Force." *Chicago Review* 18 (2): 5.

12

Telling Stories in War

Carol Burke

WITH WAR COMES A RICH BODY OF PERSONAL EXPERIENCE NARRATIVES, firsthand accounts by those who have seen war up close. These stories, sometimes irreverent and sometimes humorous, celebrate survival in the face of adversity and acknowledge the painful loss of friends not so fortunate. They tell of close calls, of extraordinary teamwork, of incompetence, and even of the mysterious or the uncanny in close proximity to death. As civilians, we often grant those who have witnessed war bragging rights to tell us of their adventures and misadventures. For soldiers, the chance to exercise these coveted rights by reliving their experiences may be one appeal of military service itself.

Shakespeare provides testimony to this allure in his account of the Battle of Agincourt, fought between English and French forces on St. Crispin's Day (October 25), 1415. In *Henry V*, young King Henry inspires his outnumbered troops by promising that their bravery and their manhood will live "from this day to the ending of the world" in the stories they tell and that others tell about them after they are gone. Welcoming those who join him in battle as his "band of brothers," he marshals support for what looks like a hopeless encounter with a superior force by imagining those who survive as aged veterans:

> He that outlives this day, and comes safe home,
> Will stand a tip-toe when this day is nam'd,
> And rouse him at the name of Crispian.
> He that shall live this day, and see old age,
> Will yearly on the vigil feast his neighbours,
> And say "To-morrow is Saint Crispian."
> Then will he strip his sleeve and show his scars,
> And say "These wounds I had on Crispin's day" . . .

DOI: 10.7330/9781607329527.c012

This story shall the good man teach his son;
And Crispin Crispian shall ne'er go by,
From this day to the ending of the world,
But we in it shall be remembered.

(Shakespeare 1598, Act IV, Scene 3, lines 2276–2283 and 2291–2294)

This stirring invitation has the desired effect. English yeomen vanquish the mighty French cavalry, and Shakespeare's version of Henry's speech survives as one of the great battle speeches in the English language. It was still being used effectively 350 years later, when Laurence Olivier delivered it in the 1944 film version of *Henry V*, a project made at the urging of Britain's Ministry of Information and intended to strengthen the morale of British soldiers preparing for the invasion of Normandy.

But Henry's speech gives a conventional picture that captures only one response of warriors to battle. In fact, the expectation that those who fight wars will go on to celebrate their actions in heroic narratives—that is, to strip their sleeves and show their scars—is not always realized. Although survivors of war win the right to tell their version of it, they also win the right to remain silent. For some, their memories of war may reside on the other side of language for years or for a lifetime, resistant to the shaping process of storytelling.

In this chapter, which draws on my experiences embedded with US troops in the conflicts in Iraq and Afghanistan, I examine some exceptions to the conventional picture of the hardened warrior proudly showing his scars. US deployments today involve a complex mix of active duty person-nel, reserve units, and civilian contractors, many of them veterans, who have been sent to play their parts in twenty-first-century wars. Listening to personal experience narratives from that arena reveals some surprising truths about who tells war stories and who does not. In the real world of today's US deployments, some storytellers have little to say about their wartime experiences, while others, in a hunger for recognition, say far too much. Here I consider examples of both these responses.

REMAINING SILENT: CENSORS AND SENSIBILITIES

It is appealing to imagine that deployment in a war zone, which entails months of confinement on base, save for infrequent missions "outside the wire," might be the perfect stage for telling war stories. One thinks of seasoned soldiers and Marines enthralling rookie privates and lance cor-porals with tales of heroic firefights and close encounters with an enemy of the most barbaric kind. But that quaint image of unit cohesion forged by legends and legacies fails to take into account the fact that all branches of the military discourage fraternization between the ranks. Officers, non-coms, and grunts sleep in separate tents, sit at different tables in the chow tent, and shield their casual conversation from outsiders. Sergeants and officers might be admired or even liked by privates, but they are never friends, and casual conversation rarely takes place across ranks. As a result, there is actually little opportunity for a "newbie" to hear old-timers' tales.

There is even less opportunity, at least in the war zone, for common soldiers to hear tales from SEALs, Special Forces, and other "special ops" personnel. These "meat eaters" or "snake eaters" as they are often called, doubtlessly could relate harrowing stories of dangerous engagements with the enemy, but while at headquarters, they typically billet in their own secured areas off-limits to other soldiers. These high-speed guys function as assets to the commanders of regular units, and they helo to remote bases to fulfill specific missions. When they do, they generally talk with the commander, the sergeants familiar with the area, and those responsible for intelligence. They rarely socialize with the rank and file and almost never share their experiences with rookie regulars. Even on small remote bases, they generally occupy their own tent. For longer stays, they may bring their own supplies and local cook. This isolation inhibits dissemination of their adventures to a wider community.

Not that there isn't an appetite for special ops narratives. On the home front, these are so much in demand that many SEAL and Special Forces memoirs have become best sellers. Among the most successful have been Doug Stanton's *Horse Soldiers*, Marcus Luttrell's *Lone Survivor*, and Mark Owen's *No Easy Day*. In the field, the special ops' derring-do is no less celebrated. The Army regulars I've spoken to regard them with awe, and on one base where a unit of Navy SEALs arrived for a few weeks, the Army privates and specialists spray-painted their black M16s beige in imitation of the SEALs they so admired. These rookies even cut a dolphin stencil and spray-painted their khaki T-shirts with the classic SEAL logo. Had the SEALs been willing to share their war stories, they would have had an eager audience, but as talkative as they can become as memoir writers, down range the SEALs, like other "quiet professionals"—Marine scout snipers, Army Rangers, and Delta Force soldiers—opted to maintain their aloofness.

If war stories are not exchanged across ranks during long deployments, are they communicated via e-mail and Skype to a home-front audience? The simple answer is No, and the reason is a variant of the World War II warning to talkative civilians: "Loose Lips Sink Ships." All deployed units today receive from their commands a similar warning about relaying war stories to their families. It's safe to assume, they are told, that the enemy intercepts all phone and online communication. So, on top of the reticence that elite units practice themselves, the services add an element of institutional censorship that further inhibits the sharing of combat experiences. This censorship can be particularly stressful, for both the deployed soldier and his or her family, when a unit sustains a loss, because that triggers a temporary blackout of all communication with home until the families of the dead or wounded have been notified.

After a combat death, soldiers try to return to what passes for normal life in a war, a battle rhythm that restores form and function over feeling. For those close to the deceased, the processing of grief must be postponed, providing yet another level of institutional silencing. Chaplains often make themselves available for grief counseling, but they must contend with their own feelings of sadness, while many of those who were closest to a fallen comrade either turn to fellow soldiers or suffer in silence. In fact, faced with obstacles to the expression of sorrow, many soldiers describe deployment itself as a death from which some are resurrected when they return home and others are not.

Finally, at the end of deployment, soldiers with unprocessed grief return home to patriotic music, cheering family and friends, celebration barbecues, and drinks with their old buddies. Their audience awaits, but they often have trouble constructing any narratives out of the images from deployment, images that, if they involved trauma or repressed fear, may hover on the other side of language, images that resist meaning, images that only those who have been there could understand. Out of curiosity or genuine concern, friends and family often pump the returnee for stories through which these loved ones can understand and share in the pathos of war, not realizing that the returnee is often not ready to assemble the pieces into narratives.

Many who step into the world of war quickly learn that only a laboriously constructed armor of numbness can shield them from the normal reactions to violence: feelings of fear, pain, and anger. Whereas the numbness during deployment may protect soldiers from pain, it can also fend off the therapy involved in cautiously reckoning with what they did, what they saw, what they felt, or what they should have felt but didn't. It also tends to push away those who could extend empathy and, perhaps, good advice on how to shed the carapace and open themselves to family and friends. Thus, for some of those who come back from a war zone, the institutional silencing that they experienced down range morphs into a silence that they impose on themselves.

There are others who return from today's wars with stories they would like to tell but that they cannot share with civilians. Macabre battlefield humor in war permits soldiers to establish an alienating distance that makes light of threat and inures them, at least temporarily, to war's carnage. Yet the same jokes that soldiers routinely exchange in deployment can fall like unexploded ordnance on civilian ears. If the soldiers don't realize that when they're deployed, they find it out quickly enough when they're back home.

For example, a Marine from one of the first units to invade Iraq in 2003 did what many soldiers and Marines did there. He took pictures of the destruction they witnessed and wrought, laid these images down against a track of heavy metal, and produced a "trophy video," a new genre that celebrates a unit's power to exterminate the enemy. In Iraq, he told me, he had played this video often to laughter and cheers. One Monday night back home in California, he invited a few fellow Marines with whom he had deployed to come over and watch a football game and enjoy a few beers. At the end of the game, he decided to play the DVD trophy video for them, as a way of retelling their common story. While it was screening, the Marine's wife came into the room carrying their baby daughter. Seeing the destruction, she asked, "What *are* you watching?" It was only then, when he saw the video through his wife's eyes, that he realized he had really come home, a place where such stories must remain unspoken.

If the "trophy video" was too violent for domestic consumption, other retellings of the deployment experience are left unspoken because they violate the heroic model from the other direction: they are seen as too tame to count as warriors' tales. Consider, for example, the tens of thousands of American and allied troops who are stationed inside the wire on large air bases such as Balad in Iraq and Bagram in Afghanistan. On any given day, typically fewer than 5 percent of these military personnel would venture beyond the HESCOs, the stone- and sand-filled perimeter walls that surround them. Many only leave the base to fly abroad for R&R or to return home at the end of their deployments.

Combat soldiers refer to these relatively protected individuals as "fobbits" because they are safely confined throughout their tours to a FOB, or Forward Operating Base. When these individuals return home, what stories do they have to tell? Maybe a story about a favorite prostitute who offered a "happy ending" to any massage for an extra ten bucks? Or a story about winning the Halo 3 video game competition on base? Would they tell about the crushed rock that covered every pathway of the base and posed the biggest source of nonlethal injury, the sprained ankle? Or would they complain about a fastidious commander of a base that hadn't been attacked in the last decade, a commander who made all soldiers caught without proper "eyepro" (goggles) stand outside the chow hall during the evening meal and recite the Army's "Soldier's Creed"? These were the personal narratives available to many on the bases I visited. Not surprisingly, few soldiers were eager to draw on them to exercise bragging rights.

TALKING TOO MUCH: WANNABES AND CONFABULATORS

So if it's not the active-duty soldiers who regale underlings with true or exaggerated accounts of past deployments, then who, in the liminal world of deployment, do relate narratives of their past adventures? In my experience, the people most ready to invoke their bragging rights—sometimes bragging about things that never happened—are the civilian contractors who have been as numerous in our recent wars as have our official fighting forces. Since 2001, to fight wars in two parts of the globe without initiating a draft, military planners have been augmenting our all-volunteer active duty forces with reserve units in unprecedented numbers and with civilian contractors. In 2011, when American troops were pulling out of Iraq and the Afghanistan surge was under way, there was a rough parity between the military and paramilitary groups: 150,000 troops to 155,000 contractors.

Contractors hired by the notorious Black Water firm and other defense specialists served as security forces, but that was only the most celebrated of their endeavors. In addition to security contractors, DynCorp sent former American police officers to train local police in Iraq and Afghanistan. Kellogg, Brown and Root (KBR), a subsidiary of Halliburton, employed civilians to clean the latrines; keep the generators running so that the tents could be warm in the winter and cool in the summer; drive the buses and vans to shuttle personnel from one side of a large base to the other; launder soldiers' uniforms and bedding; deliver pallets of bottled water; and man the omelet, pasta, and ice-cream sundae stations in the large chow halls. Military contractors, many of them veterans, also piloted personnel between bases; conducted lie detector tests; ran the post exchange (PX), bank, and gym on large bases; operated heavy equipment; interrogated prisoners; served as interpreters; and aided in what would prove to be budget-busting reconstruction projects.

Contractors pulled down hefty salaries. Consider an American in a job that pays $40,000 a year. With no food, lodging, or transportation costs to cover, this same worker could take home $200,000 a year as a defense contractor. Some contractors in that position explained their large salaries as adequate compensation for the hard work they did and the dangers they faced. Many did do valuable work and many faced danger, with some being wounded or killed while deployed. Others, though, were just there for the cash, and some of them inflated their military pasts in part, I believe, to justify the windfall they received from American taxpayers.

Take, for example, a gentleman I met while waiting at Ali Al Salem, the Army way station in Kuwait where Army troops and the civilians attached to them waited for a flight to Iraq or Afghanistan. Assigned to one of the 260 sandy tents, they waited to be called to board a large troop transport and make their way down range. It wasn't unusual to appear in the middle of the night for a flight and sit for hours only to be told to come back the next night and the next and the next. A friend of mine and fellow war traveler spent fifteen nights doing this in the Twilight Zone that is Ali Al Salem with nothing but rolling sand in all directions. One felt the irony of this place of comings and goings when sitting still night after sleepless night for hours. Most people one encountered at Ali Al Salem looked blankly and straight ahead as if refusing to admit that the base was a real place and its inhabitants were anything other than shades slipping through the rows of tents in the beastly hot days and the chilly nights. If you were there long enough, you started to doubt your own existence. So when you met someone who was friendly and wanted to talk, you paid attention.

The man who chatted me up that November day in 2010, when there was nothing to do but listen, said that he was a contractor and a Vietnam War veteran. He was eager to tell me about his days in "Nam." I knew that the average infantry soldier in the Vietnam War saw over 200 days of combat during a 365-day deployment, so I wasn't surprised to hear about the jungle fighting the genial gentleman had endured. But then he explained that though a soldier was required to head for home after receiving three Purple Hearts, he had, in fact, stayed on to receive a fourth. That claim sounded suspicious, but I let him go on with his story.

He complained about Army officers today who care more about their advancements than about those who serve under them. As evidence of his loyalty down the chain of command, he insisted that he had never asked anyone he commanded to do anything he wouldn't do himself. He said, "When I was a captain and got my own squad, I went out with my men." Thinking I had misheard him or that he had misspoken, I said, "Did you say when you were a corporal?" "No," he said, "I was an officer, a captain." The four Purple Hearts had been questionable, but when he said he'd gotten his own squad as a captain, I could smell the stink of his story. A sergeant and on occasion a corporal, but not a captain, typically commands the 8–10 soldiers in a squad. A lieutenant leads a platoon (15–30 soldiers), and a captain generally leads a company of 60–120 individuals, not a single squad. Only Special Forces have captains commanding small units, and had this man been a Green Beret, I'm certain he would have told me.

War stories that are too good to be true usually come apart when a single thread is pulled, causing the whole garment to unravel. With this guy, I saw two threads in ten minutes. It seemed clear that he was if not simply a liar, at least the type of "inventive" storyteller that folklorists call a confabulator (Long 1973). There are plenty of these wannabe heroes around—so many, in fact, that in 2013 Congress felt obliged to pass a law, the Stolen Valor Act, that makes it a crime to lie about receiving military awards to obtain money, property, or other benefits, particularly veteran benefits.

For several years I followed VWAR, a listserv created by folklorist Lydia Fish at SUNY Buffalo State, that allowed Vietnam veterans to reconnect with buddies and exchange reminiscences of their in-country experiences. From time to time a fake would be exposed. Typically, he had been a regular on the site for a long time but in just a single post would make a mistake about a piece of equipment, a type of ordnance, or the name of a particular village that shattered his disguise, and the vets on the list would shame him off the site.

I often wondered why the fake wouldn't just trot out his stories in the civilian world where the disguise could be maintained, but I answered my own question when writing an article about a fake veteran who pretended to be "Hank Higgins," a pilot who had been decorated in the Vietnam War and who was still alive when the imposter "adopted" his war record (Burke 2006). For several years, almost every day, this wannabe joined his online friends, many of them retired from the Air Force, some of them Air Force or Navy pilots, and almost daily he risked discovery. I'm convinced that the imposter took that risk because he needed affirmation from real veterans, those who could be persuaded that he was the person he pretended to be. As long as the disguise worked, as long as he passed, he could see himself as a member of the band of brothers whose acceptance he so desperately craved. In fooling them, he could go on fooling himself.

Sometimes a confabulator is so polished that he even fools an experienced professional. In his well-known article "The Perfect Informant," Marine Corps veteran and seasoned fieldworker Bruce Jackson (1990) shows how he was taken in by "Jim," an excellent storyteller who also masqueraded as a Vietnam vet. Jackson's experience with Jim sets him on a new trajectory and to the publication of his book *The Story Is True*, in which he seeks to resolve the dialectic between what Tim O'Brien in his famous work of fiction *The Things They Carried* calls "story-truth" and "happening-truth." O'Brien's narrator explains the difference:

> I want you to feel what I felt. I want you to know why story-truth is truer sometimes than happening-truth.
>
> Here is the happening-truth. I was once a soldier. There were many bodies, real bodies and real faces, but I was young then and I was afraid to look. And now, twenty years later, I'm left with faceless responsibility and faceless grief.
>
> Here is the story-truth. He was a slim, dead, almost dainty young man of about twenty. He lay in the center of a red clay trail near the village of My Khe. His jaw was in his throat. His one eye was shut, the other eye was a star-shaped hole. I killed him. ([1990] 1998, 179–180)

O'Brien's work never claims to record the exact details of lived experience; rather it presents a collection of stories that convey the absurdity, the loss, and the guilt of war. Jackson's "perfect informant," on the other hand, claims the ethos of a legitimate Vietnam War veteran and a Special Forces soldier, when he has actually spent his service in Germany not in Vietnam, has never seen combat, and has never been a member of the Special Forces. He recounts his experiences to Jackson and others with such skill and energy that even those who suspect that he never set foot in Vietnam still delight in his tales.

Jackson understands that "our stories are always in flux," that they are not very good at telling us "exactly what happened at that moment" in the past, and that the most we can expect is that stories can serve as "a primary indicator of what's happening now" (2008, 36). O'Brien's stories were created; Jim's were pieced together from the told stories of veterans, from their written accounts, and even from scenes in feature films. Both the crafted stories by the skilled author and the orally narrated accounts of the confabulator meet the audience's desire to know a little of the "story-truth" of an inscrutable war.

Not all confabulators focus on combat experience. Embedded with combat units in Iraq and Afghanistan, I have encountered deployed veterans who claimed to be completing doctoral degrees from universities that did not even grant doctorates. Others said they had earned bachelor's degrees when they had, in fact, dropped out of college after a year. In such cases the "worked material" is different, but the motivation seems the same. The dropout who wants to be thought intelligent, like the fobbit who wants to be thought courageous, uses "resume enhancement" to acquire the qualities he lacks.

I saw an interesting variant of this process when I interviewed a contractor who had served in Afghanistan on one of the Army's first Human Terrain Teams. These were small groups of contractors hired to embed with a regular Army unit and go "outside the wire" at the commander's behest to interview the civilians about issues of importance to them: the local economy, education, public health, and security. On every team a social scientist designed the projects the team conducted, determined the questions to be asked in interviews, and analyzed the data collected. The social scientist on one of the first teams was a young Army veteran I'll call Amy, who after a few months in Afghanistan returned to train others at the Human Terrain System training site in Leavenworth, Kansas. I interviewed her there on July 31, 2008.

When I asked Amy about her educational background, she said that she had graduated from West Point, served as an Army officer, and had subsequently received her PhD. She explained that she withheld the detail about her PhD from her resume in order to "protect my mentors." I asked her who directed her dissertation and the topic she investigated, but she told me that she couldn't answer any questions about what she called her "lineage," implying clearly that her research, the professor who supervised it, and even the institution who granted her doctoral degree were too secret to divulge.

I had been on the faculty of three major research universities, but this was the first time I had heard of a graduate student engaged in such a top secret dissertation. Although Amy wouldn't give me any details of her graduate career, she stated emphatically more than once, "There are very few women with my skill set. They are in the single digits." It was never really clear to me what skills made up her "skill set." They were, I surmised, as top secret as the title of her dissertation. A month later, in a phone interview with Dr. Montgomery McFate, the DOD senior social scientist who had helped create the Human Terrain System, I mentioned that I had interviewed Amy and understood that she held a doctoral degree. McFate stopped me: "Oh, she doesn't have a PhD."

Lying about academic credentials may seem quite different from lying about combat experience, but Amy was doing a dance that was similar in spirit to that of the military imposters I've encountered. Some of these were veterans who never deployed but who touted their Ranger and SEAL pasts and invoked secrecy when my questions sought too much detail. They would insist, "I was black ops" or respond with a knowing smirk and the cliché, "If I told you, I'd have to kill you." Amy did not embroider her military past, but in fabricating her civilian credentials, she too characterized her work as cloaked in secrecy. In her embroidered narrative, she was protecting the black ops of academia.

REMAKING THE SELF

American identity has always been mutable. We are a nation deeply committed to the notion that if we don't like our social status, our job, the side of the tracks we grew up on, we can always remake ourselves—by going West, by getting more education, by joining the military, by liposuction here, a few tucks there, by inventing a new online self. Or, like a former president, by remaking himself as a fighter pilot coming in for an impressive landing on an aircraft carrier.

Six weeks after US forces rolled into Iraq in March 2003, President George W. Bush staged a made-for-the-media "tailhook landing" on the *USS Abraham Lincoln*, which was moored off the coast of San Diego. As a huge crowd awaited his arrival, he emerged from a jet aircraft that had his name stenciled under the pilot's window, dressed not as a distinguished guest but as the pilot himself. Those unfamiliar with his military past might have reasonably assumed that he had managed the daring carrier landing himself. As he stood in front of an enormous banner that read "Mission Accomplished" and declared an end to combat operations in Iraq, the visual message was clear: the commander in chief was a high-speed warrior himself.

Only he wasn't. The carrier landing was a bit of patriotic theater that told an inspiring but inflated story about the president's abilities. In the Vietnam War era, Bush had learned to fly in the Texas National Guard, but he had never qualified to make carrier landings, and his flight status was revoked during his service when he failed to show up for a physical. His dramatic exit from the fighter jet onto the carrier deck was a visual story that did more than celebrate American might and masculinity. It deflected questions about why he had served in the Guard rather than in Vietnam and about whether he had actually completed his service duty.

Without saying so outright, Bush presented himself as a combat veteran and sold that story to a public hungry for reassurance from such triumphalist displays. His tailhook landing stunt wasn't lying, exactly. But it was media-supported confabulation at the highest level. A little digging would easily have revealed that George Bush was no more a fighter pilot than the veteran I met at Ali Al Salem had been a captain commanding a "squad." But that fiction captivated an audience, at least temporarily, for the same reason that Jim's fictions captivated Jackson: it was a story too appealing to be undone by mere facts.

Creative manipulation of the past, as I've been indicating, is more common and easier to pull off when you are at some distance from the events you wish to embellish. Uniformed military personnel, both active duty and reserve, wear their rank on their uniforms and often deploy with others familiar with their pasts, so for them fabrication and embellishment are pretty difficult. For the nonuniformed contractor, on the other hand—or for those reimagining a war that ended decades ago—contemporary conflicts offer a screen upon which one can project a past one wishes had been true and become, in the telling as least, "All One Can Be" in the armed services.

WORKS CITED

Burke, Carol. 2003. "Soldiers Real and Imagined and the Stories They Tell." *Contemporary Legend New Series* 6: 146–156.

Jackson, Bruce. 1990. "The Perfect Informant." *Journal of American Folklore* 103 (410): 400–416.

Jackson, Bruce. 2008. *The Story Is True*. Philadelphia: Temple University Press.

Long, Eleanor. 1973. "Ballad Makers, Ballad Singers, and Ballad Etiology." *Western Folklore* 32 (4): 225–236.

Luttrell, Marcus. 2007. *Lone Survivor*. New York: Little, Brown.

O'Brien, Tim. (1990) 1998. *The Things They Carried*. New York: Broadway.

Owen, Mark. 2014. *No Easy Day*. New York: Dutton.

Shakespeare, William. 1598. *History of Henry V*. Accessible at Open Source Shakespeare. www.opensourceshakespeare.org.

Stanton, Doug. 2010. *Horse Soldiers: The Extraordinary Story of a Band of US Soldiers Who Rode to Victory in Afghanistan*. New York: Simon & Schuster.

Conclusion

Discipline and the Limits of Unit Cohesion

Tad Tuleja

IN MY OPENING REMARKS ON THE MYTH of the robot soldier, I suggested that military discipline fosters unit cohesion in two interlocking ways: by regulating physical activity and by encouraging attachment. Here I want to return to this distinction and to reflect on how the chapters in this volume reveal the various ways in which discontent may arise in military units both as a reaction against cohesive strictures that are felt as stifling and as a defense of cohesive bonds that are seen as threatened. Let me begin by defining more fully the two modes of cohesion.

OPERATIONAL AND EMOTIONAL COHESION

On its simplest, functional level, discipline ensures that members of an armed force, when given an order, will respond with the speed and reliability that joint action requires. While such a response is deemed desirable generally, as an index of obedience to the chain of command, in combat it can become literally lifesaving, as a bulwark against distraction and disorder. The undisciplined soldier, the soldier burdened with an "individual-type attitude," is a danger to himself and every member of his unit. Recognizing that, military organizations train their members to perform every action unquestioningly and predictably, so the unit as a whole functions, if not robotically, at least with the machinelike precision that will guarantee success. Seen in this light, unit cohesion, instilled by discipline, is the enforced regulation of individual actions to serve a corporate goal that has been defined from above. We may call this mission-oriented type of regulation *operational cohesion*.

In a combat zone, such regulation may be seen by all but the occasional malcontent as necessary, even salutary. But, as I have suggested, the

DOI: 10.7330/9781607329527.c013

control of subordinates' behavior tends toward metastasis. In a military organization—a totalizing if not total institution—what begins as a protective mechanism may expand into a demand that all behavior, however trivial, conform to the same predictability, so that everything from belt feeding a gun to shining a shoe must be "obedient" to the regime called the Army way. At that point the value of top-down, operational cohesion may become less obvious, and soldiers may respond to it with creative insubordination.

Several chapters in this book reveal the variety that such relatively benign pushback may take. As Angus Gillespie shows in his reading of World War II griping in chapter 1, it may appear as grunts' good-natured complaints against indignities that the grunts know they cannot change. The resistance may take the form of "back chat" against officers, as displayed in the wartime cartoons discussed both by Gillespie in chapter 1 and by Christina Knopf in chapter 2. My essay (chapter 7), on "café colonel" trench songs reveals a similar humorous resistance to top-down cohesion among British soldiers in World War I. Studying a more contemporary context, in chapter 3 Jay Mechling and John Paul Wallis describe the ways in which American Marines today use their own regulated bodies to offer "microresistance" to the Corps' restrictions on expression.

In all of these cases, warriors who are aware that they cannot change the system—perhaps do not even wish to—draw on "weapons of the weak" to offer gentle disruptions to the sometimes picayune extensions of military authority. Their actions, I suggest, should not be construed as rebellious, and far less as antimilitary, but as judicious sorties into the world of folk expression. These sorties imply that the value of operational cohesion notwithstanding, some efforts to enforce top-down discipline spread it so thin that even the lowest-ranking soldier can see that it's not essential to accomplishing an objective.

The second purpose served by military discipline is to ensure harmonious interaction among the individuals who comprise the group performing the operation. It is to instill in the members of a military unit—no matter its size—that sense of common purpose and shared destiny that historians commonly identify as esprit de corps. Here again the elimination of the "individual type attitude" is critical, for the goal is to create a force in which each individual is able to see himself or herself not as a distinct body, but as part of the corporate body—in French, the *corps*—that he or she serves and that, in a sense, make him or her the person he or she is. If operational cohesion defines soldiers who work well together, the cohesion that creates esprit de corps defines soldiers who *feel* well together, who feel themselves connected like family members or, to use the most common analogy, like a "brotherhood of arms." This second type of cohesion may have a strong, indeed indispensable, impact on operational success, but that is not what makes it vital. The goal of operational cohesion is to protect the mission. The goal of this second type of cohesion is to protect the group—to keep the group "sticking" with each other. Because the bonding effect of that condition is so palpable, we may call this second type of solidarity *emotional cohesion.*

It is possible, as I acknowledged in the introduction, to see this bonding effect as "a romanticized means of making regimentation attractive." That emotional cohesion has this effect is undeniable. Yet the power of this social "glue" is also undeniable. As many students of military culture have noted, people may go to war for a principle or a flag, but in the thick of battle they fight and die for each other. Cynics may see this sacrifice as proof they have been manipulated. But the testimony of the battlefield is beyond dispute. Emotional cohesion, as a product of discipline, may be manufactured. But manufactured is not the same thing as unreal. Certainly not the same thing as unfelt.

Given the investment that soldiers make in this attachment to each other, it's not surprising that while operational cohesion often elicits pushback, this seems to be rarely the case with emotional cohesion. Indeed, in many cases when soldiers question or resist a disciplinary regime, it is because they believe that other members of the organization—typically, superior officers—are neglecting or subverting the "band of brothers" ideal. We see this in part II of this volume, where active-duty officers in charge of others' welfare perform acts of creative insubordination against unresponsive systems. When (see chapter 4), Navy psychologist Mark Russell "jumps the chain" of his command to secure better treatment for returning combat vets, when (see chapter 5) Special Forces officer Ronald Fry in effect refuses an order he thinks will get his men killed, they do so in defiance of strict discipline but in deference to a higher military principle: the idea that the band is just as important as the mission.

To a traditional strategist, this idea would be anathema, since nothing should be valued as highly as a mission's success. If men fight for each other, the traditional reasoning goes, that is to be encouraged not because of any inherent value to comradeship but because those who fight for each other are more likely to win. To the common soldier, though, this reasoning is questionable. It runs the risk of seeing a mission's success as a goal that is to be achieved at any cost. When that is the generals' thinking, one result is "glorious" tragedies such as Thermopylae, Balaclava, the Alamo, and the Somme.

Another result may be disillusionment with the leadership, with the immediate mission, and even with the wider national mission that the war is promoting. The essays by Matthew Perry (chapter 6), James Deutsch (chapter 8), and myself (chapter 7) in part III of this volume provide evidence of this disillusionment. E.E. Cummings's disdain for kneejerk jingoism, the wry disillusionment evident in Tommy's tunes, and the image of deserters rejecting the call of nationalism—all of these suggest a world in which human connections have been suppressed and soldiers have responded to the suppression by questioning its premises. The "discontents" remembered in these three chapters are doing more than griping at nonsensical restrictions; they are rejecting a disciplinary regime that transcends the battlefield to regulate, and to distort, patriotism itself.

INTERNALIZED DISCIPLINE: A VIRTUOUS TRIAD

I have noted elsewhere (Tuleja 2014) that "contented" soldiers, those who embrace their soldierly identities with enthusiasm, seem to swear allegiance—often but not necessarily overtly—to a code of conduct that elevates three martial qualities: toughness, devotion to the band, and self-sacrifice. These virtues are so central to the soldiers' sense of themselves that they constitute implacable "folk ideas" that function, unconsciously and explicitly, as "units of worldview" (Dundes 1971). I suspect that similar values have infused military cultures down the centuries and that some permutation of these folk ideas may have been honored by warriors as superficially different as the Roman legionnaire, the Christian knight, and the Japanese samurai. There is no doubt, in any case, that elite American warriors today are overtly, and zealously, dedicated to this triad of values. I want to suggest here that devotion to these values constitutes an internalized discipline that is more important in the regulation of behavior than any number of directives from the chain of command.

Not that these values are unknown to the chain of command. They are in fact lauded in official documents, and though they are not spelled out as a "triad," they figure frequently and prominently in recruiting and training literature. One example is the "Soldier's Creed," the US Army's most succinct version (121 words) of its warrior's code. When a soldier recites the creed, he or she pledges, "I am disciplined, physically and mentally tough"; "I will never accept defeat, I will never quit, I will never leave a fallen comrade"; and "I am a guardian of freedom and the American way of life" (US Army, n.d.). Dedication to toughness, to the band, and to the nation are explicit here, and though self-sacrifice is not mentioned by name, never leaving a fallen comrade certainly allows for that implication.

But it is in soldiers' own accounts, rather than this recruiting mantra, that the power of the triad shines through. In saying this, I'm thinking particularly of first-person accounts from the War on Terror. One representative example is the memoir *Lone Survivor*, which is Navy SEAL Marcus Luttrell's account of the 2005 Operation Redwing disaster. This best-selling book provides vivid evidence that for this elite warrior, the virtues of toughness, devotion to others, and self-sacrifice have become a fully internalized, and fiercely defended, personal discipline.

TOUGHNESS

By toughness I mean not the active qualities of aggressiveness or machismo, but the passive virtue of being able to "take it," to withstand aggression from assailants such as neighborhood bullies, Taliban attackers, or Marine Corps drill instructors. Celebrating that form of toughness, Luttrell spends the first chapters of *Lone Survivor* recounting the rigors of SEAL training and celebrating those who, like himself, prove strong enough to survive it. Reflecting on the elite unit's philosophy, he says, "My Nation expects me to be physically harder and mentally stronger than my enemies. If knocked down, I will get back up, every time . . . I am never out of the fight" (2007, 235).

The goal here is not victory but endurance. However hopeless the odds, the virtuous soldier keeps going. This trait is applauded throughout Luttrell's books and in many other accounts from Afghanistan. In *War*, for example, Sebastian Junger's record of his embedding with an Army platoon, a young grunt complains about another who is showing exhaustion: "He *can't* be smoked here. He doesn't have the *right* to be" (2011, 76). In *Outlaw Platoon*, Sean Parnell refers to his fellow Army Rangers as "indomitable": "We will always stay and finish the fight" (2013, 171). He doesn't mean that his comrades are immortal or invincible but that they are literally "unable or unwilling to be dominated."

DEVOTION: THE BAND OF BROTHERS ETHOS

The reason that Junger's young soldier doesn't have a right to be exhausted speaks to the second governing value of the virtuous triad: devotion to others. Junger describes beautifully why this matters:

> Good leaders know that exhaustion is partly a state of mind . . . and that
> the men who succumb to it have on some level decided to put themselves

above everyone else. If you're not prepared to walk for someone else,
you're certainly not prepared to die for them, and that goes to the heart of
whether you should even be in the platoon. (2011, 76–77)

Indomitability, in other words, is not a private accomplishment. In combat
units, soldiers demonstrate the never-give-up attitude not as individuals but
as members of a group whose strength derives from their connectedness.
And that connectedness means an allegiance to something larger than oneself. On the macrolevel, that something is the nation. On the more immediate level it's the team, the band of brothers, each other.

In SEAL training, Luttrell notes, the value of teamwork is not so much
"instilled" in candidates as "ram[med] home with a jackhammer" (2007,
81). Future SEALS, for example, do water training with a "swim buddy,"
and "if one of you falls over the side into the freezing ocean, the other
joins him. Immediately" (81). In combat, SEALs must be able to move
undetected across enemy terrain, where, as Luttrell writes, "the slightest
mistake might mean instant death or, *worse*, letting your team down" (156;
emphasis added). Sebastian Junger suggests that this devotion to the unit
serves as a defense against fear, particularly the fear of abandonment, of
being the man left behind (2011, 124). "The thing you were most scared
of was failing your brothers when they needed you, and compared to that,
dying was easy" (210). He pushes this insight to a logical conclusion by
saying that military brotherhood is "a form of love that even religions fail
to inspire" (239).

SACRIFICE: "MAKING HOLY"

The ultimate test of that love is the warrior's willingness to die for his
"brothers." Hence the third element of the virtuous triad: sacrifice. The
Latin source of this word, the verb *sacrificare*, means "to make holy" (Barton
2001, 30), and it is this sacred-making commitment to others' welfare that
pulls indomitability and brotherhood together, that displays the preferred
model of behavior in its most elevated form.

To illustrate this value, Luttrell cites the sacrifice of Lawrence Oates,
a Royal Navy officer who accompanied Robert Falcon Scott on his 1912
expedition to the South Pole. Believing that his frostbite was "hindering
the entire team," he left his tent to walk out into a blizzard, uttering what
Luttrell calls "the immortal words": "I am going outside now. I may be gone
for some time" (cited in Luttrell with Robinson 2007, 80). Luttrell cites too
the sacrifice of his best friend, Michael Murphy, who exposes himself to

enemy fire in a desperate attempt to call in air support—"the one chance, he believed, to save us" (363).

In a community governed by the value of self-sacrifice, Junger writes, "Who you are entirely depends on your willingness to *surrender* who you are" (2011, 276). If this makes surrender sound like a spiritual choice, that's not accidental. The most frequently quoted line in the New Testament, John 15:13, is a popular choice for a tattoo among American servicemen. One Airborne veteran, ensuring that the fraternal reference will not be missed, displays this version on his arm: "Greater love hath no man than this, that he lay down his life for his bro." (Cassidy 2012, 94, 174)

Indomitability, brotherly devotion, sacrifice: this is the triad of virtues that I see always implicit and often explicit in many of the war stories from Afghanistan and Iraq. If we were to construct out of this virtuous triad a master narrative describing "proper" soldiering, it would sound something like this:

> I was once a weak civilian, unable and unwilling to endure the stress
> of combat. Then professional warriors transformed my weakness into
> strength, my timidity into courage, my selfishness into devotion to my
> comrades. Thanks to the warrior spirit that they instilled in me, I faced
> danger disciplined and unafraid. Prepared if necessary to die for my broth-
> ers, I embraced my duty willingly and acquitted myself honorably.

I'm not suggesting that you will hear this explicit story line in any contemporary memoir. It is less a standardized plot than an ideal-typed representation of a preferred self. But it does describe the behavior that veterans such as Marcus Luttrell enthusiastically endorse. It is a template, therefore, for the story that citizens want to believe about soldiers, that soldiers want to believe about themselves, and that the military institution promotes as a normative script.

NARRATIVE LEAKS: THE UNSPEAKABLE

But such templates are not watertight. Languages, as the linguist Edward Sapir noted a century ago, are subject to "drift," and their grammars have a tendency to "leak" (1921). If we think of the warrior's normative tale as a grammar—that is, as a description of "proper" structure—we can say that it too has the tendency to leak. For a military system that asks soldiers to live by the master narrative, this leakage is problematic—and not only for the soldier who cannot live up to the code. Given the emotional invest-ment in a cohesive narrative, when a platoon mate fails to be tough enough, brotherly enough, or self-sacrificing enough, he disrupts and "discontents" the very integrity of the band. Rather than playing forward the band's collective honor, he "messes with the narrative" and thus invites censure.

The four essays in part IV all reveal some level of "messing" with a dominant narrative by folks whose military experiences have left them discontent. The Vietnam veterans interviewed by Rick Burns, as described in chapter 9, even as they honor a fallen comrade, acknowledge that their memories of his death are at variance with the government's official account. Catherine Calloway's essay (chapter 10), in pointing to another disjunction between official and personal story lines, reminds us that, for female soldiers, the "band of brothers" ideal can be at best problematic, at worst marginalizing and sexually hostile. Ron Ben-Tovim's study of Gerardo Mena's poetry (chapter 11) reveals an internal tension in this Iraqi War veteran, which reminds one of that other "good" soldier Siegfried Sassoon. And Carol Burke, in her report from today's front lines (chapter 12), shows that the war stories we expect to hear often remain unspoken, while those that fit the derring-do template are sometimes embellished by fabrication.

These chapters suggest only four of the many ways in which a messed-with narrative may threaten discipline. A unit's grammar may leak when a dutiful soldier feels cheated by his war experience: Marine sniper Anthony Swofford, for example, who is denied the "kill shot" he believes his service has earned him, concludes that he belonged to a "fucked situation" (2003, 254). It may leak when a soldier unhappy with his command under-performs his duties or goes AWOL: Bowe Bergdahl is a notorious example of this type of discontent (Farwell and Ames 2019). It may take the form of an insider's whistleblowing, as when Daniel Ellsberg—a Marine veteran turned RAND Corporation analyst—leaked the Pentagon Papers to the *New York Times*. It may appear as an attack on fellow soldiers—not just the normal pugnacity of young men in groups, but fratricidal assaults such as fragging, murder, and rape. And it may appear as a kind of attack on oneself, in the increasingly common and yet routinely misread soldierly syndrome known variously down the years as shell shock, battle fatigue, and PTSD.

The military's response to this most grievous form of discontent has, with only a few exceptions, been remarkably consistent for generations. It has been to deny or minimize the reality of combat stress and to marginalize service members who have been undone by war as malingerers, as weaklings, or simply as cowards. This institutional attitude is now "under review," and steps are being taken by the VA and the Department of Defense to provide appropriate treatment for combat stress victims. But the old "suck it up" attitude has a long history, and as Mark Russell shows in chapter 4, it is not one that responds with alacrity to psychological insight.

One infamous moment in that history occurred in August 1943, as the US Seventh Army was fighting its way across Sicily. The army's commander was Lieutenant General George S. Patton, the legendary leader who, as Angus Gillespie's essay (chapter 1) indicates, felt that Bill Mauldin's cartoons were an affront to discipline. Twice that month Old Blood and Guts encountered soldiers suffering from what was then called battle fatigue. One told Patton that he "couldn't take it," the other that he "couldn't stand the shelling." Infuriated, Patton slapped both men, accused them of cowardice, and ordered that they be immediately returned to the front. Although the incidents embarrassed the Army and earned Patton a reprimand, they also elicited widespread sympathy for the general. Many Americans felt, as he did, that the best way to handle victims of combat stress was to ridicule them into recovering their "hardihood." In other words, by mocking these lying discontents back into toughness (Axelrod 2006; Blumenson 1974).

In these kinder and gentler times, this response may sound harsh. But if we consider the soldier who "can't take it" as a member of the band, Patton's refusal to "coddle" becomes understandable. Like the Marine who says his platoon mate "doesn't have the right" to be exhausted, Patton was making the case that once you put on a uniform, you have pledged yourself to go the distance for the team. If you couldn't demonstrate toughness, devotion to your mates, and a willingness to die for them, you were by definition a traitor to your friends.

But the real problem wasn't that two rattled GIs were malingering; it was that their refusal to fight threatened discipline and cohesion. In refusing to mouth the implicit master narrative, they had replaced it with a "leaked" narrative of incapacity. To the official ideal of brotherly indomitability and self-sacrifice, their personal stories said, "I give up. I'm not your brother, and I won't die for you." If you are trying, as Patton was, to hold an army together, that assault on the proper worldview must be suppressed.

This assessment is not to say that in discouraging soldiers from admitting mental "weakness," the military was (or is) behaving simply in a callous fashion. There's ample evidence that "Blood and Guts" soldiers like Patton care deeply about their men and weep for their sacrifice. Rather, what today's Pattons are doing when they minimize the "invisible wounds of war" (Tanielian and Jaycox 2008) is defending a threatened master narrative that sees "taking it"—the toughness component of the virtuous triad—as essential to military preparedness. When a soldier says, "The military trained me to take it but I couldn't," the dangerous hidden message is

"The story that they told me wasn't true." To maintain morale (so goes the official line), this admission that discipline is fragile—that the disciplined *self* is fragile—must remain unspoken. That is why, decades after we first heard the term Post-Vietnam Syndrome, and a century after Siegfried Sassoon was sent to Craiglockhart Hospital, recruiting literature continues to promise aspirants that military training will perfect their better natures, turning weak and "nasty" civilians into men and women of honor.

It is a noble and intoxicating promise. But like all glimpses of elevation, it sometimes fails. When that happens, we may sense for a sobering moment that good soldiers are not born but made and that, in the alchemy of fortune, they can be unmade. For any number of reasons—not all of them "unheroic"—soldiers may slough off the armor of training or crack with the strain. If we look at this fact as patriots, it may distress us. But if we remember we are none of us robots, it should not surprise us.

WORKS CITED

Axelrod, Alan. 2006. *Patton: A Biography*. New York: Palgrave Macmillan.

Barton, Carlin. 2001. "Honor and Sacrifice in the Roman and Christian Worlds." In *Sacrificing the Self: Perspectives on Martyrdom and Religion*, edited by Margaret Cormack, 23–28. New York: Oxford University Press.

Blumenson, Martin. 1974. *The Patton Papers: 1940–1945*. Boston: Houghton Mifflin.

Cassidy, Kyle. 2012. *War Paint: Tattoo Culture, and the Armed Forces*. Atglen, PA: Schiffer Publishing.

Dundes, Alan. 1971. "Folk Ideas as Units of Worldview." *Journal of American Folklore* 84 (33, January–March): 93–103.

Farwell, Matt, and Michael Ames. 2019. *American Cipher: Bowe Bergdahl and the U.S. Tragedy in Afghanistan*. New York: Penguin Press.

Junger, Sebastian. 2011. *War*. New York: Twelve.

Luttrell, Marcus, with Patrick Robinson. 2007. *Lone Survivor: The Eyewitness Account of Operation Redwing and the Lost Heroes of SEAL Team 10*. New York: Little, Brown.

Parnell, Sean, with John R. Bruning. 2013. *Outlaw Platoon: Heroes, Renegades, and the Brotherhood of War in Afghanistan*. New York: William Morrow.

Sapir, Edward. 1921. *Language: An Introduction to the Study of Speech*. New York: Harcourt, Brace and Company.

Swofford, Anthony. 2003. *Jarhead: A Marine's Chronicle of the Gulf War and Other Battles*. New York: Scribner.

Tanielian, Terri L., and Lisa Jaycox, ed. 2008. *Invisible Wounds of War: Psychological and Cognitive Injuries, Their Consequences, and Services to Assist Recovery*. Santa Monica, CA: RAND Corporation: Center for Military Health Policy Research.

Tuleja, Tad. 2014. "When Master Narratives Leak." Panel presentation, American Folklore Society annual meeting, November 8. Santa Fe.

US Army. n.d. "Soldier's Creed." Accessed May 9, 2020. https://www.army.mil/values/soldiers.html.

Contributors

Tad Tuleja is a folklorist and writer whose books include *American History in 100 Nutshells*, *The New York Public Library Book of Popular Americana*, and *Usable Pasts: Traditions and Group Expressions in North America*. He collaborated with Eric A. Eliason on *Warrior Ways: Explorations in Modern Military Folklore* and with Ronald Fry on *Hammerhead Six*. Tuleja has given American Folklore Society presentations on military slang, Vietnam "memory narratives," and Barry Sadler's "Ballad of the Green Berets." With a PhD in folklore and anthropology from the University of Texas at Austin, he has taught writing and American studies at several universities, including Harvard, Princeton, and the University of Oklahoma. He is the recipient of a Puffin Foundation grant for his song cycle "Skein of Arms" and the author of the essay "Brotherhood of the Sea," which appears in *War, Literature, and the Arts* (2018).

Ron Ben-Tovim is a lecturer in Tel Aviv University's Department of English and American Studies, where he works primarily on contemporary soldier writing. He is currently working on his first book, an adaptation of his PhD thesis, "War and the Undoing of Language," which analyzed contemporary online war poems as "poetic prostheses" that enable soldiers to reconnect with language after wartime violence has disrupted their ability to communicate with their communities. By examining war writing through the prism of the prosthesis, Ben-Tovim's work is informed by poetics, linguistics, trauma theory, and disability studies. His work has been published or is forthcoming in *Philosophy and Literature*, *symplokē*, and *South Atlantic Review*.

Carol Burke, a professor of English at the University of California, Irvine, is a folklorist and ethnographer whose work has produced books that document the lives of Midwestern farm families (*Plain Talk* and *Back in Those Days*), female inmates in US prisons (*Vision Narratives of Women in Prison*), and members of the armed services (*Camp All-American, Hanoi Jane, and The High-and-Tight*). In December 2008, she embedded with a combat unit in Iraq and published articles on the dangers faced by local Iraqi interpreters working for American military units, on the threats to the few remaining independent journalists working in northern Iraq, and on the US Army's controversial Human Terrain System. In 2010–2011, she took a year's leave from her academic position and embedded with two US Army combat units in Afghanistan. She is currently writing a book on her experiences in America's longest war.

Richard Allen Burns earned his PhD in folklore and anthropology at the University of Texas at Austin after an honorable discharge from the Marines in 1973. He taught anthropology at Austin Community College and then at the University of Houston at Clear Lake and at two Texas prison farms. While a student at UT-Austin, Burns conducted research in material folk culture, which he continued as an intern at the Institute of Texan Cultures. Since 1993, Burns has been at Arkansas State University, where he is an associate professor of folklore and anthropology. While teaching courses as part of ASU's folklore minor as well as courses in the Heritage Studies Doctoral Program, Burns has published articles on Southern, prison, and military folklore. He is currently completing a book on Southern prison folklore as well as one on folk art in the Arkansas Delta.

Catherine Calloway is a professor of English at Arkansas State University, where she directs the English graduate program and teaches courses in contemporary literature. She specializes in war literature, especially that of Vietnam and later conflicts, and is the former National Area Chair of the Vietnam War section of the Popular Culture Association. The coeditor of *Approaches to Teaching the Works of Tim O'Brien* (Modern Language Association 2010), she is also a regular contributor to *American Literary Scholarship, an Annual,* and to Oxford University Press's Online Bibliography series. She has also published in *Critique: Studies in Contemporary Fiction, Tampa Review, Arkansas Review: A Journal of Delta Studies,* and *War, Literature, and the Arts,* among other forums.

James I. Deutsch is a curator and editor at the Center for Folklife and Cultural Heritage at the Smithsonian Institution in Washington, DC, Since 2003, he has helped plan and develop public programs on California, China, Hungary, the Peace Corps, the Apollo Theater, Circus Arts, the National Aeronautics and Space Administration, the Mekong River, the US Forest Service, World War II, the Silk Road, and White House workers. In addition, he serves as an adjunct professor—teaching courses on American film history and folklore—in the American Studies Department at George Washington University. Deutsch has also taught American Studies classes at universities in Armenia, Belarus, Bulgaria, Germany, Kyrgyzstan, Norway, Poland, and Turkey. He has earned academic degrees from Williams College, the University of Minnesota, Emory University, and George Washington University. His doctoral dissertation was entitled "Coming Home from 'The Good War': World War II Veterans as Depicted in American Film and Fiction."

Ronald Fry is a third-generation veteran who, as a US Army captain, served as an infantry officer in the Eighty-second Airborne Division and as a Special Forces team leader in Afghanistan. Fry commanded Operation Detachment Alpha 936, a Special Forces (Green Beret) unit sent to the Pech Valley of Afghanistan in 2003 with orders to set up an A-Camp modeled on those used in Vietnam. His 2016 memoir *Hammerhead Six* recounts that successful unconventional warfare experiment in "winning hearts and minds." Since leaving active duty in 2005, Fry has built a successful career in medical sales and as an entrepreneur. He lives with his wife and five children in St. George, Utah.

Angus Kress Gillespie is a professor of American studies at Rutgers—The State University of New Jersey. He has a PhD in American civilization from the University of Pennsylvania. He has published broadly on iconic works of civil engineering. The great-grandson of a brigadier general in the US Army Ordnance Corps, he is especially interested in military history. He currently team-teaches a course at Rutgers on the Global War on Terror with Colonel James M. Robertson, US Army (retired). This course covers the NATO-led international involvement in Afghanistan from 2001 to 2014, as well as the Iraq War from 2003 to 2011. It also deals with the insurgency in Yemen from 1992 to the present, as well as the war in northwest Pakistan from 2004 to the present. The course culminates with a mock session of the National Security Council with students taking the roles of government and military officials.

Christina M. Knopf is an associate professor in the Department of Communication and Media Studies at the State University of New York (SUNY) Cortland. She earned her PhD in (cultural) sociology and (political) communication at the University at Albany in 2005. She is the author of *The Comic Art of War: A Critical Study of Military Cartoons, 1805–2014* (2015) and has chapters in *Cultures of War in Graphic Novels: Violence, Trauma, and Memory* (2018), *The 10 Cent War: Comic Books, Propaganda, and World War II* (2017), and *Horrors of War: The Undead on the Battlefield* (2015), among others. She has also published in various journals, including *Political and Military Sociology: An Annual Review* and *Air & Space Power Journal-Africa & Francophonie*. From 2006 to 2017, she taught communication at SUNY Potsdam.

Jay Mechling is Professor Emeritus of American Studies at the University of California, Davis, having retired in 2009. In 2004 he created and taught each year before he retired the course War in American Memory, which launched him into reading and writing about warriors and veterans. Meanwhile, he spearheaded a project at his alma mater, Stetson University (Florida), creating a Stetson Alumni Vietnam Veterans Remembrance Site; it was dedicated in November of 2015. He and John Paul Wallis are coauthors of *PTSD and Folk Therapy: Everyday Practices of American Masculinity in the Combat Zone* (2019).

Matthew David Perry is an associate professor of English and chairperson of the Department of English and philosophy at Del Mar College in Corpus Christi, Texas. His research and teaching interests include American and British Modernism, film studies, and twentieth- and twenty-first-century war literature. "'(De)composing the 'Machine of Decomposition' Creative Insubordination in E.E. Cummings's *The Enormous Room*" is excerpted from his book manuscript on retreat from war in Modern American literature, which he is currently revising for publication.

Mark C. Russell is a retired navy commander and board-certified clinical psychologist with over twenty-six years of military experience. He is coauthor of *Treating Traumatic Stress Injuries in Military Personnel* and has published extensively on military mental healthcare. Commander Russell's embattled efforts as a reluctant military whistleblower to prevent a self-inflicted mental health crisis has been chronicled by

USA Today and centrally featured in the award-winning documentary film by Tom Donahue, *Thank You for Your Service*. He is the recipient of the 2006 Distinguished Psychologist Award from Washington State and the 2018 award for outstanding service to the field of trauma by the American Psychological Association.

John Paul Wallis is a lawyer and veterans' advocate. Raised in a family of veterans in Hawaii, he grew up immersed in military culture. He served as an enlisted infantryman in the United States Marine Corps, with two deployments to Iraq, in 2007 and 2008–2009. In 2014, he worked with the San Francisco Bar Association and the Department of Defense to combat military sexual assault by recommending reform of commanders' convening authority under the Uniform Code of Military Justice. He and coauthor Jay Mechling work together to examine folklore, memory, and masculinity among warriors.